INFORMATION SECURITY MANAGEMENT, EDUCATION AND PRIVACY

IFIP – The International Federation for Information Processing

IFIP was founded in 1960 under the auspices of UNESCO, following the First World Computer Congress held in Paris the previous year. An umbrella organization for societies working in information processing, IFIP's aim is two-fold: to support information processing within its member countries and to encourage technology transfer to developing nations. As its mission statement clearly states,

> *IFIP's mission is to be the leading, truly international, apolitical organization which encourages and assists in the development, exploitation and application of information technology for the benefit of all people.*

IFIP is a non-profitmaking organization, run almost solely by 2500 volunteers. It operates through a number of technical committees, which organize events and publications. IFIP's events range from an international congress to local seminars, but the most important are:

- The IFIP World Computer Congress, held every second year;
- Open conferences;
- Working conferences.

The flagship event is the IFIP World Computer Congress, at which both invited and contributed papers are presented. Contributed papers are rigorously refereed and the rejection rate is high.

As with the Congress, participation in the open conferences is open to all and papers may be invited or submitted. Again, submitted papers are stringently refereed.

The working conferences are structured differently. They are usually run by a working group and attendance is small and by invitation only. Their purpose is to create an atmosphere conducive to innovation and development. Refereeing is less rigorous and papers are subjected to extensive group discussion.

Publications arising from IFIP events vary. The papers presented at the IFIP World Computer Congress and at open conferences are published as conference proceedings, while the results of the working conferences are often published as collections of selected and edited papers.

Any national society whose primary activity is in information may apply to become a full member of IFIP, although full membership is restricted to one society per country. Full members are entitled to vote at the annual General Assembly, National societies preferring a less committed involvement may apply for associate or corresponding membership. Associate members enjoy the same benefits as full members, but without voting rights. Corresponding members are not represented in IFIP bodies. Affiliated membership is open to non-national societies, and individual and honorary membership schemes are also offered.

INFORMATION SECURITY MANAGEMENT, EDUCATION AND PRIVACY

IFIP 18th World Computer Congress
TC11 19th International Information Security Workshops
22–27 August 2004
Toulouse, France

Edited by

Yves Deswarte
LAAS-CNRS, France

Frédéric Cuppens
ENST-Bretagne, France

Sushil Jajodia
George Mason University, USA

Lingyu Wang
George Mason University, USA

KLUWER ACADEMIC PUBLISHERS
BOSTON / DORDRECHT / LONDON

Distributors for North, Central and South America:
Kluwer Academic Publishers
101 Philip Drive
Assinippi Park
Norwell, Massachusetts 02061 USA
Telephone (781) 871-6600
Fax (781) 681-9045
E-Mail <kluwer@wkap.com>

Distributors for all other countries:
Kluwer Academic Publishers Group
Post Office Box 322
3300 AH Dordrecht, THE NETHERLANDS
Telephone 31 78 6576 000
Fax 31 78 6576 254
E-Mail <services@wkap.nl>

Electronic Services <http://www.wkap.nl>

Library of Congress Cataloging-in-Publication Data

A C.I.P. Catalogue record for this book is available from the Library of Congress.

Information Security Management, Education and Privacy
Edited by Yves Deswarte, Frédéric Cuppens, Sushil Jajodia, and Lingyu Wang
ISBN 1-4020-8144-8
ISBN 1-4020-8145-6 (eBook)

Printed on acid-free paper.
Printed in the United States of America.

Contents

Preface

This volume gathers the papers presented at three workshops that are embedded in the IFIP/Sec Conference in 2004, to enlighten specific topics that are currently particularly active in Security.

The first one is the 10th IFIP Annual Working Conference on Information Security Management. It is organized by the IFIP WG 11.1, which is itself dedicated to Information Security Management, i.e., not only to the practical implementation of new security technology issued from recent research and development, but also and mostly to the improvement of security practice in all organizations, from multinational corporations to small enterprises. Methods and techniques are developed to increase personal awareness and education in security, analyze and manage risks, identify security policies, evaluate and certify products, processes and systems. Matt Warren, from Deakin University, Australia, who is the current Chair of WG 11.1, acted as the Program Chair.

The second workshop is organized by the IFIP WG 11.8, dedicated to Information Security Education. This workshop is a follow-up of three issues of the World Conference on Information Security Education (WISE) that were also organized by WG 11.8. The first WISE was organized by Louise Yngstrom in 1999 in Stockholm, and the next one, WISE'4, will be held in Moscow, Russia, 18-20 May 2005. This year, the workshop is aimed at developing a first draft of an international doctorate program allowing a specialization in IT Security. The draft will be based upon both selected papers from individuals or groups (from academic, military and government organizations), and discussions at the workshop. This draft will be further refined and eventually published as an IFIP Report. The Program Committee was chaired by Helen Armstrong, from Curtin University, Australia, who is also the Chair of the IFIP WG 11.8.

Finally, the last workshop is the 3rd Working Conference on Privacy and Anonymity in Networked and Distributed Systems (I-NetSec04), organized by the IFIP WG 11.4 on Network Security. The purpose of the workshop is to bring together privacy and anonymity experts from around the world to discuss recent advances and new perspectives on these topics, that are increasingly important aspects in electronic services, especially in advanced distributed applications, such as m-commerce, agent-based systems, P2P, etc. The Program Committee was co-chaired by Bart De Decker, from the Catholic University of Leuven, Belgium, who is also chairing the IFIP WG 11.4, and by Els Van Herreweghen, from IBM Research Lab, Zurich, Switzerland.

The carefully selected papers gathered in this volume show the richness of the information security domain, as well as the liveliness of the working groups cooperating in the IFIP TC-11 on Security and Protection in Information Processing Systems.

Yves Deswarte
General Chair

10th IFIP WG 11.1 Annual Working Conference on Information Security Management Program Committees

Program Committee Chair
Matt Warren, Deakin University, Australia

Program Committee
William Hutchinson, Edith Cowan University, Australia
Steven Furnell, Plymouth University, UK
Jill Slay, University of South Australia, Australia
Craig Valli, Edith Cowan University, Australia
Rossouw von Solms, Port Elizabeth Technikon, South Africa

IFIP TC11 WG 11.8 Information Security Education Workshop Program Committees

Program Committee Chair
Helen Armstrong, Curtin University, Australia

Program Committee
Colin Armstrong, Curtin University, Australia
William Caelli, Queensland University of Technology, Australia
Steven Furnell, Plymouth University, UK
Simone Fischer-Hubner, Karlstad University, Sweden
William Hutchinson, Edith Cowan University, Australia
Cynthia Irvine, Naval Postgraduate School, Monterey, CA, USA
Sokratis Katsikas, University of the Aegean, Greece
Natalia Miloslavskaia, Moscow State Engineering Physics Institute, Russia
Gerard Quirchmayr, University of Vienna, Austria
Corey Schou, Idaho State University, USA
Jill Slay, University of South Australia, Australia
Matthew Warren, Deakin University, Australia
Louise Yngstrom, Stockholm University, Sweden

I-NetSec04 – 3rd Working Conference on Privacy and Anonymity in Networked and Distributed Systems
Program Committees

Program Committee Co-chairs
B. De Decker, K.U.Leuven, Belgium
E. Van Herreweghen, IBM Research Lab, Zurich, Switzerland

Program Committee
S. De Capitani, Univ. of Brescia, Italy
Y. Deswarte, LAAS-CNRS, Toulouse, France
H. Federrath, Univ. of Regensburg, Germany
S. Fischer-Hübner, Karlstad Univ., Sweden
U. Gattiker, EICAR, Aalborg Univ., Denmark
K. Martin, Royal Holloway, Univ. London, UK
R. Molva, Eurécom, France
K. Rannenberg, Goethe Univ. of Frankfurt, Germany
P. Ryan, Univ. of Newcastle, UK
P. Samarati, Univ. of Milan, Italy
V. Shmatikov, SRI International, USA

PART ONE

10TH IFIP WG 11.1 ANNUAL WORKING CONFERENCE ON INFORMATION SECURITY MANAGEMENT

CORPORATE INFORMATION SECURITY EDUCATION:

Is Outcomes Based Education the Solution?

Johan Van Niekerk [1] And Rossouw Von Solms [2]

Department of Business Information Systems, Port Elizabeth Technikon[1]; Department of Information Technology, Port Elizabeth Technikon[2]

Abstract: Today's global economy is increasingly dependent on the creation, management, and distribution of information resources. Information and its use permeate all aspects of modern society. Most modern organizations need information systems to survive and prosper. Information has become a valuable commodity and as such needs to be protected. This protection is typically implemented in the form of various security controls. In order for these controls to be effective, the users in the organization need to be educated regarding these controls. Recent studies have indicated that current user education programs fail to pay adequate attention to behavioral theories. This paper examines the educational principles an information security user education program should adhere to. It then introduces outcomes based education (OBE) and finally argues that OBE is ideally suited for the needs of information security.

Key words: Information Security, Information Security Culture, Outcomes Based Education, Awareness

1. INTRODUCTION

In today's business world, information is a valuable commodity and as such, needs to be protected. Information affects all aspects of today's businesses, from top management right down to the operational level (Turban, et al., 2002. pp 3-37). In order to avoid loss or damage to this valuable resource, companies need to be serious about protecting their information. This protection is typically implemented in the form of various security controls (Barnard & Von Solms, 2000). However, it is very difficult to know exactly which controls would be required in order to guarantee an acceptable minimum level of security. Furthermore, managing these controls to see that they are always up to date and implemented uniformly throughout the organization is a constant headache to organizations.

When selecting the controls to implement in an organization, it is important to refer to accepted international standards (Von Solms, 1999). There exist several internationally accepted standards and codes of practice to assist organizations in the implementation and management of an organizational information security strategy. Some of the better known examples would include the ISO/IEC 17799 (British Standards Institute (BSI), 1999) and ISO/IEC 13335 also known as GMITS (Guidelines to the Management of Information Technology Security (GMITS), 1995).

These standards and codes of practice provide organizations with guidelines specifying how the problem of managing information security should be approached (Von Solms, 1999). One of the primary controls identified by many of the major IT security standards published to date is the introduction of a corporate information security awareness program (BSI, 1999; GMITS, 1995). The purpose of such a program is to educate the users about information security or, more specifically, to educate users about the individual roles they should play in the effective execution and maintenance of these controls. Most security controls, whether physical, technical, managerial or administrative in nature, requires some form of human involvement. This paper will examine this dependence of information security on human involvement with specific emphasis on the role user education has to play in a corporate information security strategy. It will then propose outcomes based education (OBE) as a pedagogical methodology suitable for the information security education needs of organizations.

2. THE HUMAN SIDE OF INFORMATION SECURITY

Information security controls can generally be sub-divided into three categories: Physical controls, Technical controls and Operational controls (Thomson, 1998, p. 29). Physical controls deal with the physical aspects of security, for example; the lock on the door of an office containing sensitive documents. Technical controls are controls of a technical nature, usually software based, for example; forcing a user to authenticate with a unique username and password before allowing the user to access the operating system. The third category, operational controls, collectively including business-, administrative-, managerial-, and procedural controls, consist of all controls that deal with human behavior in one form or another. These controls would include those that deal with the creation of information security policies and procedures, and administration of other controls. Both physical and technical controls, even though they do not deal directly with operational issues, usually require some form of human involvement. In an organizational context, these controls would thus have to be supported by procedures outlining the employee's involvement in the use of these controls.

Employees, whether intentionally or through negligence, often due to a lack of knowledge, are the greatest threat to information security (Thomson, 1998, p. 12, Mitnick & Simon, 2002, p. 3). Operational controls rely on human behavior. This means that these controls are arguably some of the weakest links in information security. Unfortunately, both physical and technical controls rely to some extent on these operational controls for effectiveness. As an example, an operational control might state that a user leaving his/her office must logoff from the operating system and lock his/her office door. If a user were to ignore this procedure, both the technical control forcing authentication and the physical control of having a lock on the door would be rendered useless. Thus, anyone who thinks that security products, i.e. technical and physical controls, alone, offer true security is settling for the illusion of security (Mitnick & Simon, 2002, p. 4).

Siponen (2001) describes this tendency of organizations to settle for the illusion of security as a general human tendency to often blindly ignore complications in IT related issues. Without an adequate level of user co-operation and knowledge, many security techniques are liable to be misused or misinterpreted by users. This may result in even an adequate security measure becoming inadequate (Siponen, 2001) Organizations **cannot** protect the integrity, confidentiality, and availability of information in today's highly networked systems environment without ensuring that each person involved understands his/her roles and responsibilities and is adequately trained to perform them (National Institute of Standards and Technology (NIST), 1998, p. 3).

Teaching employees their roles and responsibilities relating to information security requires the investment of company resources in a user education program. However, budgetary requirements for security education and training are generally not a top priority for organizations (Nosworthy, 2000). Organizations often spend most their information security budget on technical controls and fail to realize that a successful information security management program requires a balance of technical and business controls (Nosworthy, 2000). Business controls in this sense refer to operational controls. According to Dhillon (1999), increasing awareness of security issues is the most cost-effective control that an organization can implement. However, in order to ensure that the maximum return on investment is gained, special care should be taken to ensure the success of the user education programs used. For **educational** programs this would mean ensuring adherence to proper pedagogical principles when these educational programs are compiled.

Most current user education programs fail to pay adequate attention to behavioral theories (Siponen, 2001). The emphasis of user education programs should be to build an organizational sub-culture of security awareness, by instilling the aspects of information security in every employee as a natural way of performing his or her daily job (Von Solms, 2000). Recent studies have indicated that the establishment of an information security "culture" in the organization is desirable for effective information security (Von Solms, 2000). Such a culture should support all business activities in such a way that information security becomes a natural aspect in the daily activities of every employee (Schlienger & Teufel, 2003). A detailed examination of how such a culture could be established in an organization falls outside the scope of this paper. Instead this paper will focus only on user education, one of the cornerstones required for the establishment of such a culture. For more information on the establishment of such a culture see e.g. (Van Niekerk & Von Solms, 2003; Schlienger & Teufel, 2003).

3. ELEMENTS OF INFORMATION SECURITY EDUCATION

The user education programs needed for information security purposes differ from traditional educational programs. Unlike traditional educational programs, these programs will primarily be aimed at teaching adults. Adults have well established, not formative, values, beliefs, and opinions (NIST, 1998, p. 20). The educational methodology used should thus be suitable for adult education. Furthermore, there are several other requirements specific to the role that such a program will play in the overall organization's information security efforts. In the following sections, this paper will suggest and attempt to motivate some of the features that should typically constitute such an information security education program.

3.1 Everyone should be able to "pass" the course.

Nosworthy (2000) states that each person in the organization from the CEO to House Keeping staff must be aware of, and trained to exercise their responsibilities towards information security. However in traditional educational models there are usually a percentage of the learners who do not pass the course, or in other words, successfully meet the assessment criteria. In order for an organization's information to be secure, everyone needs to not only be trained, but to "pass" the training. Unlike traditional education, failing an information security educational program cannot be accepted. Workers at every level, even those who do not use a computer, are liable to be targeted (Mitnick & Simon, 2002, p. 39). This means that having even a single person who does not know his/her information security responsibilities should be unacceptable.

3.2 Employees must know why information security is important and why a specific policy or control is in place.

Recent studies have suggested that current information security awareness programs are failing (Siponen, 2001). This failure is due to many reasons. Schlienger & Teufel (2003) have shown that even employees who know their responsibilities with regards to information security will still disobey security policy if they disagree with the policy. They suggest that the mere awareness of the policies and procedures is in fact not sufficient, the users also need to know why a specific policy or control is in place (Schlienger & Teufel, 2003). In information security, being taught why a specific policy or control is in place is generally considered to be a feature of education, and not of awareness (Schlienger & Teufel, 2003; NIST, 1998, pp. 16-17). Information security "education" is generally sub-divided into three levels, namely; awareness, training and education. Awareness simply focuses attention on information security. Training is more interactive and tries to instill the necessary skills and competencies. Education integrates all of the security skills and competencies of the various functional specialties into a common body of knowledge and adds a multi-disciplinary study of concepts, issues, and principles (NIST, 1998, pp. 15-16). A feature of the educational level is that the user must understand why information security is important (Schlienger & Teufel, 2003; NIST, 1998, pp. 16-17). Obviously end-users do not require the same level of understanding as information security professionals (NIST, 1998, p. 14). You don't need to understand why procedures are in place or how the technologies work to use them effectively (Tripathy, 2000; NIST 1998, p. 15). However, in information security, if a user asks why, it should always be explained (Tripathy, 2000).

3.3 Learning materials should be customized to the needs of individual learners.

In an organizational context, users of information exist at several levels. There are essentially three categories of users that need to be educated in information security awareness namely: The End User, IT Personnel and Top Management (Thompson, 1998). The National Institute for Science and Technology (NIST) expands on this classification by stating that training and education are to be provided selectively, based on individual responsibilities and needs. Specifically, training is to be provided to individuals based on their particular job functions (NIST, 1998, p. 43). The ISO/IEC 17799 states that the information security policy should be communicated throughout the organization to users in a form that is relevant, accessible and understandable to the intended reader (BSI, 1999, p. 3). According to NIST, individuals learn in several ways, but each person, as part of his/her personality, has a preferred or primary learning style. Instruction can positively, or negatively, affect a student's performance, depending on whether it is matched, or mismatched, with a student's preferred learning style (NIST, 1998, p. 19). Thus, what should be taught to a specific individual user and how it should be taught, will depend on both the user's preferred learning style, and the specific role that user plays within the organization.

3.4 Users should be responsible for their own learning.

In today's organizations it is crucial to maximize return on investment. Through its very nature classroom training requires the availability of highly trained specialists to present the courses. It also requires that the learners take time off from their regular duties to attend classes. These factors make classroom training very expensive. One of the most cost-effective substitutes for traditional classroom training is to provide employees with intranet-based instruction (O'Brien, 1999, p.361). Such web-based instructional programs require individual learners to be responsible for their own acquisition of knowledge instead of being passive receptors in the process (ITiCSE Working Group on the Web and Distance Learning, 1997). Self-driven learning also enables organizations to make learning material available in a variety of formats. This is turn means users will have a choice of how they are taught, which has already been shown to be a necessary feature of information security education.

3.5 Users should be held accountable for their studies.

Most information security standards make it clear that users should be held accountable for their information security **responsibilities** (BSI, 1999, pp. 8-10). These responsibilities are normally spelt out in the organization's information security policies and procedures. In an organization, policies function in a similar fashion to laws. For laws, ignorance is not a valid defense. However ignorance of policy **is** an acceptable defense (Whitman & Mattord, 2003, p. 93). Thus, to be able to hold employees accountable for their **actions**, the organization should have proof, normally in the form of a signed form, that the employees have been educated regarding their responsibilities and that they understand and accept these responsibilities as laid out in the policies (Whitman & Mattord, 2003, p. 93). Wood (1997) suggests that all employees should be required, on an annual basis, to sign a statement saying that they have read and understood the information security policy manual. It should thus be clear that self-driven learning for information security purposes, as discussed previously, could only be used if the employees are also held accountable for their learning. Otherwise the organization could not legally hold the employees accountable for their actions.

Many organizations have realized that their own employees are the biggest threat to their information systems (Von Solms, 2000). However, through the establishment of a culture of information security, users can become a security asset instead of being a threat (Von Solms, 2000). Education of employees plays a very important role in the establishment of such a culture. It is paramount that the people are educated to want to be more secure in their day to day operation (Nosworthy, 2000). Such a change of attitude is of utmost importance, because a change in attitude automatically leads to a subsequent behavioral change (Nosworthy, 2000). The employees can then become the organization's most valuable assets. Current programs used to educate employees, fails to pay sufficient attention to aspects related to the behavioral sciences (Siponen, 2001).

It would make sense to adhere to a formal educational methodology when constructing such educational programs. The methodology used should be suitable for the specific needs of an information security user education program. Since the aim of the user education program is not to prepare the users for further levels of formal education, but rather to help them achi information security know-how for use in their everyday jobs, the educational methodology used should be chosen accordingly. Outcomes Based Education (OBE) is an educational methodology that might in fact be ideally suited for use in such programs. The aim of OBE is to help learners achieve a specific outcome, in this case information security awareness and know-how.

4. OUTCOMES BASED EDUCATION

OBE is defined as an approach to teaching and learning which stresses the need to be clear about what learners are expected to achieve. The educator states beforehand what "outcome" is expected of the learners. The role of the educator is then to help the learners achieve that outcome (Siebörger, 1998).

Outcomes can be defined as either cross-curriculum (general outcomes) or specific outcomes. A cross-curriculum outcome can be seen as the desired effect that attaining a specific competency should have within the general environment within which the learner operates. A specific outcome is one that directly demonstrates the mastery of the appropriate skill that the learner should gain from the OBE program.

For each outcome an assessment standard should be defined. These standards are necessary in order to provide feedback to the learners. According to Siebörger (1998) assessment is essential to OBE to measure the degree to which a learner has achieved an outcome. In fact being able to assess progress and provide feedback to the learner is a prerequisite for any educational program to be successful. Fingar (1996) states that feedback, specifically in the form of knowledge regarding the outcomes of the learners' actions, is required for learning to take place. Furthermore this feedback should be continuous and constructive (Department Of Education (DOE), 2001).

The educational process in general can be viewed as a system of teaching and learning activities that are tied together via various feedback loops. It also includes other functions such as assessment, admission, quality assurance, direction and support (Tait, 1997). All of these components can, and should, play a role in the creation of an effective information security education program. OBE can be viewed in three different ways: as a theory of education, a systematic structure for education, or the creation of educational material, and lastly as a classroom practice (Killen, 2000). OBE can thus be seen as a complete educational system, which contains all the components such a system should have.

According to Killen (2000), OBE is based upon three basic premises, namely:

1. All students can learn and succeed, but not all in the same time or in the same way.
2. Successful learning promotes even more successful learning.
3. Schools (and teachers) control the conditions that determine whether or not students are successful at learning.

From these basic premises four essential principles of OBE were developed (Killen, 2000). They are:

1. Clarity of focus, which means that all teaching activities must be clearly focused on the desired outcome that the learners should achieve.
2. Designing back, which means that the starting point for an OBE program's design should be a clear definition of the desired results. The rest of the curriculum should be designed according to this desired outcome.
3. High expectations for all students. OBE not only assumes that everyone can attain the desired outcomes, it also requires that high standards should be set. This is based on evidence that learners are more likely to attain high standards when they are challenged by what is expected from them.
4. Expanded opportunities for all learners. This final principle of OBE is based on the idea that not everyone learns the same way or at the same pace. Thus, in OBE, learners are given many opportunities for learning. Achieving the desired outcome is deemed more important than how that outcome was reached.

In order for an educational program to be classified as being outcomes based, it has to adhere to all four of these principles.

5. OUTCOMES BASED EDUCATION FOR INFORMATION SECURITY

Up to this point this paper has shown the requirements an educational methodology would have to meet in order for it to be suitable for information security education. It has also introduced OBE and briefly outlined the basic premises and the principles of this educational methodology. It will now attempt to show that OBE is in fact well suited to the needs of information security.

The first requirement listed for information security education was that everyone should be able to "pass" the course. Clearly OBE fulfils this requirement since the first premise upon which OBE is based is the assumption that all students can succeed and learn.

Secondly, for information security education to be successful, employees must know why information security is important and why a specific policy or control is in place. Course developers should be aware that adults have well-established values, beliefs, and opinions. Adults relate new information and knowledge to previously learned information, experiences, and values which might result in misunderstanding (NIST, 1998, p. 20). It is even possible that they understand correctly but still don't adhere to a security policy because it conflicts with their beliefs and values (Schlienger & Teufel, 2003). One of the fundamental differences between OBE and traditional educational models is the fact that rote learning is completely unacceptable in OBE. OBE requires the learner to identify and solve problems in which responses display that responsible decisions using critical and creative thinking have been made (Olivier, 1998; Pretorius, 1998). This type of thinking requires not only knowledge but also insight. Insight requires the learner to know why they are doing something (NIST, 1998, p. 18). According to Killen (2000) each outcome based educational program must have a rationale to explain why the program exists.

The third requirement of information security education identified was that learning materials should be customized to the needs of individual learners. The first basic premise of OBE not only states that all students can learn and succeed, but it also states that all students cannot necessarily do this in the same time or in the same way. This premise is also expanded on in the fourth principle of OBE, which states that learners should be given many opportunities for learning. OBE thus recognizes that individuals learn in different ways and at different paces. For a program to be truly outcomes based it is vital that learning materials are provided in as customized a format as possible for individual learners. However, according to Killen (2000) the practical difficulties of providing expanded opportunities must be weighed against the long-term benefits of enabling all learners to be successful.

The fourth and fifth suggested requirements of information security education state that users should be both responsible and accountable for their own learning. In other words, the users should take ownership of their own learning. Ownership of their learning and self-driven learning are central concepts to OBE. Because OBE recognizes that different students will learn at a different pace, OBE encourages self-driven learning. The ability to effectively manage one's own time, and learning abilities, are one of the critical cross curriculum outcomes identified for all South African students (South African Qualification Authority (SAQA), 2000). The OBE model strives to move away from teacher centeredness, towards learner-centered education (Malan, 2000). Thus, responsibility for their own studies can be seen to be central to OBE. Hand in hand with responsibility is accountability. OBE places major emphasis on assessment as a tool to provide feedback on progress to the learner, and as a tool for measuring whether the desired outcomes have been reached (Killen, 2000; Malan, 2000). Assessment makes students accountable for their studies.

The following is a brief summary of the relationships between OBE and information security education concluded thus far:

1. In terms of an organization's overall information security effort it is vital for all users to ultimately pass the information security course. OBE requires a high expectation for all learners to do well, and additionally requires that learners be given multiple opportunities to prove that they have achieved the desired outcomes.
2. Employees should be told why a specific information security policy, or control, that applies to them, is in place. In OBE memorization of concepts is not sufficient, OBE requires learners to have insight and thus to understand why they are doing something.
3. Due to the different levels of prior education, different organizational roles and different individual preferences of employees in an organization, learning materials used in an organization should be customized to the needs of individual learners. Recognizing that individuals learn in different ways and at different paces are concepts central to OBE. Flexible learning material, to suit individual needs, is a pre-requisite in an outcomes based program.
4. In order to control costs, and to provide the above-mentioned flexibility in learning materials, organizational learners should be responsible for their own learning. The organization should supply the learning materials in formats that support as many learning styles as possible, but responsibility for using those materials should ultimately rest with the individual employees. Employees should thus take ownership of their learning. This concept of ownership and self-driven learning are central to OBE, which is essentially a learner centered educational methodology

5. Hand-in-hand with ownership and responsibility is accountability. Organizations need to make employees accountable for their own learning, otherwise, they would not be able to hold them accountable for negligence stemming from a lack of education. In OBE, and other educational methodologies, assessment plays a vital role. Learners must be held accountable for their learning in order to get them to accept ownership of their learning.

OBE can thus be seen to match all of the requirements for information security education identified by this paper. In fact, a closer examination of the "results-based" educational framework advocated by NIST (1998) for information security programs will reveal many elements that are common to OBE as well. For example, NIST argues that information security education programs should be "results-based" and should focus on job functions, or roles and responsibilities specific to individuals (NIST, 1998, p. iii). OBE aims to help learners achieve a specific outcome or attain a specific skill. These outcomes should reflect the complexities of the real life and the roles the learners would have to fulfill (Killen, 2000). In an organizational context this would mean that the outcomes would have to reflect skills needed in the individual's day-to-day job functions. Several other such similarities exist, but a detailed examination of these falls outside the scope of this paper. Instead, the contextual role of OBE in the establishment of a corporate culture of information security will be briefly examined.

According to Van Niekerk and Von Solms (2003), establishing a corporate culture will have to start with top management, who has to show commitment to information security via vision statements, policies and their own behavior. Secondly, a user education program should be constructed to educate the users about these policies and the behavior expected from them. Thirdly, middle management will have to positively reinforce any learning that took place by giving continuous feedback to the users. This feedback could take the form of performance metrics, e.g. key performance indicators, for individual employees. Ultimately, it will be this continuous reinforcement by middle management that produces the change in behavior.

If OBE is to be used in this process, the cross-curriculum outcomes and measurables for these outcomes would have to be clearly defined. The programs to teach employees the necessary skills to attain these outcomes would then have to be drawn up and made available in a variety of learning formats. These could for example include a set of online tutorials, security manuals, videos or even lunch-hour workshops. This will ensure that each user has a choice in terms of *how* they learn, which satisfies the third requirement as outlined previously. Part of these programs would have to discuss the possible consequences to both the individual and the organization as a whole, should an employee fail to comply to the taught procedures. This will satisfy the requirement that user should know why they are taught a skill.

Finally, to ensure that the users take ownership of their own learning, and to hold them accountable for their own learning, compliance metrics should be gathered. These metrics could then be used as part of individual user's key performance indicators. This can fulfill the role of the continuous feedback from middle management that is required to change behavior. These metrics could be gathered per department, branch, etc. and can then also be made part of the key performance indicators for the appropriate middle level manager. The old adage that what you measure is what you get will then play its part by ensuring that the appropriate line managers will feed this statistics back to their staff since it impacts on their own performance evaluations. Since the learning material should always be available and the employees are measured against their compliance, eventually all the users should reach a level of compliance that indicates they have "passed" the course. It should thus be very possible to integrate all the requirements of information security education, as identified in this paper, into the process aimed at introducing a change in the organizational culture, as outlined by Van Niekerk and Von Solms (2003).

6. CONCLUSION

Humans today live in an emerging global information society, with a global economy that is increasingly dependent on the creation, management, and distribution of information resources. Information and its use permeate all aspects of modern society. Today, most organizations need information systems to survive and prosper. It is therefore imperative that modern organizations, operating in this global information society, take the protection of their information resources seriously.

This paper has pointed out that this protection of information resources are to a large extent dependent on human co-operated behavior. It also pointed out that this dependence on human behavior makes it necessary to have a user education program to educate users regarding their roles and responsibilities towards information security. This paper proposed several "elements", or properties such an information security education program should have in order for it to suit the needs of modern organizations. These included:

- Everyone should be able to "pass" the course.
- Employees must know why information security is important and why a specific policy or control is in place.
- Learning materials should be customized to the needs of individual learners.
- Users should be responsible for their own learning.
- Users should be held accountable for their studies.

Each of these proposed elements were argued in earlier sections of this paper.

The same elements were shown to be present in OBE, an existing pedagogical methodology. The possible role of OBE in the context of attempting to change organizational culture, were also briefly examined. This paper argued that OBE could be seen to be an excellent fit for the needs of information security education and is definitely **a** solution to these needs. It has been suggested that information security, because it depends on human behavior, should look at the human sciences when attempting to solve problems relating to the roles humans play in information security. This paper aims to reinforce that suggestion. Educationalists spend many years developing models such as outcomes based education (OBE). These models have been extensively tested and critically examined in the literature. It is the contention of this paper that instead of "re-inventing the wheel" when designing user education programs, information security practitioners should "borrow" methodologies, like OBE, from the educational sciences. Future researchers who wish to solve information security education problems should be basing their work on sound pedagogical models.

REFERENCES

Barnard, L., Von Solms, R. (2000). A Formalized Approach to the Effective Selection and Evaluation of Information Security Controls. Computers and Security, 19(2): pp. 185-194.

British Standards Institute (BSI) (1999), BS 7799 Part 1: Code of Practice for Information Security Management (CoP), BSI, UK.

Dhillon, G. (1999) Managing and controlling computer misuse, Information Management & Computer Security, 7 (4), pp. 171-175.

Department of Education (DOE). (2001) Draft Revised National Curriculum Statement: Technology Learning Area. Department of Education. Available at:
http://education.pwv.gov.za/DoE_Sites/Curriculum/New_2005/draft_revised_national_curriculu.htm

Fingar, P. (1996). The blueprint for business objects. New York, New York : SIGS Books & Multimedia

Guidelines to the Management of Information Technology Security (GMITS). (1995). Part 1, ISO/IEC, JTC 1, SC27, WG 1.

ITiCSE Working Group on the Web and Distance Learning (1997). The Web and distance learning:what is appropriate and what is not. ITiCSE'97 Working Group Reports and Supplemental Proceedings, pp. 27-37.

Killen, R. (2000). Outcomes-Based education: Principles and Possibilities. Unpublished manuscript, University of Newcastle, Faculty of Education. [WWW document]. URL http://www.schools.nt.edu.au/curricbr/cf/outcomefocus/killen_paper.pdf. Sited 20 August 2003.

Laudon, K. C., Laudon, J. P. (2002). Management Information Systems: Managing the Digital Firm (7th ed). New Jersey, USA: Prentice Hall.

Malan, S.P.T. (2000) The 'new paradigm' of outcomes-based education in perspective. Tydskrif vir Gesinsekologie en Verbruikerswetenskappe (28), South Africa.

Martins, A., Eloff, J.H.P. (2002) Assessing Information Security Culture. ISSA 2002, Muldersdrift, South Africa, 10-12 July 2002.

Mitnick, K.D., Simon, W.L. (2002) The art of deception: Controlling the human element of security. United States of America : Wiley Publishing, Inc.

National Institute of Standards and Technology (NIST). (1998). Information Technology Security Training Requirements: A Role- and Performance-Based Model. NIST Special Publication 800-16. U.S. Government Printing Office, Washington.

Nosworthy, J. D. (2000) Implementing Information Security In the 21st Century – Do You Have the Balancing Factors? Computer & Security (19), pp. 337- 347. Elsevier Science Ltd.

O'Brien, J. A. (1999) Management Information Systems: Managing Information Technology in the Internetworked Enterprise (4th ed.). United States of America : Irwin/McGraw-Hill.

Olivier, C. (1998), Educate and Train : Outcomes-Based. Pretoria, South Africa. J.L. van Schaik.

Pretorius, F. (1998). Outcomes-based Education in South Africa. Randburg, South Africa: Hodder and Stoughton Educational.

South African Qualifications Authority (SAQA) (2000). The National Qualifications Framework and Curriculum Development. Retrieved on 10 September 2003 from URL http://www.saqa.org.za

Schlienger, T., Teufel, S. (2003) Information Security Culture – From Analysis to Change. Proceedings of the 3rd Annual Information Security South Africa Conference, 9-11 July 2003, Sandton, South Africa, pp. 183-196.

Siebörger, R. (1998). Transforming Assessment: A guide for South African teachers. Cape Town, RSA : JUTA.

Siponen, M.T. (2001). Five Dimensions of Information Security Awareness. Computers and Society, June 2001. Pp. 24-29.

Tait, B. (1997). Object Orientation in educational software. Innovations in Education and Training International, 34 (3). Pp. 167-173.

Thomson, M. (1998). The development of an effective information security awareness program for use in an organization. Unpublished master's thesis. Port Elizabeth Technikon, Port Elizabeth, South Africa.

Tripathi, A. (2000) Education in Information Security. IEEE Concurrency, October-December 2000, pp. 4-8.

Turban, E., Mclean, E., Wetherbe, J. (2002). Information technology for management: Transforming business in the digital economy (3rd Ed).United States of America. John Wiley & Sons, inc.

Van Niekerk, J., Von Solms, R. (2003). Establishing an Information Security Culture in Organisations: An Outcomes Based Education Approach. Proceedings of the 3rd Annual Information Security South Africa Conference, 9-11 July 2003, Sandton, South Africa, pp. 3-12.

Von Solms, B. (2000) Information Security – The Third Wave? Computers & Security, 19 (7), pp. 615-620.

Von Solms, R. (1999) Information Security Management: why standards are important. Information Management & Computer Security, 7 (1), pp. 50-57.

Whitman, M. E., Mattord, H. J. (2003) Principles of Information Security. Canada: Thomson Course Technology.

Wood, C.C. (1997) Policies alone do not constitute a sufficient awareness effort. Computer Fraud & Security, December 1997, pp. 14-19.

ACKNOWLEDGEMENTS

The financial assistance of the National Research Foundation (NRF) towards this research is hereby acknowledged. Opinions expressed and conclusions arrived at, are those of the author and are not necessarily to be attributed to the National Research Foundation.

TOWARDS CORPORATE INFORMATION SECURITY OBEDIENCE

Kerry-Lynn Thomson and Rossouw von Solms
Port Elizabeth Technikon, South Africa
{kthomson; rossouw}@petech.ac.za

Abstract: All organisations possess a corporate culture, whether they are aware of it or not. This culture determines, to a large extent, the effectiveness of an organisation and the behaviour of employees within an organisation. As part of its corporate governance duties, senior management is responsible for the protection of the assets of its organisation. And as information is a vital asset to most organisations, senior management is ultimately responsible for the protection of information assets. An ideal corporate culture, in terms of information security, would be one where the second-nature behaviour of employees, determined by the culture, is to protect information assets. This paper will provide initial guidelines as to how to establish this culture by examining Schein's model and by investigating how to start implementing Corporate Information Security Obedience.

Key words: Information Security; Corporate Governance; Corporate Culture; Goal Consensus; Corporate Information Security Obedience.

1. INTRODUCTION

Information is a vital asset and it is often described as the lifeblood of organisations (Gordon, 2002, online). It is, however, difficult to measure the exact value of the information that an organisation possesses. Still, it is evident that any breach in the confidentiality, integrity or availability of information could result in devastating consequences for an organisation (Gordon and Glickson LLC, 2001, online). Information security practices, together with other physical and technological means, therefore, need to be implemented and managed within the organisation to ensure that the information is kept safe and secure (Krige, 1999, p 7).

As information is a fundamental organisational asset, its security must be integrated into the organisation's overall management plan (Lane, 1985, pp 2-3; Smith, 1989, p 193). This plan should be guided by good corporate governance practices. Corporate governance is one of the significant issues in business at present. Corporate governance is there to endorse the competent use of resources and to involve accountability for the management of those resources (Gaines, 2002, online; World Bank Group, 1999, online).

Senior management, as part of its corporate governance duties, should encourage employees to adhere to the behaviour specified by senior management to contribute towards a successful organisation. Senior management should preferably not autocratically enforce this behaviour, but encourage it as naturally as possible, resulting in the correct behaviour becoming part of the corporate culture. Corporate culture is the outcome of all the collective, taken-for-granted assumptions that a group has learned throughout history. It is the residue of success (Schein, 1999, p 29).

The purpose of this paper is to detail the ideal corporate culture that should exist for it to be effective in protecting information. The paper initially investigates the role senior management should play in protecting information assets and how the creation and execution of the Corporate Information Security Policy could play a part in cultivating an information security conscious culture. The emphasis of this paper is to start investigating how to implement Corporate Information Security Obedience through expanding Schein's model of corporate culture into a two-dimensional model representing both management and employee dimensions.

2. MANAGING AN ORGANISATION

Corporate governance is extremely important for managing the operation of organisations. Senior management, through effective corporate governance practices, must lead its organisation through 'direction giving' and strategy implementation (Planting, 2001, online). In order to implement this management strategy, the King Report recommends that four central pillars of corporate governance are visible in an organisation, namely; accountability, responsibility, fairness and transparency (2001, p 17).

Accountability provides assurance that individuals and groups in an organisation are accountable for the decisions and actions that they take (King Report, 2001, p 14). The pillar of *responsibility* indicates that corrective action should be taken against negligence and misconduct (King Report, 2001, p 14). The third pillar, *fairness*, attempts to ensure that there is a balance in an organisation, in terms of the recognition various parties should receive. The final pillar, *transparency*, is the measure of how effective management is at making necessary information available in an open, precise and timely manner (King Report, 2001, pp. 13-14). These four pillars contribute to the overall goal of proper corporate governance.

Through effective corporate governance, senior management is accountable and responsible for the wellbeing of its organisation and must ensure that the assets of its organisation are well protected. One such asset is information, and, therefore, it is the responsibility of senior management to protect the information assets of its organisation (King Report, 2001, p 17; Deloitte & Touche, 2002, online). Another responsibility of senior management is to cultivate and shape the corporate culture of its organisation.

3. CORPORATE CULTURE

Organisations develop cultures whether they want to or not. The culture of an organisation operates at both a conscious and unconscious level and if management does not understand the culture in its organisation, it could prove to be fatal in today's business world (Hagberg Consulting Group, 2002, online). Edgar H. Schein defines three levels of culture.

3.1 The three levels of corporate culture

One of the problems when trying to understand culture is to oversimplify this complex field. Culture exists at several levels, which range from the very visible to the tacit and invisible. Furthermore, it is imperative that these levels are managed and understood (Schein, 1999, p 15).

The first level of corporate culture is the *Artifacts Level*. This is probably the easiest level to observe as it consists of the visible behaviour of individuals (Hagberg Consulting Group, 2002, online; Schein, 1999, p 15). At this level, it is still not clear as to why employees of an organisation behave in this way and why each organisation is constructed as it is (Schein, 1999, p 16). This leads to an investigation of the second level of culture. The *Espoused Values Level* of corporate culture is the level where the values an organisation is promoting are outlined in the organisation's policies (Schein, 1999, p 17).

There could be a few noticeable inconsistencies between some of the *Espoused Values* or goals of an organisation and the visible behaviour of individuals as seen at the *Artifacts Level*. These inconsistencies indicate that a deeper level of thought is driving the obvious behaviour of the employees (Schein, 1999, p 18). To truly understand the visible behaviour and culture of an organisation, the *Shared Tacit Assumptions Level* of culture must be understood (Schein, 1999, pp 18-19).

This *Shared Tacit Assumptions Level* represents the core of corporate culture. This core is the mutually learned beliefs and assumptions that become taken for granted as the organisation continues to be successful. The beliefs and values found at this level are second-nature to employees and influence the decisions and actions that they take (Schein, 1999, p 21). The corporate culture of an organisation should assist senior management in enforcing and ensuring good information security practices. Together with corporate culture, good corporate governance practices are essential for successful information security.

4. INFORMATION SECURITY AND CORPORATE GOVERNANCE

Information security transcends many facets of an organisation and is one of the most significant policy and structure decisions in an organisation (Spafford, 1998, online). It is becoming progressively more obvious that access to correct information at the right time is imperative to gaining competitive advantage or simply remaining in business (PriceWaterhouseCoopers, 2002, p 1). Policies and procedures are the responsibility of senior management as part of their corporate governance duties. Therefore, it follows that senior management should be responsible for setting strategic direction regarding the protection of information. One of the ways for management to express its commitment to information security in its organisation is to provide support towards a documented Corporate Information Security Policy, as it is one of the controls considered common best practice in terms of information security (BS 7799-1, 1999, p 4).

5. CORPORATE INFORMATION SECURITY POLICY

The Corporate Information Security Policy is a direction-giving document and should define the objectives and boundaries of the information security program. The main aim of any policy is to influence and determine decisions, actions and other issues, by specifying what behaviour is acceptable and what behaviour is unacceptable. The behaviour and actions of employees often represents the weakest link in the information security process (Martins & Eloff, 2002, p 203). Policies and procedures are, therefore, organisational laws that determine acceptable and unacceptable conduct within the context of corporate culture (Whitman & Mattord, 2003, p 194). Additionally, it should indicate management's commitment and support for information security and should describe the role that the policy plays in reaching the organisation's vision (Höne, 2003, CD-ROM; BS 7799-1, 1999, p 5). The correct behaviour, as envisioned in the Corporate Information Security Policy, should become second-nature to employees and the corporate culture should adapt to reflect this.

6. THE NEED TO CHANGE THE CORPORATE CULTURE

The acceptable actions and behaviour of employees towards information as outlined in the Corporate Information Security Policy should become the behaviour that employees demonstrate in their daily activities. Physical and technical controls are tangible controls that attempt to enforce compliance with information security practices and procedures in an organisation, but it is really operational controls and the resulting behaviour and actions of the employees and the processes they use that can sustain information security practices (Deloitte & Touche, 2002, online). As seen previously, the corporate culture of an organisation largely determines the behaviour of employees. Therefore, for the acceptable behaviour to become the *de facto* behaviour of employees, the corporate culture must be changed.

Apprehension arises when there is the prospect of a big change in the environment that employees know so well (Drennan, 1992, p 9). The power to change corporate culture lies principally in the hands of senior management and transforming the culture takes vision, commitment and determination. Without this combination it will not happen, and it certainly will not last (Drennan, 1992, p 3-4). Employees of an organisation may be coerced into changing their obvious behaviour, but this behavioural change will not become established until the deepest level of culture, the *Shared Tacit Assumptions Level*, experiences a transformation (Schein, 1999, p 26).

A new corporate culture cannot simply be 'created'. Senior management can demand or encourage a new way of working and thinking, management can monitor the changes to make sure that they are done, but employees of the organisation will not internalise the changes and make it part of the new culture unless they understand the benefit of these changes. It is senior management's responsibility to highlight that the changes needed in the current culture are worthwhile and important (Schein, 1999, p 187). Senior management, through effective corporate governance practices, must ensure that the policies of the organisation are in line with the vision for the organisation. Senior management should then enforce these policies so that they become part of the way things are done in the organisation and ensure that employees understand the benefits to their organisation. However, it is not enough for senior management to only enforce its policies - it is important for the attitudes of senior management to encourage this change in the corporate culture. If nothing changes in the procedures of the organisation or the attitudes of its management, employee attitudes will not change either (Drennan, 1992, p 3).

7. ORGANISATIONAL ENVIRONMENTS

There are three key environments that could exist in organisations. These environments dictate how the organisation is run and how employees react in certain circumstances. These environments are Coercive, Utilitarian and Goal Consensus (Schein, 1992, online).

The Coercive Environment is one where employees feel alienated in their environment and seek to leave this environment if possible. Peer relationships in this environment develop in defence of the authority in the organisation, in other words, senior management. These employees perform tasks because they must, rather than because they agree with the actions and decisions of senior management (Schein, 1992, online). The Utilitarian Environment is one where employees participate in their organisation by evolving workgroups based on an incentive system. In this environment employees will do as senior management wishes because of the rewards that they will receive. They still do not necessarily agree with senior management (Schein, 1992, online).

Figure 1 illustrates the Coercive and Utilitarian Environments mapped onto Schein's model of corporate culture. It shows that, in the Coercive and

Utilitarian Environments, the *Artifacts Level* of both management and employees are in concurrence with one another. In the Coercive Environment this indicates that there is stringent management control and employees adhere to the behaviour specified by management, or else harsh corrective action will be taken against them. In the Utilitarian Environment this concurrence indicates that employees will do as management wishes in return for a reward. As indicated in the Figure, the *Shared Tacit Assumptions Level* in both environments is not in line at all – the beliefs and values of management and employees are not the same. Without either strict management or incentives, the correct behaviour of employees would fade.

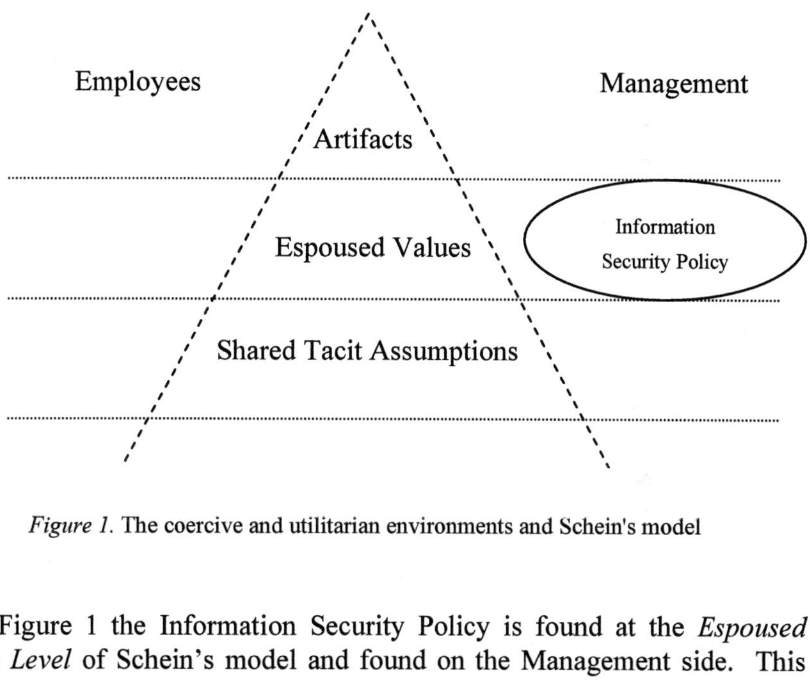

Figure 1. The coercive and utilitarian environments and Schein's model

In Figure 1 the Information Security Policy is found at the *Espoused Values Level* of Schein's model and found on the Management side. This indicates that the contents of the policy are in agreement with what management wishes, but not at all in line with the beliefs and values of the employees. It is vital that employees are in agreement with their work policies, as it is indicated that productivity and performance will increase by 30% to 40% if employees are satisfied with the policies (Schafer, 2003, online). Consequently, employees should be satisfied with the Corporate Information Security Policy. If the Information Security Policy is not discussed, supported and evaluated by management and employees, the Policy may remain a 'piece of paper' (Canadian Labour Program, 2003, online).

The third organisational environment, the Goal Consensus Environment, is one where employees are morally involved with the organisation. They identify with the organisation and share the same beliefs and values of senior management and they are striving towards the vision of senior management. In this environment, employees' actions are not as a result of being forced to do so or because of a reward, but because they are in agreement with the way things are done in the organisation (Schein, 1992, online). This Goal Consensus Environment could be seen as a corporate culture which is in line with the vision of senior management. This would mean that 'right' decisions and actions of employees become second-nature and part of their culture (Schein, 1999, p 15-17).

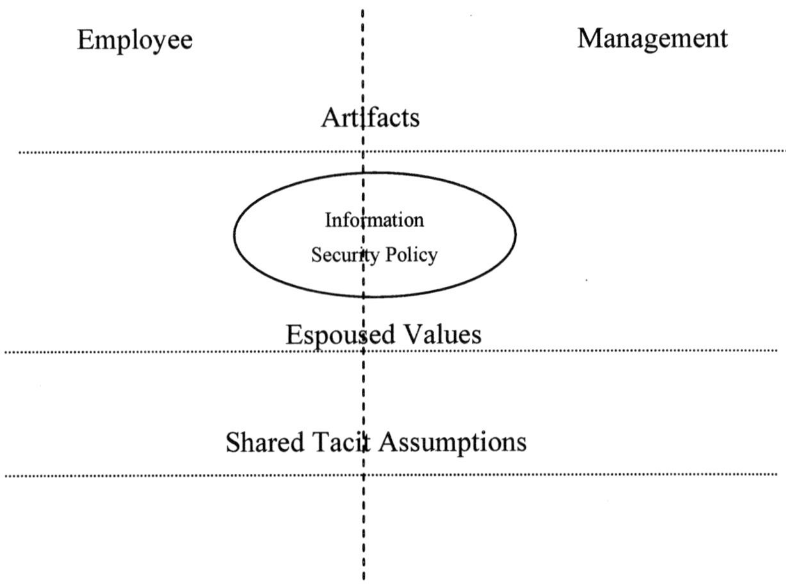

Figure 2. The goal consensus environment and Schein's model

Figure 2 illustrates that in the Goal Consensus Environment, all three levels of corporate culture in Schein's model are in agreement. This is an ideal corporate culture, in terms of information security, as the information security vision expressed at the *Espoused Values Level* by senior management is supported by the actions and behaviour of employees at the *Artifacts Level*. This level is determined by the *Shared Tacit Assumptions Level* of corporate culture. In the Figure, the Corporate Information Security Policy is found at the intersection of management and employees. This indicates that the beliefs and values of the employees are in agreement with senior management's vision for information security. This would indicate that Corporate Information Security Obedience has been implemented in this organisational environment (Thomson & von Solms, 2003, p 107).

8. IMPLEMENTING CORPORATE INFORMATION SECURITY OBEDIENCE

As seen previously, corporate culture is the residue of success. In other words, it is the set of procedures that senior management and employees of an organisation follow in order to be successful. For information security practices to be successful, it is important for Corporate Information Security Obedience to be implemented in an organisation.

By implementing Information Security Obedience, the *de facto* behaviour of employees towards information security should be the correct behaviour outlined in the Information Security Policy. In order to do this, the *Espoused Values* and *Shared Tacit Assumptions Level* of Schein's model must be addressed. Senior management must have a very clear vision as to what correct behaviour is in terms of information security. Management should then analyse its current corporate culture and identify the cultural elements that need to change (Spotlight, 2002, online). The *Espoused Values Level* is where the organisational policies, including the Corporate Information Security Policy, of an organisation are created by senior management. In order for Information Security Obedience to be implemented, the Information Security Policy contents must be drafted and communicated in a way that is acceptable in terms of the employees' beliefs and values. One way to do this is to involve employees in decision-making processes, taking into account employee welfare. If employees do not agree with the Corporate Information Security Policy or do not understand the benefits of the change in behaviour they will not adhere to the correct behaviour (Goal/QPC, 2003, online).

Correct behaviour should be encouraged and displayed by senior management, which will, to a large extent, shape the corporate culture (Hagberg Consulting Group, 2002, online). If this new, correct behaviour is an improvement on the current behaviour it should begin to influence the beliefs and values of employees found at the *Shared Tacit Assumptions Level*. This in turn should begin to shape the corporate culture (Schein, 1999, p 23). This would mean that the *Espoused Values Level* and the associated Information Security Policy is in line with the *Shared Tacit Assumptions Level* of employees and Corporate Information Security Obedience has been achieved.

9. CONCLUSION

Information is a vital asset in most organisations and as such should be well protected through effective information security practices. One of the problems facing the protection of information is the actions and behaviour of the employees in an organisation. If correct information security practices could become second-nature to employees and part of the way they conduct their daily activities, it would, to a large extent, eliminate this problem. This would assist in the creation of an environment of Corporate Information Security Obedience, where the information security procedures outlined by senior management in the Corporate Information Security Policy is the behaviour displayed by employees.

In order to implement Information Security Obedience the beliefs and values of employees, in terms of information security, must be addressed at the root level of *Shared Tacit Assumptions*. This level must be aligned with the contents of the Corporate Information Security Policy found at the *Espoused Values Level.* If these two levels are in concurrence with one another, it will mean that the information security practices employed by employees is the same as the correct information security practices outlined at the *Espoused Values Level.* This paper has outlined the reason that Corporate Information Security Obedience is necessary for employees to fully understand the role they must play in information security in their organisation. This should, to a large extent, eradicate the incorrect information security practices performed by employees and further research will continue to investigate the action that should be taken to firmly entrench correct information security practices in an organisation through Corporate Information Security Obedience.

At present, the concept of implementing Corporate Information Security Obedience is being researched. Therefore, there are no further recommendations on how to accomplish this implementation included in this paper. These recommendations will form part of further research.

10. REFERENCES

BS 7799-1. (1999). *Code of practice for information security management (CoP).* DISC PD 0007. UK.

Canadian Labour Program. (2003). *Work-life balance in Canadian workplaces.* [online]. [cited 20 February 2004] Available from Internet: URL http://labour.hrdc-drhc.gc.ca/worklife/moving-beyond-policies-en.cfm

Deloitte & Touche. (May, 2002). *Management briefing – information security.* [online]. [cited 13 January 2003] Available from Internet: URL http://www.deloitte.com/dtt/cda/doc/content/info_security(1).pdf

Drennan, D. (1992). *Transforming company culture.* Berkshire, England : MacGraw-Hill.

Gaines, C. (2002, April 22). The benefits of the BS7799 certification with particular reference to e-commerce applications. *IT Security* [online]. [cited 4 August 2002] Available from Internet: URL http://www. itsecurity.com/papers/insight1.htm

Goal/QPC (2003). Journal of innovative management [online]. [cited 4 February 2004] Available from Internet: URL http://www.goalqpc.com/ 2003/Journalfiles/currentissue.htm

Gordon, G. (May 12, 2002). Dozens of threats beset your data. *Sunday Times, Business Surveys* [online]. [cited 17 July 2002] Available from Internet: URL http://www.suntimes.co.za/2002/05/12/business/surveys/ internet/survey10.asp

Gordon and Glickson LLC. (2001). *Comprehensive information security policies: meeting an organisation's privacy and security needs.* [online]. [cited 23 March 2003] Available from Internet: http://www. ggtech. com/

Hagberg Consulting Group (2002). *Corporate culture/organisational culture: understanding and assessment* [online]. [cited 25 January 2003] Available from Internet: URL http://www.hcgnet.com/html/ articles/understanding-Culture.html

Höne, K. (2003). *Abstract of 'effective information security policies – the why, what and how'.* [CD-ROM]. South Africa: ISSA 2003.

King Committee on Corporate Governance. (2001). *King report on corporate governance for South Africa 2001.* [online]. [cited 3 March 2002] Available from Internet: URL http://www.iodsa.co.za/ IoD%20 Draft%20King%20Report.pdf

Krige, W. (1999). *The usage of audit logs for effective information security management.* Unpublished master's thesis. Port Elizabeth Technikon, Port Elizabeth, South Africa.

Lane, V.P. (1985). *Security of computer based information systems.* London: Macmillan.

Martins, A. & Eloff, J. (2002). *Information Security Culture.* IFIP TC11, 17th International Conference on Information Security, Ain Shams University, Cairo, Egypt, Kluwer Academic Publishers Group.

Planting, S. (2001, March 9). Giving boards a workout - the fish rots from the head. *Future Organisation* [online]. [cited 27 April 2002] Available from Internet: URL http://www.futureorganisation.co.za/2001/03/09/reviewb.htm

PriceWaterhouseCoopers (2002). *Information security breaches survey technical report.* [online]. [cited 5 January 2003] Available from Internet: URL http://www.security-survey.co.uk

Schafer, M. (February 2003). The human-capital balancing act. *Optimize Magazine: issue 16* [online]. [cited 13 February 2003] Available from Internet: URL http://www.optimizemag.com/issue/016/culture.htm

Schein, E.H. (1999). *The corporate culture survival guide.* San Francisco, California, United States of America : Jossey-Bass Publishers.

Schein, E.H. (1992). Organisational leadership and culture. [online]. [cited 12 January 2004] Available from Internet: URL http://www.tnellen.com/ted/tc/schein.html

Smith, M.R. (1989). *Commonsense computer security.* London: McGraw-Hill.

Spafford, E.H. (1998). It's about more than computers. *CERIAS* [online]. [cited 12 February 2003] Available from Internet: URL http://www.cerias.purdue.edu/training_and_awarness/products/brochure_001.pdf

Spotlight (2002). *Schein interview.* [online]. [cited on 12 February 2004] Available from Internet: URL http://www.boys-camp-southafrica.de/files/ Edgar%20Schein.pdf

Thomson, K-L & von Solms, R. (2003). *Integrating information security into corporate culture.* Unpublished master's thesis. Port Elizabeth Technikon, Port Elizabeth, South Africa.

Whitman, M.E. & Mattord, H.J. (2003). *Principles of Information Security.* Kennesaw State University : Thomson Course Technology.

World Bank Group. (September 20, 1999). *Corporate governance: a framework for implementation – overview.* [online]. [cited 23 December 2002] Available from Internet: URL http://www.worldbank.org/html/fpd/privatesector/cg/docs/gcgfbooklet.pdf

CIIP-RAM - A SECURITY RISK ANALYSIS METHODOLOGY FOR CRITICAL INFORMATION INFRASTRUCTURE PROTECTION

T. B. Busuttil[1], and M. J. Warren[2]
[1]School of Information Technology, Deakin University, Australia; [2]School of Information Systems, Deakin University, Australia
{tbb; mwarren}@deakin.edu.au

Abstract: Critical Information Infrastructure has become a priority for all levels of management, It is one of the key components of efficient business and business continuity plans. There is a need for a new security methodology to deal with the new and unique attack threats and vulnerabilities associated with the new information technology security paradigm. CIIP-RAM, is a new security risk analysis method which copes with the shift from computer/information security to critical information infrastructure protection. This type of methodology is the next step toward handling information technology security risk at all levels from upper management information security down to firewall configurations. The paper will present the methodology of the new techniques and their application to critical information infrastructure protection. The associated advantages of this methodology will also be discussed.

Key words: Critical Information Infrastructure, Security Risk Analysis and Information Security.

1. INTRODUCTION

Understanding and managing Critical Information Infrastructure (CII) security risks is a priority to most organisations dealing with Information Technology (IT) and Information Warfare (IW) scenarios today (Libicki 2000). Traditional security risk analysis was well suited to these tasks within the paradigm of computer security where the focus was on securing tangible items such as computing and communications equipment (NCS 1996, Cramer 1998). With the growth of information interchange and reliance on information infrastructure, the ability to understand where vulnerabilities lie within an organisation, regardless of size, has become extremely difficult (NIPC 1996). To place a value on the information that is owned and used by an organisation is virtually an impossible task (Busuttil and Warren 2001a). The suitability of risk analysis to assist in managing Critical Information Infrastructure-related security risks is unqualified, however studies have been undertaken to build frameworks and methodologies for modelling Information Attacks (Beer 1984, Molander et al. 1996, Johnson 1997, Busuttil and Warren 2001b, Hutchinson and Warren 2001) which will assist greatly in applying risk analysis concepts and methodologies to the burgeoning information technology security paradigm, Information Warfare. The concept of behind this unique method of security risk analysis takes the form of the conceptual model of layered logical transformation models (LTMs) (Busuttil and Warren 2002). These models allow stakeholders to apply risk analysis to traditional IW scenarios so as to deal with the problems of scalability and inaccurate cost analysis as well as being dynamic enough to keep up with the constant changes occurring in information infrastructure and information attacks.

2. A NEW METHOD OF SECURITY RISK ANALYSIS AND INFORMATION INFRASTRUCTURE PROTECTION

Third generation security risk analysis methodologies, LTMs, were designed to work well when built into information system security risk analysis scenarios from the beginning (Baskerville 1993). The major characteristics of IW and CII Protection which set them apart from information security (IS) are the need to take (1) organisational scalability, (2) flexibility and (3) difficulty in cost evaluating of threats, vulnerabilities and attacks into account when considering CII Issues. So to adapt LTM security risk analysis technology from IS to CII protection these issues of scalability and adaptability must first be dealt with.

One of the major advantages of LTMs are the ability to build security into information systems in an adaptable manner (Baskerville 1993). The flexibility of control that is possible when designing security using LTMs is a definite strength when dealing with IW concerns as threats, vulnerabilities and targets are constantly changing. The problem of scalability is the need to deal with infrastructure at many (Global, National, Organisational etc) levels. This can be dealt with by bringing forward the concept of layering the LTMs so that each level of information infrastructure can have one-to-many LTMs that each depicts a security-based problem/solution pairing. Any number or level of information infrastructures can be included in the overall model. This way of dealing with issues allow the entire organization to deal with security as a cultural issue rather than leaving the task up to management armed with baseline methodologies, and an ever increasing work load.

The problem of cost evaluation influencing critical system security is solved, as

LTMs do not make cost evaluation a major part of the decision making process. CII-based cost evaluation is virtually impossible, so factoring it in but at a lower level is a way of making sure security is built well over the breadth and depth of the system. Focusing on one seemingly major, but, actually minor area to secure can often be a downfall of organisations (Cramer 1997). The only minor difficulty is the need to classify which information infrastructure level contains particular entities, problems etc. A proposed solution to this problem is to also include scope in the modelling methodology to handle infrastructure interfaces. This would be where security issues regarding physical and/or logical links between two infrastructure levels would be discussed.

The proposal of the idea of a new LLTM-based security risk analysis model comes about as a result of the lack of suitability of the aforementioned security risk analysis methodologies to Information Warfare and CII protection (Busuttil and Warren 2002). The lack of suitability of SRA methodologies comes about due to insufficiencies in the current standards and guidelines that current infrastructure security professionals are required to work within. This next generation will involve the application of logical transformation methods across the layers of information infrastructure discussed in table 1.

3. CRITICAL INFORMATION INFRASTRUCTURE PROTECTION - RISK ANALYSIS METHODOLOGY

When building an information security system using logical transformation models there are a number of steps that need to be followed. Firstly, a system implementation participation group representing a large cross-section of the involved system users should undertake the approach as this will assist in the exposition of infrastructure definitions, vulnerabilities and countermeasures. For each defined piece of the information infrastructure the following information needs to be stored:

- Infrastructure definitions;
- An Infrastructure vulnerability assessment on each infrastructure level.

Once a vulnerability assessment has been completed the group can then attempt to map the vulnerabilities to areas of infrastructure and organisational responsibility so as to get an overall understanding of the problems that face the organisation undertaking this risk analysis approach. The following formal stages are required for completing this new method of security risk analysis:

1. Form system implementation participation group;
2. Define Infrastructure;
3. Complete vulnerability assessment on each infrastructure level;
4. Derive countermeasures based on findings from steps 2 and 3.

Stage 1 should be completed once at the beginning of the lifecycle of the risk analysis process. Stage 2 should be completed once for each piece of infrastructure that is introduced to the overall system. Stages 3 and 4 should be completed once at the beginning of the analysis to cover all the parts that exist at this time within the infrastructure system and should be updated regularly for both new and previously integrated infrastructure entities. A step-by-step description of each of the aforementioned stages follows.

3.1 INTRODUCTION TO STAGE 1 OF CIIP-RAM

The first stage in CIIP-RAM (Critical Information Infrastructure Protection – Risk Analysis Methodology) was originally to construct a committee with a wide cross-section of understanding regarding the current computing environment within the organisation in which the risk analysis is being undertaken. This committee was designed to encompass people from all levels of the organisation e.g. management to clerks, and also different areas of expertise e.g. computing to accounting. The reason for this diversity to be inherent within the panel undertaking the analysis is that the organisation are looking for all information infrastructure security risks and the wider the net is cast the more likely each ensuing stage will be completed to an efficient level.

The concept of bringing people's concerns to the discussion table or at least voicing opinions is believed to be an important step in constructing systems that are efficient (Mumford and Henshall 1979). However, the major goals of forming a committee are often not met if a leader champions the group with strong views toward an issue or with a preconceived and/or stubborn approach to the process (Davey 2002). In view of this situation, a more effective approach to the first stage of the methodology is to accept representative views in electronic form and allow computing technology and a system operator to take the form of a trusted third party which offers pre-programmed cataloguing and indexing of the problems and formulates them in a way so as to allow easy understanding of where the problem lies, who is affected and also when and how the problem occurs or has occurred in the past. This approach offers two major advantages over the original committee-based approach. Firstly it allows issues to be raised in an unfettered manner by the system implementation participation group and secondly, the results are stored in an easy to read and recall environment which can be access controlled. This method of system development has been characterised by the Joint Application Development (JAD) methodology originally employed in the early 1970's by IBM as a way of designing systems which fit requirements of all the users. JAD required a number of participants from all areas within the project scope as well as outsiders to discuss and document the system requirements whilst also communicating with those who would ultimately use, implement and maintain the system (Hoffer et al 2002). It was originally designed to cater to the creation of computing and information systems. The creation and implementation of a security policy is similar as there is a final goal and an ongoing, sign-posted, evolutionary process to achieve this goal.

3.2 CIIP-RAM Stage 1 – Form system implementation participation group

Stage 1 of CIIP-RAM is described in detail within sections 3.2.1 – 3.2.3.

3.2.1 CIIP-RAM Stage 1.1 - Assemble Group of Stakeholders

The first step toward the application of the CIIP-RAM methodology is the assembly of a system implementation participation group. The main focus of this group is to collect and present, without prejudice or bias, the concerns of the stakeholders, users, developers etc. of the new security culture. Using either a manual or computer-based system, depicted in figure 1, as a tool for information collection this group should see the first implementation cycle through whilst also ensuring that new system entities be they human or non-human are kept informed, updated, secured and involved with new and changing policy.

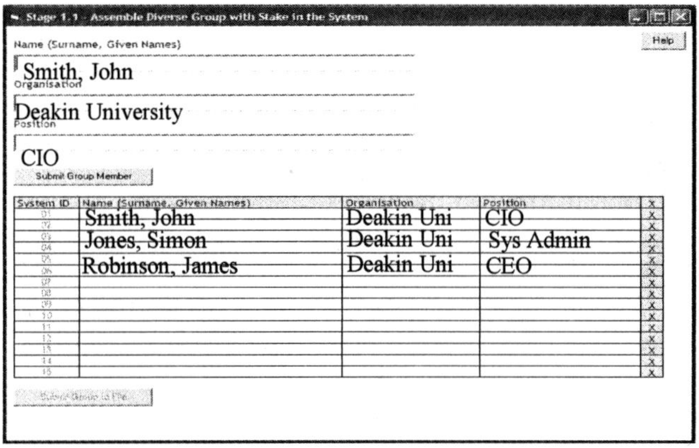

Figure 1 : Screenshot depicting CIIP-RAM System Step 1.1 (Section 3.2.1)

3.2.2 CIIP-RAM Stage 1.2 - Instruct Group as to the Goals of the Exercise

The instruction of the group as to the goals of this new exercise is a crucial step in the creation and sustainability of new policy and culture. It is important that the group members can understand the need for change in security policy and culture through training with regards to goals of this exercise. It is also important that group members are able to communicate to other members of the organisation in a concise manner what changes will be put in place and the reason for these changes. The ability to put forward new and unforeseen issues and problems is also a key task for system implementation participation group members. The overall goal of the exercise is to eradicate information infrastructure vulnerability whilst taking into consideration stakeholders within the system. This should not only be the goal of the exercise but also the goal of each member of the group and in turn the organisation.

3.2.3 CIIP-RAM Stage 1.3 - Instruct Group on the steps involved

The CIIP-RAM system is a methodology which is designed to be followed stage-by-stage. It is important that the group knows what each of the steps are, what they must do singularly and as a team to fulfil each step. Most critically, the maintenance of the culture change that the use of this methodology will likely invoke must be taken into consideration at this stage. Each group member should be given information on the process as well as step-by-step instructions on how to manage and execute the methodology. At the point where all group members have read and understood what the process will entail, group consensus should be reached with regard to any perceived problems or ambiguities.

3.3 INTRODUCTION TO STAGE 2 OF CIIP-RAM

This stage requires the committee to classify what sort of CII it is dependent on. An organisation makes use of an organisational CII that administers personal IIs whilst being reliant on a NII. At this stage the system boundaries (Vidalis and Blyth 2002) should be mapped so as to understand where different LTM's are required for different layers of II. The total OII should be broken down into sections that can be defined, classified and analysed separately. This definition of infrastructure entities may include a mapping to the infrastructure, including its interfaces to other infrastructure within and outside of the organisation as well as the current security measures currently in place. Previous security incidents (if any) and the relevant countermeasures taken (if any) would also assist in the further steps in the model. It is important to remember that the focus of stage 2 is to derive the organisational CII and despite the use of PIIs, NIIs and GIIs to derive the scope of the organisational CII these other IIs are not really important to the undertaking of the CIIP-RAM.

3.4 CIIP-RAM Stage 2 – Define Critical Information Infrastructure

Stage 2 of CIIP-RAM is described in detail within sections 3.4.1 – 3.4.5.

3.4.1 CIIP-RAM Stage 2.1 - Define the Information Infrastructure

The definition of the information infrastructure should be completed using two basic methods. Firstly, a diagrammatic depiction of the Information infrastructure should be derived, perhaps using UML or some other information-rich graphical representation. The diagram should show, to the greatest possible detail, systems, entities, links etc. The diagram should deal with multiple infrastructure levels from high-level (offices in London and New York) to low-level (computers linked in room x of building y via null modem cable). The depiction of these scenes helps in the understanding of networked infrastructure.

It is also an extremely important part of this step to textually show relationships between network infrastructures. Once again this should focus across the width and breadth of the organisation and should be completed with as much detail as possible.

The completion of both the diagram and the written form will allow for the system implementation participation group to have a clear and detailed view of their organisational world. The group should review the two depictions and clear up ambiguities and imperfections before moving on to the next step.

3.4.2 CIIP-RAM Stage 2.2 - Define the System Boundaries

In defining the system boundaries the group must work toward understanding which infrastructural entities they do or do not own and control. Demarcation of the boundaries helps the group understand the scope of the information infrastructure they are working within. The group should then review the information infrastructure definition they have derived so as to exclude all infrastructure entities outside these new boundaries.

3.4.3 CIIP-RAM Stage 2.3 - Define Manageable CII Sub-Systems

At this stage the group will have a reasonable understanding of the infrastructural entities they must protect as well as a pre-existing knowledge of the organisational processes that are undertaken by them and their colleagues. The next task is to break down the newly defined information infrastructure into more manageable and critical subsystems. The splitting of these systems can be done in numerous ways but, the simplest ways are grouping by physical location (systems in London and New York become sub-systems) or by logical connection (payment systems and database systems become sub-systems) or a mixture of both. These newly derived sub-systems should be of manageable size. If this has not been reached then further division of systems shall be done by the group until this requirement is met. This information should be entered into the CIIP-RAM system step 2.3 as depicted in Figure 2.

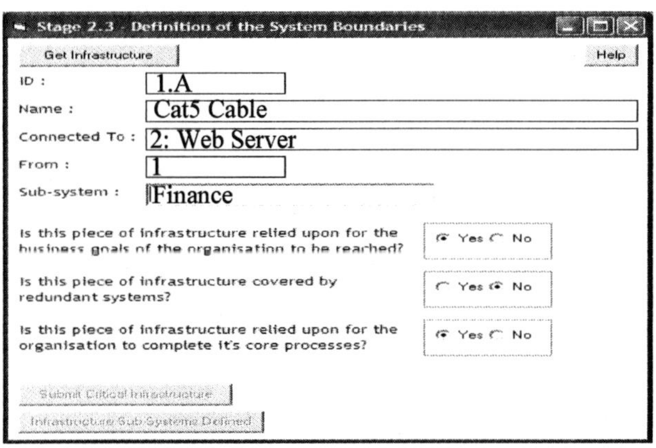

Figure 2: Screenshot depicting CIIP-RAM System Step 2.3

3.4.4 CIIP-RAM Stage 2.4 - Breakdown Sub-Systems into Classifiable Infrastructure Entities

Considering now the derived information infrastructure sub-systems, it is an important next process to further break down these systems into the entities that make up the system. In the case of this review an entity is defined as any infrastructural hardware device, information store, connection mechanism or person. These entities should be mapped out both textually (Figure 3) and diagrammatically as was completed in the previous step and using similar methods and syntax to show relationships.

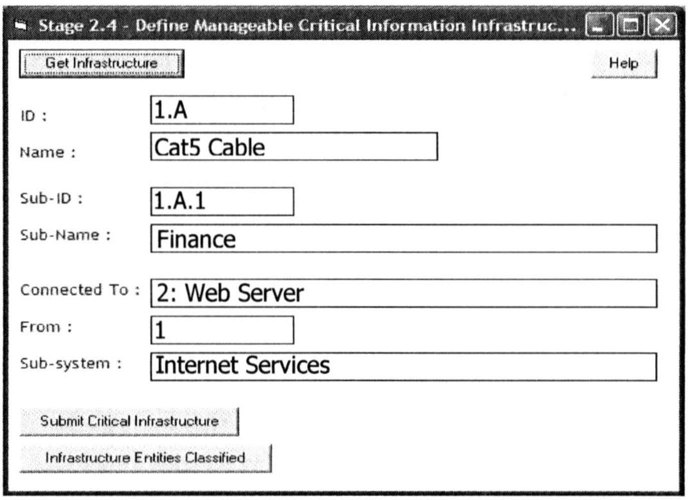

Figure 3: Screenshot depicting CIIP-RAM System Step 2.4

3.4.5 CIIP-RAM Stage 2.5 - Enter Information about Each Entity

The entering of information captured within this phase is an important step in the infrastructure definition process. The major goal of this exercise is to capture the information that is currently known about the entity in question. The required information and a method for capturing that information is shown in Table 1.

Table 1. An example of a classification table

Classification	Explanation
Sub-System	Payment Systems Support
Entity	Workstation 6
Connections	Payment Systems Support LAN via CAT5 cabling
Security in Place	Dumb terminal status, password access
Past Security Problems	(July 1997) Subversion of password controls
Solutions Applied	(July 1997) Changed password

It is noticeable that the sub-system, Entity and connection fields have different colours applied to them. The blue depicts a subsystem name, red depicts an entity name and green depicts a connection mechanism. It is crucial that differences between these three are noted and marked in some way. Doing this makes the understanding of the model easier to derive information from at a later date. At the completion of this step the system implementation participation group should have a compiled list of entities and the information known about each. It is important that this information is conserved for use in further steps and also as a reference.

3.5 INTRODUCTION TO STAGE 3 OF CIIP-RAM

The third stage requires the completion of a vulnerability assessment which should include a thorough rundown of likely vulnerabilities within the organisation as a whole and also any known vulnerabilities within its connection scope to particular entities within the OII. A method of vulnerability assessment within the scope of electronic payment systems (EPS) named 'Threat Assessment Model for EPS' (TAME) (O'Mahony et al. 1997) shows a loosely coupled decision loop that allows for on-the-fly adjustment to system threats and inputs and outputs (Vidalis and Blyth 2002). The steps involved in this system are useful; however it is important to know where an organisation is in the security process. The TAME system also focuses greatly on assessing threat which takes impetus away from finding vulnerabilities within the organisation. Concentration on threat as opposed to vulnerability can cause security weaknesses to go unnoticed as there may be a threat that can never be prepared for. If the organisation attempts to keep vulnerabilities to a minimum then it is not overly important to know the nature of the threat agent (Malone 2002).

The new methodology takes into account the following contiguous stages:

- Assessment Scope;
- Scenario Construction and Modelling;
- Vulnerability Analysis;
- Evaluation.

The stages consist of a number of steps which should be completed in turn so as to be easier to follow and keep track of. The concepts covered in the new methodology are similar to those discussed in the TAME system.

3.6 CIIP-RAM Stage 3 – Complete Vulnerability Assessment on Infrastructure Levels

CIIP-RAM's third stage is described in more detail in sections 3.6.1 – 3.6.4.2.

3.6.1 CIIP-RAM Stage 3.1 - Prepare an Assessment Scope

The preparation of an assessment scope is a two step process which consists of the completion of a Business Analysis and a Stakeholder Identification.

3.6.1.1 CIIP-RAM Stage 3.1.1 - Complete a Business Analysis

A basic business analysis in accordance with (Nosworthy 2000) involves the process of business goal and business process identification. In addition to undertaking the basic business analysis the inclusion of an environmental analysis should also take place as a means of examining the environment within which the organisation exists.

3.6.1.1.1 CIIP-RAM Stage 3.1.1.1 - Identification of Business Goals

The identification of business goals is of key importance in any risk analysis application as it allows the system implementation participation group to bring major issues requiring review to the forefront of the risk analysis (Forte 2000). The identification of the business goals can be determined by stakeholders of the organisation that is the subject of the analysis.

3.6.1.1.2 CIIP-RAM Stage 3.1.1.2 - Identification of business processes

With the identification of an organisation's critical business processes we are able to bring to the surface more assets and vulnerabilities. A number of organisational primary and support processes could be identified (Johnson and Scholes 1999) at this time and should be updated as conditions and processes change. Depending on the size of the organisation under analysis three to eight organisational processes could be identified and should be noted. These processes can later be used as scenarios in the system modelling step. An in depth description of these processes should be produced. From these details the system implementation participation group will be in a position to identify and note more assets and vulnerabilities to add to the database.

3.6.1.1.3 CIIP-RAM Stage 3.1.1.3 - Environmental Analysis

The completion of an environmental analysis is based on Porter's five forces approach of examining the business environment at the strategic level (Johnson and Scholes 1999). Three environments are identified as targets for this analysis, technical environment; business environment and; physical environment.

The environmental analysis is a reasonably basic step which consists of breaking down the three environments mentioned via discussion and getting a feel for the organisations position with regards to each of the five forces in each of the organisational environments and noting down findings. This step will further help in the fleshing out of the issues affecting the organisation.

3.6.1.2 CIIP-RAM Stage 3.1.2 - Identify Stakeholders

Each infrastructure entity will have a set of stakeholders that can be questioned in an effort to define its function, nature and scope. There are three distinct classes of stakeholder within systems according to Sutcliffe (1988), The management stakeholders; The user stakeholders and the development stakeholders.

How ever customised stakeholder classifications can be used in each case. This would be dependent on the type of business the organisation is involved in. A list of each stakeholder should be constructed and each entry on the list is required to give input on assets and vulnerabilities that they can identify. The invocation of infrastructure protection should be looked at as an entire-organisation initiative rather than a one person job for the computer security guru. In the current environment it is important that all stakeholders in an organisation form a formidable information infrastructure protection team (Wood 1997).

3.6.2 CIIP-RAM Stage 3.2 - Scenario Construction and Modelling

Scenario construction and modeling is made up of the following steps; (1) Scenario Generation; (2) System Modeling; (3) Asset Identification.

3.6.2.1 CIIP-RAM Stage 3.2.1 - Scenario Generation

In this step the parties involved in the system implementation participation group are required to come up with a scenario involving the organisation and its use of the particular infrastructure entity under discussion. The parties that should be involved predominately at this step are the management of the company along with the stakeholders in cooperation with organisational security staff. The scenario should describe a real world application of the organisation. Risk assessment should be conducted with this, and similar, scenarios in mind. This step goes a long way toward helping all members of the system implementation participation group understand the nature of vulnerabilities across the organisation. Getting all members involved in the discussion of an area that is not necessarily within their jurisdiction can assist in the uncovering of widespread, endemic or multi-organisational vulnerabilities.

Although probably not necessary at this stage, more assets and vulnerabilities are likely to be identified. The more a particular scenario is refined and understood the more likely the group is to continue to uncover hidden aspects and vulnerabilities of a system. In addition, because each stakeholder is constructing a scenario, all likely to be from differing standpoints, it would be difficult for the system implementation participation group to not uncover the majority of the issues regarding the system under review. These scenarios are then filtered for similarities to provide a less cluttered view of the reviewed system.

3.6.2.2 CIIP-RAM Stage 3.2.2 - System Modelling

This step involves the system as a whole being modeled. All its aspects, procedures resources and transactions will be analysed in great detail. The system implementation participation group should try and take a high level view of the system. The more complete and detailed the model is at the completion of this step, the more successful the further stages are likely to be. Once again, further issues, assets and vulnerabilities are expected to be identified. If these new found attributes fall within the scope of the assessment they should then be included in the appropriate list.

The method that the user will employ to model the CII of the organisation is to enter the names of each of the infrastructure components into the data collection mechanism and also mention connections that each infrastructure entity has with other entities in the system. With the group working toward this system comprehension it is unlikely that systems and entities will be overlooked.

3.6.2.3 CIIP-RAM Stage 3.2.3 - Asset Identification

The entries of the asset list, relevant to the scope under which we see the critical information infrastructure and its components, as well as the system procedures involved in the system transactions that we want to examine, should be included and denoted. The user should identify all examinable assets at this stage. Further assets will be identified during other steps.

The assets uncovered at all stages up to this point should then be entered under the following categories in the asset table (Nosworthy 2000), Software, Hardware, Data, Administrative, Communications, Human Resources and Physical. It is not necessary for the table to contain all the asset categories. The selection and inclusion of categories is dependent on the scope of the CII.

3.6.3 CIIP-RAM Stage 3.3 - Vulnerability Analysis

The 'CIIP-RAM Stage 3.3 - Vulnerability Analysis' stage requires users to complete stages 3.3.1-2 for each vulnerability.

3.6.3.1 CIIP-RAM Stage 3.3.1 - Vulnerability Type Identification & Selection

Vulnerability can be noted as a weakness in the security system that might be exploited to cause harm or loss (Pfleeger 1997). So with that we can safely say that a CII vulnerability is a weakness in a CII security system that might be exploited to cause harm or loss. This methodology will focus on the CII vulnerabilities. The vulnerability list structure put forward by Neumann (1995) is the method of reporting that will be used (Table 2).

Table 2. An example excerpt from an entity-vulnerability list

Entity	**Vulnerability**
1.4 - Web Server	Software not up to date
	Virus signature file out of date

With systems such as CIIs with so many aspects, variables and hierarchical levels it is important that we complete the step of vulnerability selection so as to make the methodology easier to follow and more usable. The completion of a vulnerability selection can help simplify and tailor the system so that it is more manageable. The user can select the vulnerabilities of one type e.g. web server vulnerabilities and tailor the system to deal with the focused problem.

However, this step could also be avoided entirely so as to give an extremely detailed look at the system from all points of view. The final vulnerability list needs to be combined with the entity list in order to get a matrix which depicts all the vulnerabilities for each entity. By doing this the user sets-up a link between entities, vulnerabilities and countermeasures. Within the computer-based CIIP-RAM management tool being developed currently, the procedure of linking the entities, vulnerabilities and countermeasures (Figure 4) will be automated to deal with complexity on-the-fly

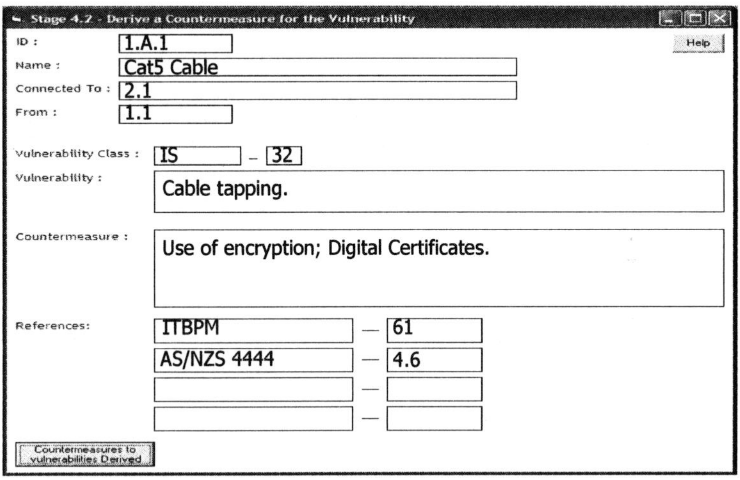

Figure 4: Screenshot depicting automated data entry from the CIIP-RAM System

3.6.3.2 CIIP-RAM Stage 3.3.2 - Vulnerability Complexity Analysis

It is important that for each entity/vulnerability pair, a certain amount of analysis be done on how many levels of security a threat agent would need to go through to exploit a vulnerability. If multiple vulnerabilities need to be exploited before a particular database server is compromised then these vulnerabilities need to be broken down into their composite vulnerabilities. These 'new' vulnerabilities should then be fed back into the matrix for further assessment.

3.6.4 CIIP-RAM Stage 3.4 - Evaluation

The 'CIIP-RAM Stage 3.4 - Evaluation' stage requires users to complete stages 3.4.1-2 for each vulnerability.

3.6.4.1 CIIP-RAM Stage 3.4.1 - Stakeholder Evaluation

In this step the stakeholders of the Critical Information Infrastructure under discussion should review the outputs of all the other stages. As with any computing related system it is important to the success of the project for the developers to stay in close contact with the client (Pressman 2001). In all cases the developers will be the system implementation participation group and the clients are representatives of the stakeholders of the CII under discussion.

Entities and vulnerabilities are expected to be introduced, or excluded, not fr the model, but from further investigation from the current iteration of the system. Once an entity or vulnerability has been introduced to the system it is important that it not be taken out. Entities and vulnerabilities may, at the first iteration, seem trivial, however due to the dynamism of computing, they may come into play during a later iteration.

3.6.4.2 CIIP-RAM Stage 3.4.2 - Vulnerability Statement Generation

After the completion of the previous step in the methodology, the output will be a number of vulnerabilities related to an entity of a critical Information Infrastructure. In this step we will produce a final table which categorises entities, vulnerabilities and a list of associated countermeasure option/recommendations. As each infrastructure entity is denoted as critical it is important that each vulnerability is dealt with as though its exploitation could be fatal to the system infrastructure.

3.7 INTRODUCTION TO STAGE 4 OF CIIP-RAM

The final stage in this security risk analysis is to derive countermeasures for the vulnerabilities that were identified in the vulnerability assessment. These countermeasures should attempt to solve the security problem being faced whilst also attempting to maintain a reasonable degree of subjective cost benefit. The derivation of countermeasures can be done in many ways including the concurrent application of bug fixes, patching, staff training new software solutions etc.

The formal presentation of these countermeasures should be delivered as shown in table 3 in the instance of each vulnerability:

Table 3. Basic example of a countermeasures table

Vulnerability	**Derived Countermeasures**
Apache Server security hole	Install and correctly configure firewall to assist halting of DOS attacks

3.8 CIIP-RAM Stage 4 – Derive, Apply and Analyse Countermeasures

Based on the recommendations put forward as an output from the previous stage the system implementation participation group should at this stage research the countermeasure solution space. The group should provide a selection of a finite list of possible countermeasures and should work toward an efficient solution to the problem.

From the short list of solutions provided as output from the previous task, a counter measure should be derived and formally described so as to provide a non-ambiguous process of countermeasure application.

Users then apply the countermeasure that is the output from the previous task in a correct, thorough and compatible manner. It is important that the informing and training of staff that are required to deal with the newly implemented countermeasure be completed in an efficient and thorough manner also.

After an agreed upon period of time after the application of the countermeasure it is extremely important to complete an analysis of the applied countermeasure. This analysis should include:

- Testing of the functionality of the system post-implementation;
- Mock exploitation of the originally perceived vulnerability in the post-countermeasure environment;
- User training comprehension of the new environment.

These three analyses sequences respectively should ensure that the system:

- Still does the job it designed to do in light of the newly applied countermeasures;
- Is more robust in a security sense post-implementation and;
- Is fully understood by the users of the system.

4. FUTURE RESEARCH

The major direction of this research at the current point is to derive a web-enabled version of CIIP-RAM which can be put into place to allow the security risk analysis process to be undertaken in an online environment. This product would allow for a more easily workable and hence more efficient final methodology.

5. CONCLUSIONS

CIIP-RAM is a move toward dealing with scalability issues that have meant that RA was not immediately adaptable to information warfare and other information infrastructure protection requirements. This methodology would prove to be helpful to organisations with mid-level infrastructure such as an organisational information infrastructure if undertaken in solitude however the true benefits of this methodology would be seen if it was put into practice by higher level infrastructure stakeholders. This uptake by higher-level infrastructure would lead to higher dependability and reliability being built into infrastructure system from the outset. Information warfare needs a unique security methodology that is useful at dealing with all the previous concerns that Computer Security and Information Security dealt with along with the ability to be adaptable and scalable also. When researching existing methodologies, logical transformation models proved to be a suitable method for coping with adaptability issues. The scalability issues are dealt with through the application of multiple layers of LTMs. Cost evaluation has been found to be an outdated function when analysing IW risks, LTMs have the added feature of being solution-oriented and independent of any cost evaluation procedures.

5. REFERENCES

Baskerville, R. (1993). Information Systems Security Design Methods: Implications for Information Systems Development. *ACM Computing Surveys* 25(4): 375-414.

Beer, S. (1984). *The Viable System Model: its provenance, development, methodology and pathology.*, Eds. Espejo, R. and Harnden, R., John Wiley, Chichester, UK.

Busuttil, T. B. and Warren, M. J., (2001a). An Information Warfare Protection Method. *Conference Proceedings of EUROMEDIA 2001*, SCS, Valencia, Spain.

Busuttil, T. B. and Warren, M. J. (2001b). Intelligent Agents and Their Information Warfare Implications. *Conference Proceedings of the 2nd Australian Information Warfare & Security Conference 2001*, We-Bcentre, Perth, Australia.

Busuttil, T. B. and Warren, M. J. (2002). A Conceptual Approach to Information Warfare Security Risk Analysis, *Conference Proceedings of the 2nd European Conference on Information Warfare*, London, UK.

Cramer, M. L. (1997). Measuring the Value of Information. *NCSA InfoWarCon 97*, USA.

Cramer, M. L. (1998). Information Warfare: A Consequence of the Information Revolution. *The Information Revolution: Current and Future Consequences.* A. L. Porter and W. H. Read, Ablex Publishing Corp, USA.

Davey, J. (2002). Comment made at *'Information Warfare'* Workshop, 3rd Australian Information Warfare & Security Conference 2002, We-Bcentre, Perth, Australia.

Forte. (2000). "Information Security Assessment: Procedures and Methodology." *Computer Fraud & Security* 2000(8): 9-12.

Hoffer, J. A., George J. F., Valacich, J. S., (2002), *Modern Systems Analysis and Design*, Prentice Hall, New Jersey, USA.

Hutchinson, W. and Warren, M. J., (2001). *Information Warfare - Corporate Attack and Defence in a Digital World.* Butterworth-Heinemann, Oxford, UK.

Johnson, L. S., (1997). Toward a Functional Model of Information Warfare. Studies in Intelligence 1(1).

Johnson and Scholes (1999). *Exploring corporate strategy*, Prentice Hall Europe.

Libicki, M., (2000). *The Future of Information Security*, Institute for National Strategic Studies: 10, USA.

Malone, J., (2002). Comment made at *'Information Warfare'* Workshop, 3rd Australian Information Warfare & Security Conference 2002, We-Bcentre, Perth, Australia.

Molander, R. C., Riddile, A. S. and Wilson, P. A., (1996). *Strategic Information Warfare: A New Face of War.* RAND Corporation, Washington, USA.

Mumford, E., Henshall, D., (1979), *A Participative Approach to Computer Systems Design*, Associated Business Press, London, UK.

NCS., (1996). *Risk Assessment: A Nation's Information at Risk.* Arlington, Virginia, National Communications System, USA.

Neumann, (1995). Computer Related risks, Addison-Wesley.

NIPC., (1996). *Critical Infrastructures*, National Infrastructure Protection Center - US Government. USA.

Nosworthy (2000). "A Practical Risk Analysis Approach: managing BCM risk." *Computers & Security,* 19(7): 596-614.

O'Mahony, D., Peirce, M. and Tewari, H. (1997), *Electronic Payment Systems*, Artech House Inc.

Pfleeger (1997). *Security in Computing*, Prentice Hall Int.

Pressman (2001). *Software engineering: A practitioner's approach*, McGraw-Hill.

Sutcliffe (1988). *Human-Computer Interface Design*, Macmillan Education.

Vidalis, S. and Blyth, A. (2002). Understanding and Developing a Threat assessment Model, *Conference Proceedings of the 2nd European Conference on Information Warfare, London, UK.*

Wood (1997). "Policies alone do not constitute a sufficient awareness effort." *Computer Fraud & Security* 1997(12): 14-19.

A FRAMEWORK FOR ROLE-BASED MONITORING OF INSIDER MISUSE

Aung Htike Phyo, Steven M. Furnell, and Francisco Portilla
Network Research Group, School of Computing, Communications and Electronics, University of Plymouth, Drake Circus, Plymouth, PL4 8AA, United Kingdom, nrg@plymouth.ac.uk

Abstract: Many security incidents involve legitimate users who misuse their existing privileges, such that they have the system-level right to perform an action, but not the moral right to do so. Current Intrusion Detection Systems (IDSs) are ineffective in this context, because they do not have knowledge of user responsibilities, normal working scope of a user for a relevant position, or the separation of duties that should be enforced. This paper considers examples of the forms that misuse may take within typical applications, and then outlines a novel framework to address the problem of insider misuse monitoring. The approach argues that users with similar roles and responsibilities will exhibit similar behaviour within the system, enabling any activity that deviates from the normal profile to be flagged for further examination. The system utilises established access control principles for defining user roles, and the relationships between them, and proposes a misuse monitoring agent that will police application-level activities for signs of unauthorised behaviour.

Key words: Misuse Detection, Insider Misuse, Intrusion Detection, Role-based Monitoring.

1. INTRODUCTION

The need for information security is increasing as organizations depend on IT infrastructures for the smooth functioning of their businesses. While the media has highlighted the threat brought about by external intruders and viruses, it has not promoted the awareness of the threat to the organization's IT infrastructure from its own employees. In reality, however, insiders are very often the cause of the most significant and costly security incidents, and a significant proportion of cybercrime can be attributed to them.

This paper examines the problem of insider misuse, and outlines a framework for monitoring of user activity in order to detect potential misuse. The literature review section examines the scale of insider misuse and explains why current Intrusion Detection Systems are unable to detect some of the insider misuses, particularly improper data access and fraud. In the methods section, the common forms of application-level misuse are listed, and the abuse of features within database applications is analysed as a more specific example. The detection strategies employed by current intrusion detection systems are evaluated, and the requirements for effective inside misuse monitoring are identified. The results section presents a conceptual framework that would allow role-based monitoring of insider misuse. This framework would allow the detection of users violating the principle of least privileges and separation of duties.

2. INSIDER MISUSE AND DETECTION ISSUES

Examining computer crime literature and surveys dating up to the mid-90s, suggests that the main threat was to be found from one's own staff (with as much as 80% of computer crime believed to be the result of insider activity). For example, in discussing the findings of the 1995 survey from the Computer Security Institute (CSI), Power (1995, p.5) observes that "the greatest threat comes from inside your own organisation". Although more recent years have revealed a different picture in terms of the incident proportions (e.g. by 2002, the CSI results reported that, for the fifth year running, more respondents had cited their Internet connection as a frequent point of attack (74%), than had cited internal systems (33%) (Power, 2002)), the financial impact of insider incidents is still clearly greater. Table 1 presents the figures from these CSI/FBI surveys, and compares the dollar amount lost due to outsider attacks to that of insider net abuse and unauthorised insider access. The figures relating to insider abuse of network access clearly suggest that, as well as bringing considerable advantages in terms of web and email communication, Internet access has also ushered in a whole range of new problems. This can be further evidenced by a survey of 544 human resources managers, conducted in 2002 and targeting large UK companies (i.e. employing an average of 2,500 people). The results revealed that almost a quarter (23%) had felt obliged to dismiss employees in relation to Internet misconduct (with the vast majority of these cases – 69% - being linked to the downloading of pornographic materials) (Theregister, 2002). Many other cases resulted in less severe courses of action, such as verbal warnings or a discreet word in the ear of the person concerned, and in total the results indicated that 72% of respondents had encountered Internet misuse in some form.

Table 1. Annual losses for selected incidents from CSI/FBI surveys

Year	System penetration by outsider	Insider abuse of Net access	Unauthorised insider acess
1998	$1,637,000	$3,720,000	$50,565,000
1999	$2,885,000	$7,576,000	$3,567,000
2000	$7,104,000	$27,984,740	$22,554,500
2001	$19,066,600	$35,001,650	$6,064,000
2002	$13,055,000	$50,099,000	$4,503,000
2003	$2,754,400	$11,767,200	$406,300
Total	$46,502,000	$136,148,590	$87,659,800

The main difference between insider misuse and outsider attacks is that the insiders have legitimate access to the system and resources, but abuse their privileges by using the resources in an inappropriate manner or for an unapproved purpose. Anderson (1980) classifies such users as 'misfeasors'. The fact that insiders are already within the organisation often puts them in an ideal position to misuse a system if they are inclined to do so, as they have insight knowledge of what security mechanisms are employed and how to evade detection. Current Intrusion Detection Systems (IDS) are geared towards detecting attacks by outsiders, as well as insiders who employ the same methods to mount an attack. The types of attacks the IDS can detect depend on the type of data collected for analysis. The data for intrusion analysis can be collected at three varying levels of the IT systems, i.e. Network, Host OS, and application (Phyo and Furnell, 2003). Different types of misuse can manifest themselves at varying levels within the system. Therefore the data needs to be collected at the appropriate level in order to detect various types of misuses. Many of the currently available intrusion detection systems are Network-based (Roesch, 1999; Paxson, 1998), and Host-based (Anderson *et al.*, 1994; Lindqvist and Porras, 2001). Previously mentioned IDSs can detect network penetrations, exploitation of network protocols, and anomalous process behaviour. However, insiders may not need to exploit network protocols or system vulnerabilities in these ways because they already have legitimate access to it (Audit Commission, 1990). In reality many security incidents involve legitimate users abusing their existing privileges, such that they have the system-level right to perform an action, but not the moral right to do so. This is especially true in database applications as database management systems are rich in functionality and varying classes of users can manipulate the data in many different ways. One of the main problems of insider misuse is the improper access of data within databases, which can result in data theft, breach of privacy, fraud, and compromised data integrity. Database level misuses can have severe impact on the organisation as many businesses employ database systems for record management, accounting, trading, business analysis and strategic planning. The authors have identified two notable approaches amongst previous work that detect anomalous behaviour at the application level. The first of these, DIDAFIT (Detecting Database Intrusions Through Fingerprinting Transactions), monitors anomalous SQL queries by generating fingerprints of authorised queries (Low *et al.*, 2002). These fingerprints are sequences of SQL queries, along with variables that the users should not change, ensuring that the queries are executed in proper order and only on the restricted range of records. Another example is (Detection of Misuse In Database Systems) DEMIDS (Chung, Gertz, and Levitt, 1999), which attempts to profile working scopes based on user access patterns in relational databases, and assumes that a user will not typically access all attributes and data in a database schema. Therefore user access patterns will form some working scopes, which are sets of attributes usually referenced together with some values. Based upon this assumption, Chung *et al.* (1999) defined the notion of a distance measure between sets of attributes that consider both the structure of the data and user behaviour. This notion is then used to guide the search for regular patterns that describe user behaviour in a relational database. However, to be able to detect, data theft and potential occurrence of fraud in complex transaction/trading systems, the detection system also needs to have the knowledge of user responsibilities, work patterns, separation of duties and organisation hierarchy. Knowledge of job positions and segregation of duties are important as the opportunity for misuse arises when the individual is in a position of trust and the controls are weak. Many of the misuses in Audit Commission (1990) survey are the result of lack of application level controls and proper segregation of duties. Therefore, there is a need to provide the detection system with knowledge of required separation of duties, business processes, and working scope in order to enable more effective monitoring.

3. OPPORTUNITIES FOR APPLICATION-LEVEL MISUSE

Commercial applications include more features than the users may actually need to perform the task, and such features may sometimes be misused. In feature rich applications where users of varying responsibilities may access different features and the mechanism to control access to the features may not be present. Again, some of the features may not be easily disabled. Therefore, the detection system needs to monitor the features/functionality accessed by each user. In order to be able to prevent and monitor insider misuse, the nature of potential misuses must firstly be identified and analysed. This section analyses how features in common applications can be misused, and suggests a functional classification. Table 2 list the possible misuses with regard to the type of application commonly available on most computers, with the right-hand column indicating the means by which misuse would be achieved (Portilla, 2003).

Table 2. Misuse of typical application features

LEGITIMATE ACTION	MISUSE
Client/Server Applications	
Message Exchange	Unusual exchange of messages hat degrades performance
Connectivity to Server	Exceeding possible number of connections to cause a denial of service
Execution of Tasks	Executing privileged procedures
Word Processors	
Writing a Document	Insertion of illegal content Insertion of malicious code
Mail Clients	
Sending and receiving emails	Distribution of illegal content Setting up remote attack Private use/gain Spamming
Browsers	
Browsing the Internet	Access to illegal content
Access to cached files and history	Displaying other user's view files and previous accesses
Programming tools	
Developing programs	Creation of malware
Debugging	Access to memory segments containing sensitive data
General purpose applications	
Input to programs	Buffer overflow for elevation of privileges Buffer overflow for cod execution Buffer overflow for denial of service
Database Applications	
Data access	Anomalous browsing of database Inference attacks Inappropriate modification of data

Despite controls established in databases, authorised users may misuse their legitimate privileges. Possible misuses associated with legitimate visualisation rights are:

- Data aggregation: users could try to collect information about one or more individuals, transactions or products for different purposes.
- Displaying data in an improper way (conditioned or sorted): when information is not displayed in a manner that exclusively serves the purpose of the database system, it can provide additional information and capabilities. For example, displaying a telephone directory sorted by number.
- Retrieval of a large amount of data: users could attempt a partial reconstruction of the database by retrieving a large amount of information. This reconstruction could possibly provide more operations over the data that were initially restricted.
- Discovering the existence of restricted information: unsuccessful attempts to display restricted fields could allow users to identify records with sensitive information or to guess part of them.
- Inference: Data within a database is semantically related. Therefore, sometimes users can come to know an unknown value without accessing it directly by inferring it from known values.

Misuses associated with legitimate creation and modification rights are:

- Deliberate insertion of false data: users can insert erroneous content in the database in order to damage its integrity or to corrupt the supported procedures.
- Misuse of coherence mechanisms: users can exploit mechanisms that check for coherence and compatibility of related values in the database. They may be able to discover the structure of the database, by displaying error messages when attempting to perform a writing operation. Besides, inserting false information into particular fields might be used to change the values of initially restricted fields.

Considering the list of potential misuses listed in the table, it is possible that appropriate controls could be used to prevent some of them, but even these will not be sufficient for all contexts (consider, for instance, the case in which the misfeasor has legitimate access to the payroll database, but modifies records to raise his own salary). In this example, even though the user has the system right to modify the data, it should require someone else to authorise the modification. Many of the insider misuse cases in Audit Commission surveys are a result of lack of separation of duties and application level control (Audit Commission, 1990). Therefore, insider misuse is not only a technical problem, but also a managerial problem, because in some cases it is the improper segregation of duties that presented the problem. One of the main problems of insider misuse is the improper access of data in database environments, which can result in data theft, breach of privacy, fraud, and compromise of data integrity, depending on the motive of the perpetrator.

4. A COMPARISON OF DETECTION STRATEGIES

IDS employ two main strategies to identify attacks, namely misuse-based and anomaly-based detection (Amoroso, 1999), and it is possible to see how each of these could be applied to the insider problem.

Misuse-based detection. This approach relies upon knowing or predicting the incident that the system is to detect. Intrusions are specified as attack signatures, which can then be matched to current activity using a rule-based approach. A similar approach could potentially be incorporated for misfeasor incidents, based upon those methods that employees have been known to exploit in the past, or those that can be anticipated they would attempt based upon the privileges and resources available to them. For example, at a conceptual level, one such misuse signature might relate to a user who is identified as attempting to modify a record about him/her in a database. The rule here is that no one should modify their own records without someone else's authorisation. The problem with applying misuse-based detection to insider misuse is that the possible misuse scenarios for insiders are wide ranging and could be extremely organisation-specific. Thus it would be difficult to catalogue them all. Misuse-based detection is only as good as the database of signatures it relies upon for detection. Therefore, the database would need to be updated constantly to detect new attack methods. This approach would not be suitable for insider misuse detection as it would be too time-consuming in person-hours to create misuse signatures for all possible scenarios and to continually keep them updated.

Anomaly-based detection. This approach relies upon watching out for things that do not look normal when compared to typical user activities within the system. In standard IDS, the principle is that any event that appears abnormal might be indicative of a security breach having occurred or being in progress. The assessment of abnormality is based upon a comparison of current activity against a historical profile of behaviour that has been established over time (Anderson *et al.*, 1994). One advantage insider misuse detection system has over outsider attacks is that it is possible to characterise normal activities of insiders according to their job position, as users with the same responsibilities should exhibit similar activities within the system and application environment to complete their daily tasks. The similarities may be profiled to represent normal behaviour for users with the same responsibilities, and different profiles for different job positions. If the user's behaviour deviates from the normal profile that represents his position, the activity should be flagged as suspicious. An example would be monitoring frequency of access to certain databases can lead to the detection of in insider who browses the database for personal use. Examples of such databases are medical records, and criminal records.

The concept of applying the techniques for the detection of misfeasor activity makes the task more difficult, because we are dealing with legitimate users who are not violating system level access controls. From a misuse-based detection perspective, it is more difficult to identify the ways in which an insider might misuse the resources to which they have legitimate access, while from an anomaly detection perspective the level of behaviour profiling would need to be more precise and comprehensive. When basing the assessment upon a comparison against their behaviour profile, a legitimate user misbehaving will almost certainly be more difficult to identify than a total impostor who is masquerading under the legitimate user's identity, because it is more likely that the impostor's behaviour would deviate by a larger margin, whereas conversely the deviation is likely to be minimal for a legitimate user who abuses existing privileges. In addition, in an adaptive system, the process of profile refinement might be exploited by wily misfeasors who gradually train the system to accept misuse behaviour as normal. Again, when users change positions within the organisation, their behaviour would change to reflect the new responsibilities assigned. A potential solution to counter the exploitation of profile refinement, and improve profile management is to profile common user behaviour based on the role the user takes up within the organisation. Another advantage of role-based profile comparison is that when the users of a particular role are assigned special assignments, the sudden change of user profile may not be considered anomalous, if the changes are similar for all users within the same role. Individual user profiles can be complemented, such that activities associated with job responsibilities are stored in the role profile and the rest in individual user profiles.

5. KNOWLEDGE OF SEPARATION OF DUTIES

Another problem associated with insider misuse detection is that current IDSs lack the necessary knowledge of business processes, organisation hierarchy, separation of duties, and the role of the users within the organisation structure. This knowledge needs to be expressed in the form that is understandable to the detection system, if effective misfeasor monitoring is to take place. Role management principles specified by (Gavrila and Barkley, 1998) are utilised in Role-Based Access Control

(RBAC) to support user role assignment, role relationships, constraints and assignable privileges. The idea of role-based access control was introduced by Ferraiolo and Khun (1992). While privileges are assigned directly to users in Discretionary and Mandatory Access Control methods, assignment of privileges is a two stage process in RBAC. Privileges are assigned to roles and the users are assigned to roles, subsequently the user inherits the privileges assigned to the role. A role can be thought as a collection of operations required to complete the daily tasks of a user. This approach simplifies the task of assigning permissions to the user, as the roles for appropriate job functions are created with the least privileges required to complete the relevant tasks and the users are assigned to the role that reflects their responsibilities. Users can be assigned from one role to another, or assigned multiple roles, and permissions can be assigned at role-level to affect all users associated with the role. This use of roles is similar to the use of groups in Discretionary Access Controls (DAC). The main focus of RBAC is to maintain the integrity of the information by defining who can perform what operations on which set of data. The type of operations and objects that can be controlled by RBAC is dependant upon the environment and the level at which it has been implemented. For example, at the OS level, RBAC may be able to control read, write, and execute; within database management systems controlled operations may include insert, delete, append, and update; within transaction management systems, operations would take the form that express the properties of a transaction. The term transaction here means a combination of operation and the data item affected by the operation. Therefore, a transaction can be thought of as an operation performed on a set of associated data items. The ability to control specific transactions, rather than restricting simple read and write operations are very important in database environments. For example, a clerk may be able to initiate a transaction and the supervisor may be able to correct the completed transactions, for which both users need read and write access to the same fields in the transaction file. However, the actual procedures for the operations and the values entered may be different. Meanwhile, the clerk may not be allowed to correct the completed transactions and the supervisor may not be allowed to initiate the transactions. The problem is that determining whether the data has been modified in the authorised manner, for it can be as complex as the actual procedures that modified the data. This is where SQL fingerprinting techniques utilised in DIDAFIT can be employed. However, transactions need to be certified and classified before associating them with the roles. To characterise the required transactions for a role, duties and responsibilities of the users need to be specified first.

The most interesting feature of RBAC is the ability to define relationships between roles and enforce separation of duties. In RBAC, separation of duties can be applied by specifying mutually exclusive roles, and allow administrators to regulate who can perform what actions, when, from where, in what order and sometimes under what circumstances. Access controls only allow or deny access to certain resources, however there is a need to monitor and analyse the user actions after the access has been gained and the operations had been carried out. In theory the idea of roles and role-management principles can be applied to misfeasor monitoring. Instead of allowing or denying operations to be performed, common user operations can be associated with roles, and the users can be assigned to appropriate roles. If the user's operations deviate from the common profile, a thorough investigation can be carried out to clarify if the user has misused the system in an inappropriate manner or for unapproved purpose.

6. PROPOSING A FRAMEWORK FOR MISUSE MONITORING

It has been mentioned previously that anomaly detection is more suitable for insider misuse detection, because employees' normal behaviour can be profiled. It is assumed that the users with the same responsibilities within the organisation will exhibit similar activities within the system, and their working-scopes may be established. The idea of establishing working-scopes for users with same responsibilities has been tested in relational database environments by Chung *et al.* (1999). However, in order to be able to detect violation of separation of duties, the detection system needs to be provided with the knowledge of organisation hierarchy and relationships between roles. RBAC utilises role-relationship management principles to define role-hierarchy and separation of duties. The authors' proposed system combines the ability of RBAC to provide knowledge of role- relationships, with intrusion detection techniques to effectively detect users who abuse their existing privileges.

Figure 1 presents the framework of the conceptual insider misuse detection system. Functional modules are explained in subsequent paragraphs.

6.1 Management Functions

All management functions, such as defining roles, characterisation of operations, association of operations to roles and user assignment to roles, are carried out from the Management Console. The working scope of a user is defined by the operations associated with the role(s) the user assumes. Once the separation of duties between roles has been defined, it is expressed in the Role-Relations Matrix, such as inheritance, static separation of duties, and dynamic separation of duties. Static separation of duties occurs at the role level by specifying mutually exclusive roles. When the two roles are in static separation of duties, a user may not be assigned both roles. Dynamic separation of duties occurs at the operations level and the conditions can be that operations within dynamically separated roles are mutually excluded, disallowed to execute concurrently, or disallowed to be performed on the same set of data.

When the two roles are in dynamic separation of duties, the user may not execute the operations that are mutually exclusive or on the same set of data. The relationships expressed in the Role-Relations Matrix are checked against the rules specified by (Gavrila and Barkley, 1998) for consistency.

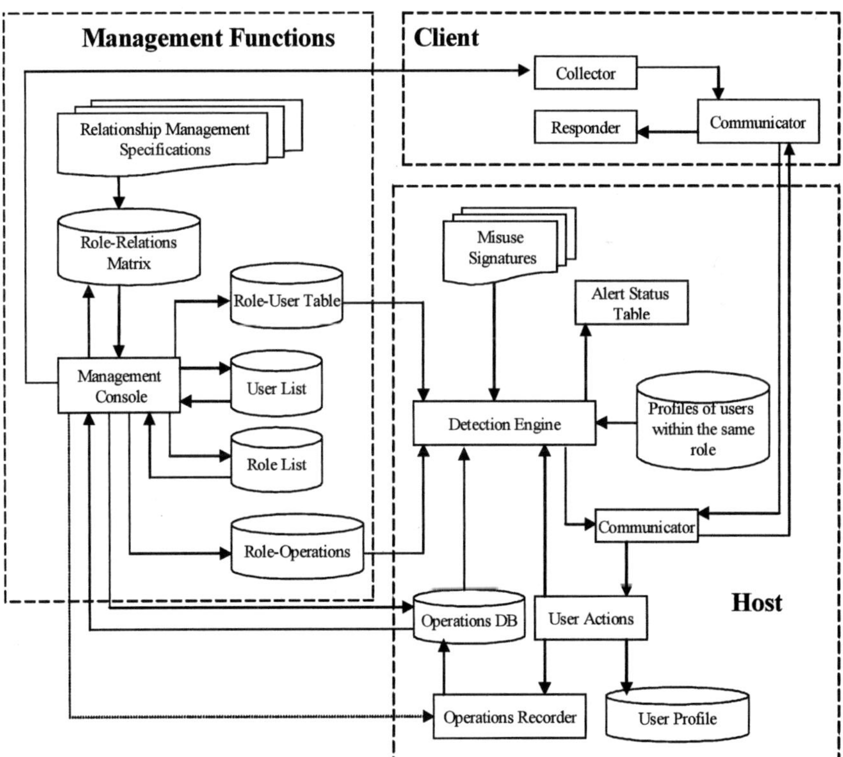

Figure 1. Conceptual Framework for Role-Based Monitoring of Insider Misuse

6.2 Host

This is where the actual profiling of user(s) and the detection process takes place. Characteristics of each operation are stored in the *Operations DB* along with an appropriate name for each operation. The characteristics are dependent upon which level of the system they are being profiled at. Characteristics of the operations may be in the form of file access, sequence of system calls, SQL queries, API calls, User interactions, and Network access. Recording the characteristics of each operation is controlled from the *Management Console*.

The profiling should be done at all three levels of the system namely: network, system, and application level. The *Detection Engine* checks the roles available to the active user, and next checks the *RoleOperations* table for the names of the operations available to the user. After this, the characteristics of the available operations from the *Operations DB* are compared to the current user actions. If current user actions do not match the characteristics of operations available to the user, the administrator is alerted. This alert may indicate the user performing a totally new operation, or performing a valid operation in the *Operation DB* but is violating separation of duties because the operation is not listed under any roles the user may assume.

The envisaged detection flow is as follows:

1. Detection Engine gets the name of the user from the Client. Looks for the roles the user's name is associated with, in the Role-User table.
2. After acquiring the list of roles for the user, the Detection Engine looks for the names of the operations associated with each role in the Operations DB (Note: only names of the operations are associated with the Roles.)
3. After acquiring the names of operations available to the user, the Detection Engine reads the characteristics of available operations from the Operations DB and they are compared against current user actions.
4. If the current user action matches with the characteristics of operations available to the user, then the user is not in breach of static separation of duties.
5. If OpA belongs to RoleA, OpB belongs to RoleB, and RoleA and RoleB are in dynamic separation of duties. Condition of the separation is checked to clarify whether the operations are: mutually

excluded; disallowed to execute concurrently; or disallowed to perform both operations on the same set of data.

If the user violated the specified condition, the system security officer is alerted. In addition, the misuse rules employed in expert systems within traditional IDSs can also be included. These rules may then be associated with an operation, such as modifying the payroll database to increase one's own wages. In this case, the process is as follows: If modification is performed on the payroll database, check that the employee ID of the user is not the same as that of the record being modified. (Note: This will require the inclusion of system user ID in the personnel records.)

6.3 Client

This is where the actual data is collected and transferred to the Host for analysis. The *Clients* can be network server systems or end-user workstations. The nature of the data collected may vary depending on the type of the *Client*. For example, mail logs can be collected from the mail server, user queries from the database server, and application logs from user workstations. The data to be collected is specified by the system administrator from the *Management Console*. The collected data can then be refined to a standard format by the *Communicator* module before sending the data to the *Host*, so that data from heterogeneous *Client* systems is in a standard format. The *Client* may also have a *Responder* module to respond to detected incidents, and the appropriate response for each incident can be specified from the *Management Console*. For example, when a misuse is detected, the *Responder* may be configured to terminate the user session, revoke privileges, deny further access, alert the security officer, or terminate the anomalous process (Papadaki *et al*., 2003).

7. DISCUSSION AND CONCLUSIONS

Insiders pose a considerable threat and organisations need to give equal priority in detecting insider abuse as well as outsider attacks. Access controls only allow or deny access; however there is a need to monitor what the user does after gaining access to the system and objects. In order to effectively monitor privilege abuse, IDS require the knowledge of organisation hierarchy, managerial controls, responsibilities and working scopes of each user. The methods employed in RBAC to express knowledge of roles, organisation hierarchy, and separation of duties can be coupled with intrusion detection techniques to detect users who abuse their existing privileges. This paper presented a framework for monitoring users who abuse their existing privileges.

In order to be able to implement the system successfully, separation of duties would first need to be defined at the organisation level. Next, the responsibilities of the users need to be defined. Then it needs to be checked that the operations a user is allowed to perform would not lead to a successful misuse. All of these are more of a managerial (rather than technical) issue. However, these are not trivial and could require considerable amount of time and labour. Again, at a technical level, monitoring of user behaviour at application level may require modification of the software package if appropriate APIs are not included.

The authors' future research will focus on developing the proposed system and testing it against a variety of simulated insider misuses, such as data theft, fraud, net abuse, sabotage, and breach of privacy.

8. REFERENCES

Amoroso, E., 1999, *Intrusion Detection: An Introduction to Internet, Surveillance, Correlation, Traceback, Traps and Response*, First Edition, Intrusion.Net books, NJ, ISBN: 0966670078.

Anderson, D. Frivold, T. Tamaru, A. And Valdes A., 1994, Next-generation intrusion detection system (NIDES): Software users manual, Technical Report. Computer Science Laboratory, SRI International. December 1994.

Anderson, J.P., 1980, Computer security threat monitoring and surveillance. Technical Report, James P Anderson Co., Fort Washington, April 1980.

Audit Commission, 1990, Survey of computer fraud & abuse: Supplement. Audit Commission, 1990.

Chung, C.Y. Gertz, M. Levitt, K., 1999, DEMIDS: A misuse detection system for database systems, in the Proceedings of the 3rd International Working Conference on Integrity and Internal control in Information Systems. 18-19 November, Amsterdam. pp. 159-178.

Ferraiolo, D. Kuhn, R., 1992, Role-based access control, In the Proceedings of the 15th National Computer Security Conference, October 1992, Washington DC. pp. 554-563.

Gavrila, S.I. Barkley, J.F., 1998, Formal specification for role based access control user/role and role/role relationship management, Third ACM workshop on Role Based Access Control, October 22-23, Fairfax, Virginia. pp 81-90.

Lindqvist,U. and Porras, P., 2001, eXpert-BSM: A host based intrusion detection solution for Sun Solaris. 17th Annual Computer Security Applications Conference, New Orleans, December 2001.

Low, W. L. Lee, J. Teoh, P., 2002, DIDAFIT: Detecting intrusions in databases through fingerprinting transactions. In the Proceedings of the 4th Internationsal Conference o Enterprise Information Systems, Ciudal Real, Spain, April 2-6, 2002.

Paxson, V., 1998, Bro: A system for detecting network intruders in real-time, In 7th Annual USENIX Security Symposium, San Antonio, Texas, January 26-29, 1998, pp.31-52.

Phyo, A.H and Furnell, S.M., 2003, Data gathering for insider misuse monitoring, In the Proceedings of the 2nd European Conference on Information Warfare and Security, pp.247-254, University of Reading, UK, 30th June-1st July, 2003.

Portilla, F., 2003, Analysis of insider misuse in commercial applications, MSc thesis, University of Plymouth, United Kingdom, September 2003.

Power, R., 1995, Current and future danger: A CSI primer on computer crime and information warfare. San Francisco, CA: Computer Security Institute.

Power, R., 2002, 2002 CSI/FBI computer crime and security survey. Computer Security Issues & Trends, Vol. VIII, No. 1. Computer Security Institute. Spring 2002.

Richardson, R., 2003, 2003 CSI/FBI Computer Crime and Security Survey, Computer Security Institute. Spring 2003.

Roesch, M., 1999, Snort - lightweight intrusion detection for networks, In the Proceedings of the 1999 USENIX LISA Conference, Seattle, Washington, November 7-12, 1999, pp.229-238.

Theregister, 2002, Leyden, J. (July 9 2002); P45s for porn surfers, http://www.theregister.co.uk/content/6/26098.html.

UPDATE/PATCH MANAGEMENT SYSTEMS:
a protocol taxonomy with security implications

Andrew Colarik, Clark Thomborson, and Lech Janczewski
The University of Auckland, New Zealand

Abstract: Software fixes, patches and updates are issued periodically to extend the functional life cycle of software products. In order to facilitate the prompt notification, delivery, and installation of updates, the software industry has responded with update and patch management systems. Because of the proprietary nature of these systems, improvement efforts by academic researchers are greatly restricted. One solution to increasing our understanding of the underlying components and processes is architectural recovery. One contribution to recreating an architecture is the examination of design specification literature, such as patents. If a sizeable amount of similar and hopefully diverse patents can be examined, then some general conclusions about the components and processes of existing systems may be formulated. In this paper, we present an analytic framework consisting of a five-phase protocol taxonomy based on thirty-three software-based update and patch management system patents and patent applications. Furthermore, we present a decomposition of the security design provisions contained within the patent literature, and provide some general trends derived from the data. We suggest that this research may be used to improve the security services aspect of update and patch management system products.

Key words: Architectural Recovery, Taxonomy, Patches, Updates, Patents, and Security Design Provisions.

1. INTRODUCTION

At the core of the maintenance phase of the software development life cycle are the issuance of patches (software fixes) and updates (a collection of fixes and improvements) to resolve system faults, flaws (bugs), and security holes in an attempt to extend the functional life of a software product. Due to the time and effort required to assess, locate, and acquire these updates, the on-going effort is often delayed or over-looked by users and system administrators until some urgency or incident occurs that prompts a swift response. In recent years, software manufacturers have typically provided access to their product updates via the Internet (i.e. website, ftp, e-mail, bulletin boards and newsgroups). Interestingly, connectivity to the Internet has also created an additional burden to the issuance of updates and patches. The CERT Coordination Center maintains statistics on the number of vulnerabilities reported that can potentially be / have been exploited through malicious acts, virus infections, and self-replicating worms, among others. For the past three years, the vulnerabilities reported have continued to nearly double from the previous year. There were 1090 reported vulnerabilities reported in 2000, 2437 in 2001, and 4129 in 2002 [CE03]. The need for systematic notification, acquisition, and deployment of patches and updates has prompted the software industry to produce update and patch management systems. There are numerous producers and products of patch and update systems (see Table 1: Examples of Patch/Update System Products).

Table 1: Examples of Patch/Update System Products

Company Name	Product
BigFix Incorporated	BigFix Patch Manager
Bindview Corporation	bv-Control
Citadel Security Software	Hercules
ConfigureSoft	Security Update Manager
Ecora Corporation	PatchMeister
Gibraltar Software	Everguard
Harris Corporation	STAT Scanner
Hewlett-Packard	Security Check Patch
McAfee Security	OilChangeOnline
Microsoft Corporation	Windows Update
PatchLink Corporation	Patchlink
Ringmaster Software Corporation	Ring Master
Shavlik Technologies	HFNetChkPro
St. Bernard Software	UpdateEXPERT
Sun Microsystems	Patch Management Module

From a design and academic perspective, a primary problem emerges: How do we, as researchers, peel away the proprietary tendencies of organizations to hide the inner designs and processes of their products in order to better understand, communicate and hopefully improve the development of such systems? In the event that the original architectural design literature is unavailable, one possible approach is to reverse engineer the architecture through the use of system code, views, and documentation [Ei98]. The authors of this paper propose a supplemental approach using the information disclosed by inventors in patents and patent application documents, and in particular when such resources are unavailable.

In section two of this paper, the authors present a discussion on the contributions of a taxonomy towards reconstructing system architectures. In sections three and four, we present our patent search criteria, and provide a protocol phase taxonomy derived from 33 update and patch management system patents and patent applications. We then re-examine the patents for security design provisions by each phase of the taxonomy in section five, and present a discussion of the security design implications and limitations of our findings in section six.

2. CONTRIBUTION OF A TAXONOMY

Before a discussion on the significance of a taxonomy towards reconstructing software architectures may occur, some basic understandings of what comprises an architecture, and some of the issues in acquiring and documenting an architecture needs to occur. Shaw & Garlan (1996) state that:

> *"The architecture of a software system defines that system in terms of computational components and interactions among those components. Components are such things as clients and servers, databases, filters, and layers in a hierarchical system. Interactions among components at this level of design can be simple and familiar."*

As academics attempting to conceptually improve on existing systems, poorly documented or non-existent architectures (in documented form) pose a significant problem. Even when architectures do exist, they may no longer be valid because many systems simply have evolved beyond their original documentation due to in-process design development, and maintenance of existing code to adapt to changing conditions [Ka99]. Thus, reverse engineering and decomposition of existing systems becomes essential. The process begins at the lowest level of abstraction with an examination of the product's source code and documentation. These are used to develop a set of software views with the use of domain knowledge by the researcher. Combining all these elements, in theory, should lead the researcher to developing a set of architectural elements that will be used to formulate the system's architectural representation [Ei98].

The discovery process of re-creating a software's architecture involves an assembly of disparate sources of information by interpretive means. It is a very subjective process that may result in substantial variation from one researcher's interpretation to another. Because the researcher's interpretation is based on available information and the researcher's own understanding of the subject matter, the process can be prone to error. It would, therefore, be reasoned that any additional contribution to clarifying the components or subsystems that comprise an architecture adds to the accuracy and consistency of its reconstruction. We propose that a taxonomy is a useful tool in architectural reconstruction, and creating a common reference point for researchers to improve existing products and processes.

The American Heritage Dictionary (2000) defines "taxonomy" as "the science, laws, or principles of classification"; and the "division into ordered groups or categories" [Jo00]. The significance to architectural discovery provided by a taxonomy lies within the context of the ordered groups. The contributions provided by a taxonomy towards understanding an underlying architecture are:

- Additional domain knowledge by which a researcher may interpret other aspects of accumulated design documentation and coding decomposition analysis [Ei98],
- Provide a visual representation as to how the components detailed are organized [Ka99] [Pa00],
- Explicitly/implicitly ask who, what, where, when, and how questions in order to provide abstractions to the corresponding categories of the taxonomy [So92], and
- Provide a means for defining what data are to be searched for and recorded, as well as a means for a comparison between specimens [La94].

In the following sections, we present our patent search criteria, the proposed, developed taxonomy, and apply the taxonomy phases to the security design provisions contained within the patent documents.

3. SEARCH CRITERIA

The original focus for this line of research was to add to our understanding of the fundamental design components and specifications that are predominant in the updating systems environment by providing a representative sample of global patents. Thus, our intention was to review the patent literature that represented complete, software-driven systems for the purpose of studying the interconnecting processes. To be eligible for our review, the literature had to involve the update of operational and/or application code excluding firmware (i.e. not processors, modems, etc). The emphasis of the search was placed on "method of" instead of "apparatus for" in order to reduce the amount of hardware dependence in the specification. Where appropriate, patent applications were also included. Lastly, due to the popularity of English regarding end-user targeted markets, and commercial development centres, our emphasis was placed on patents filed in English.

The first step was to search the patent databases' abstracts for occurrences of "patch", "update", "dissemination", etc. in order to initially narrow the volume of potential systems. This initial step reduced the possible systems to approximately 2,000. After appraising the remaining abstracts, 100 patent and patent applications were selected for detailed examination by applying the search criteria. This process resulted in 24 patents and 9 patent applications from which we formulated a better understanding of the state-of-the-art in update and patch management systems.

Because our goal is to develop a technological understanding of update and patch management systems, we examined only the descriptive matter and diagrams of each patent. We did not analyze the claims of any patent for their novelty, originality, or specificity. Such matters are of vital importance in legal proceedings, but were not a factor in our development of the taxonomy.

4. TAXONOMY PHASES PRESENTED

During the detailed examination of the patent documents, we discovered that the patents contained a sequence of communication steps for initiating a communication session, performing some exchange of information regarding updates, performing some determination as to the requirement to deliver an update, transporting the update, and initiating an installation. Within each of these protocol phases, there emerged distinct categories as to the means or methods to facilitate each phase. It is these phases and categories that we base the following taxonomy (see Table 2: Updating / Patch Management Systems Protocol Taxonomy).

Table 2: Updating / Patch Management Systems Protocol Taxonomy (5 sub-taxonomies)

	Activity Phase	Category		Count	Patents (see references)
Protocol	Contact	Client	User Defined	19	A2, A4a, A7a, A8a, A9a, P1, P2, P3, P7, P8a, P9, P12a, P13, P14, P15, P16, P20, P22a, P24a
			System Defined	19	A4b, A5, A6, A7b, A8b, A9b, P4, P5a, P6, P8b, P10, P11a, P12b, P17, P18, P21, P22b, P23, P24b
		Server	User Defined	2	A3a, P11b
			System Defined	6	A1, A3b, A7c, A8c, P5b, P22c
		Integrated / Combined		1	P19
	Selection	Client to Server		20	A2, A4, A5, P2, P3, P4, P5, P7, P8, P9, P10, P12, P14, P15, P16, P17, P18, P20, P23, P24
		Server to Client		10	A3, A6, A7, A8, A9, P6, P11, P13, P21, P22
		Integrated / Combined		2	A1, P19
		No Exchange		1	P1
	Determination	Index / Manifest / Table		28	A1, A2, A3, A4, A5, A6, A7, A8, A9, P1, P2, P3, P5, P6, P7, P9, P11, P12, P13, P14, P15, P16, P18a, P19, P20, P21a, P22, P23
		State Change		3	P10, P18b, P21b
		Configuration Information		4	P4, P8, P17, P24
	Transport	Client	Pull	25	A1a, A2, A3a, A4, A5, A6, A7a, A8a, A9, P1, P4a, P6, P9, P10, P11, P13, P14, P15, P16, P17, P18, P20a, P21a, P22a, P24a
		Server	Push	11	P2, P3, P4b, P5, P7, P8, P12, P19, P20b, P21b, P23
			Reference Location	6	A1b, A3b, A7b, A8b, P22b, P24b
	Installation	Client	Manual	11	A1, A2a, A5, A6a, P1a, P2a, P3a, P7a, P12a, P16a, P20a
			User Enabled	19	A2b, A6b, A7a, A8a, P1b, P2b, P3b, P4a, P5a, P7b, P9, P11a, P12b, P13, P14, P15a, P16b, P19, P20b
			Automated	13	A2c, A3, A6c, A9, P5b, P6, P12c, P15b, P16c, P17, P20c, P21, P23
		Server	User Enabled	3	P8a, P11b, P24a
			Automated	12	A4, A7b, A8b, P2c, P3c, P4b, P7c, P8b, P10, P18, P22, P24b

The above activity phases can best be thought of as answering the following questions:

- Contact: When is contact initiated and by whom?
- Selection: Where is the exchanged information compared?
- Determination: What is the basis for the determination of an update?
- Transport: How is the update acquired?
- Installation: Who has control of the installation?

Within each phase, there are self-explanatory categories identifying the methods discussed in the patent literature. However, we would like to clarify several categories within the Contact, Selection and Determination phases. In the Contact and Selection phases, "Integrated / Combined" designates that the processes are a combination of communications and transfers of information between the client and the server (much more than a handshake). In the Determination phase, "Index / Manifest / Table" refers to a software data list that is used for comparison with a master list. "State Change" refers to the status-data of the software. When a given state change is detected between two systems (client/server), the master system (server) restores or updates the software of the servant (client) to the new state.

It should be noted that within each patent there were variations and multiple embodiments of the claims presented. This allowed an inventor to assert variations on the approaches/methods claimed. Thus, in Table 2 there are multiple category entries within each phase for the same patent. For instance, patent P8 describes an embodiment in which a client permits the user to initiate the communication manually (P8a: user defined) or the client contacts the server on a timely/periodic basis (P8b: system defined).

5. SECURITY PROVISIONS

The term "secure" carries with it a multitude of subjective implications and exceptions. Before a software product can be identified as secure, the security objectives, i.e. "a statement of intent to counter identified threats and/or satisfy identified organization security policies and assumptions" [Co99], must be considered with regards to standard security fundamentals. Because these security objectives are either confidential, poorly documented or non-existent, we needed a way to examine each phase of the protocol taxonomy so that any security provisions contained within the design documentation (i.e. the patent) could be identified and classified. Our purpose was to facilitate the emergence of any potential design trends [Pa00].

Therefore, utilizing the The Open Group Architectural Framework (TOGAF) Security Services guidelines as a basis for considering any design considerations contained within the patents, we re-examined the documentation by each phase of the protocol. These guidelines are based on the Technical Architecture Framework for Information Management (TAFIM), developed by the US Department of Defence, and are used in the development of an IT architecture. The guidelines are outlined in Table 3.

Table 3: TOGAF Security Services Guidelines [Op03]

Service	Criteria
Identification and authentication	Identification, accountability and audit of users and their actions
	Use of authentication and account data
	Protection of authentication data
	Active user status information
	Password authentication mechanisms
System entry control	Security-aware warning to unauthorized users
	Authentication of users
	Information about login attempts
	User initiated locking of a session
Audit	Authorized control and protection of the audit trail
	Recording of security-relevant events
	Audit trail control, management and inspection
Access control	Access control attributes for subjects and objects
	Enforcement of rules of access control attributes
	Enforcement of access controls
	Control of object creation and deletion, including reuse of objects
Non-repudiation	Proof that a user carried out an action, or sent or received some information, at a particular time
Security management	Secure system set-up and initialization
	Control of security policy parameters
	Management of user registration data and system resources
	Restrictions on the use of administrative functions
Trusted recovery	Recovery facilities in ways that do not compromise security protection
Encryption	Ways of encoding data such that it can only be read by an appropriate key or other secret information
Trusted communication	A secure way for communicating parties to authenticate themselves without the risk of masquerading
	A secure way of generating and verifying check values for data integrity
	Data encipherment and decipherment
	A way to produce an irreversible hash of data for support of digital signature and non-repudiation functions
	Generation, derivation, distribution, storage, retrieval and deletion of cryptographic keys

Each patent was re-examined with regards to the TOGAF security criteria (see Table 3). An allocation to an appropriate phase was assigned if the patent provided some account of a security service or mechanism that matched at least one of the TOGAF Security Services' qualifications. An example would be that at the installation phase, a given inventor states that a digital certificate would be included with the update file to ensure the file's integrity and source of origin. The patent would be allocated to the non-repudiation and trusted communication provisions of the installation phase. Table 4 summarizes the results.

What we have attempted to provide is a classification of the assertions made in the body of patents and applications, with regards to any security design provisions that the inventor has proposed to include in their particular invention. What we have not provided in this research is any evaluation of the feasibility, reliability or efficiency of any of the specified mechanisms or systems. Such evaluations would be a fruitful, albeit difficult, subject for future research.

Our analysis of the patent literature is summarized in Table 4. We observe that inventive activity has focused mostly on the provision of security in the installation phase (75 counts in Table 4), with relatively little attention being paid to the selection and determination phases (24 and 17 counts). Frequent use was made of audit and trusted communication, but very little mention was made of security management and access control.

Overall, the patents and applications take a reasoned approach to providing security in update and patch management systems. Even so, the empty cells in Table 4 reveal security provisions that are not discussed in the patent literature we reviewed, but which we believe must be addressed at some point in the development of a truly secure patch management system.

- System Entry and Control Services, in the Determination phase (0 counts). The patent literature reveals no provision for authenticating users or objects. This may become a problem if the data to be compared is encapsulated as an object.
- Access Control, in the Transport phase (0 counts): no provision for privilege management. This function could be used as a push distribution point for malicious code in the same sense that viruses exploit E-mail address books to distribute themselves.
- Non-Repudiation, in the Contact phase (0 counts): no proof of identity, even though transactions may be audited. In the Determination phase (0 counts): a lack of non-repudiation may be a limiting factor in secure deployments where it is important to establish proof of origin, original content, delivery, and/or original content received.

Table 4: Number of Patents with Various Security Provisions, by Phase

33 Patents Total		Activity					Total Counts
		Contact	Selection	Determination	Transport	Installation	
Security Provisions	Identification and authentication	12 (E1)	5 (E2)	2 (A4, P8)	6 (E3)	8 (E4)	33
	System entry control services	7 (E5)	1 (P8)		1 (P21)	2 (P8, P21)	11
	Audit	6 (E6)	4 (E7)	4 (E8)	13 (E9)	18 (E10)	45
	Access control	1 (P8)	2 (P8, P13)	2 (P8, P13)		3 (E11)	8
	Non-repudiation		1 (P8)		2 (P13, P17)	9 (E12)	12
	Security management	2 (P8, P17)	1 (P8)			4 (E13)	7
	Trusted recovery			1 (P21)	2 (P17, P21)	17 (E14)	20
	Encryption	6 (E15)	4 (E16)	3 (E17)	10 (E18)	4 (E19)	27
	Trusted communication	6 (E20)	6 (E21)	5 (E22)	12 (E23)	10 (E24)	39
Total Counts		40	24	17	46	75	202

Entries with more than 2 patents or applications

E1: A3, A7, A8, A9, P4, P5, P8, P10, P18, P21, P22, P24

E2: P5, P8, P17, P21, P24

E3: P2, P3, P5, P7, P8, P21

E4: A7, A8, P8, P15, P16, P21, P22, P23

E5: A7, A8, P4, P5, P8, P21, P22

E6: A7, A8, P8, P10, P18, P22

E7: A7, A8, P4, P22

E8: A7, A8, P4, P22

E9: A2, A7, A8, P5, P6, P9, P13, P14, P15, P16, P20, P21, P22

E10: A2, A7, A8, P2, P3, P4, P5, P6, P7, P8, P9, P13, P14, P15, P16, P17, P20, P22

E11: P9, P13, P15

E12: P8, P9, P13, P14, P15, P16, P17, P20, P23

E13: P2, P3, P7, P16

E14: A2, A7, A8, P2, P3, P6, P7, P8, P9, P11, P14, P15, P16, P17, P19, P20, P22

E15: A7, A8, P8, P10, P18, P22

E16: A2, P8, P10, P18

E17: P10, P18, P21

E18: A2, P5, P9, P10, P14, P15, P16, P18, P20, P21

E19: A9, P10, P16, P21

E20: A2, A7, A8, P8, P10, P18

E21: A2, P8, P10, P13, P17, P18

E22: A1, P10, P17, P18, P21

E23: A1, P9, P10, P13, P14, P15, P16, P17, P18, P20, P21, P23

E24: A7, A8, P10, P14, P15, P16, P17, P18, P22, P23

- Security Management, in the Determination (0 counts) and Transportation phases (0 counts): we interpret this as an insufficiency in requirements specification, rather than as a defect in design. These forms of security are easily provided by underlying network protocols and operating systems.
- Trusted Recovery in the Contact (0 counts) and Selection phases (0 counts): no secure method is proposed to authenticate, generate and verify integrity check values. We interpret this as another insufficiency in requirements specification, rather than in design.

Our summary matrix (Table 4) can also be used to generate research questions. For instance, as noted above, we found no provision for non-repudiation in the contact phase. Two questions that come to mind are "Would there be any benefit to the server if the client initiated contact in a non-refutable manner?" and "Would there be any benefit to the client if the server initiated contact in a non-refutable manner?" We believe that the answers are "yes", and that enquiry along these lines would lead to improvements in the design, requirements specification, and other documentation for update and patch management systems.

A detailed examination or study of the subjectivity involved in conducting this research may be of value for establishing parameters for future academic research that attempts to draw conclusions about a technological field by examining the patent literature.

6. SUMMARY

In this paper, we have argued that taxonomies can be a valued contribution in the understanding and the reconstruction of system architectures, and that they may be effective in organizing system(s) design documentation. We developed an analytic framework for describing and characterizing update and patch management systems. The framework was developed from a consideration of the systems disclosed in the bodies of thirty-three (33) patents and patent applications. Our analytic framework has the following elements: a generalized update process, a decomposition of the update process into five (5) phases, several alternative methods for accomplishing each phase of the protocol, and a consideration of the security services that may be provided by each phase. We have established that when a taxonomy is combined with industry design specifications (our 5 phase protocol & TOGAF), useful trends may be inferred, and additional research questions may be developed for pursuing the improvement of system architectures [Co03].

REFERENCES

[CE03] CERT Coordination Center Statistics, http://www.cert.org/stats/cert_stats.html, 2003.

[Co99] Common Criteria Management Committee, "Common Criteria for Information Technology Security Evaluation, Part I: Introduction and general model, Version 2.1", August 1999.

[Co03] Colarik, Andrew, "A Secure Patch Management Authority", PhD Thesis, University of Auckland, November 2003.

[Ei98] Eixelsberger et al., "Recovery of Architectural Structure: A Case Study", *Proceedings of Second International ESPRIT ARES Workshop, LNCS 1429*, pp. 89-96, 1998.

[Jo00] Johnson, Samuel, "American Heritage Dictionary of the English Language, Fourth Edition", Houghton Mifflin Company, 2000.

[Ka99] Kazman, Rick, and Carriere, S. Jeromy, "Playing Detective: Reconstructing Software Architecture from Available Evidence", *Automated Software Engineering*, 6, pp.107-138, 1999.

[La94] Landwehr et al., "A Taxonomy of Computer Program Security Flaws", *ACM Computing Surveys*, 26(3), September 1994.

[Op03] Open Group, "The Open Group Architectural Framework Version 7", http://www.opengroup.org/togaf/p3/trm/tx/tx_secur.htm, 2003.

[Pa00] Payne, Christian, "The Role of the Development Process in Operating System Security", *Proceedings of the Third Information Security Workshop, LNCS 1975*, 2000.

[Sa96] Shaw, Mary, and Garlan, David, *Software Architecture: Perspectives on an Emerging Discipline*, Prentice Hall, 1996.

[So92] Sowa, J.F., and Zachman, J.A., "Extending and formalizing the framework for information systems architecture", *IBM Systems Journal*, 31(3), 1992.

<u>Patent Applications</u>

[A1] US 2002/0004402 A1, Suzuki, Naoya, Assignee: None, "Update notification system, update monitoring apparatus, mobile communication terminal, information processing apparatus, contents acquisition instructing method, contents acquiring method, and program storing medium", January 10, 2002.

[A2] US 2002/0016956 A1, Fawcett, Phillip, Assignee: Microsoft Corporation, "Method and system for identifying and obtaining computer software from a remote computer", February 7, 2002.

[A3] US 2002/0016959 A1, Barton et al., Assignee: Network Associates Technology, Inc., "Updating computer files", February 7, 2002.

[A4] US 2002/0100035 A1, Kenyon et al., Assignee: None, "Asynchronous software update", July 25, 2002.

[A5] US 2002/0112230 A1, Scott, C., Assignee: None, "Software update management system with update chronology generator", August 15, 2002.

[A6] US 2002/0184619 A1, Meyerson, M., "Intelligent update agent", December 5, 2002.

[A7] US 2003/0046675 A1, Cheng et al., Assignee: None, "Automatic updating of diverse software products on multiple client computer systems", March 6, 2003.

[A8] US 2003/0046676 A1, Cheng et al., Assignee: None, "Automatic updating of diverse software products on multiple client computer systems", March 6, 2003.

[A9] US 2003/0070087 A1, Gryaznov, D., Assignee: None, "System and method for automatic updating of multiple anti-virus programs", April 10, 2003.

Patents

[P1] US 5,577,244, Killebrew, Alice, and Mann, Charles, Assignee: International Business Machines Corporation, "Methods of applying software modifications", November 19, 1996.

[P2] US 5,586,304, Stupek, Jr. et al., Assignee: Compaq Computer Corporation, "Automatic computer upgrading", December 17, 1996.

[P3] US 5,588,143, Stupek, Jr. et al., Assignee: Compaq Computer Corporation, "Automatic computer upgrading", December 24, 1996.

[P4] US 5,619,716, Nonaka et al., Assignee: Hitachi, Ltd., "Information processing system having a configuration management system for managing the software of the information processing system", April 8, 1997.

[P5] US 5,694,546, Reisman, Richard, Assignee: None, "System for automatic unattended electronic information transport between a server and a client by a vendor provided transport software with a manifest list", December 2, 1997.

[P6] US 5,732,275, Kullick, Steven, and Titus, Diane, Assignee: Apple Computer, Inc., "Method and apparatus for managing and automatically updating software programs", March 24, 1998.

[P7] US 5,809,287, Stupek, Jr. et al., Assignee: Compaq Computer Corporation, "Automatic computer upgrading", September 15, 1998.

[P8] US 5,835,911, Nakagawa, Toru, and Yuji, Takada, Assignee: Fujitsu Limited, "Software distribution and maintenance system and method", November 10, 1998.

[P9] US 5,845,077, Fawcett, Phillip, Assignee: Microsoft Corporation, "Method and system for identifying and obtaining computer software from a remote computer", December 1, 1998.

[P10] US 5,919,247, van Hoff et al., Assignee: Marimba, Inc., "Method for the distribution of code and data updates", July 6, 1999.

[P11] US 5,933,647, Aronberg et al., Assignee: Cognet Corporation, "System and method for software distribution and desktop management in a computer network environment", August 3, 1999.

[P12] US 5,974,454, Apfel et al., Assignee: Microsoft Corporation, "Method and system for installing and updating program module components", October 26, 1999.

[P13] US 5,999,740, Rowley, David John, Assignee: International Computers Limited, "Updating mechanism for software", December 7, 1999.

[P14] US 6,049,671 Slivka, Benjamin, and Webber, Jeffrey, Assignee: Microsoft Corporation, "Method for identifying and obtaining computer software from a network computer", April 11, 2000.

[P15] US 6,073,214, Fawcett, Phillip, Assignee: Microsoft Corporation, "Method and system for identifying and obtaining computer software from a remote computer", June 6, 2000.

[P16] US 6,256,668 B1, Slivka, Benjamin, and Webber, Jeffrey, Assignee: Microsoft Corporation, "Method for identifying and obtaining computer software from a network computer using a tag", July 3, 2001.

[P17] US 6,263,497 B1, Maeda, Tetsuji, and Mori, Toshiya, Assignee: Matsushita Electronic Industrial Co., "Remote maintenance method and remote maintenance apparatus", July 17, 2001.

[P18] US 6,272,536 B1, van Hoff et al., Assignee: Marimba, Inc., "System and method for the distribution of code and data", August 7, 2001.

[P19] US 6,308,061 B1, Criss, Mark, and Cowan, Paul, Assignee: Texlon Corporation, "Wireless software upgrades with version control", October 23, 2001.

[P20] US 6,327,617 B1, Fawcett, Phillip, Assignee: Microsoft Corporation, "Method and system for identifying and obtaining computer software from a remote computer", December 4, 2001.
[P21] US 6,341,373 B1, Shaw, Robert, Assignee: Liberate Technologies, "Secure data downloading, recovery and upgrading", January 22, 2002.
[P22] US 6,457,076 B1, Cheng et al., Network Associates Technology, Inc., "System and method for modifying software residing on a client computer that has access to a network", September 24, 2002.
[P23] US 6,493,871 B1, McGuire et al., Assignee: Microsoft Corporation, "Method and system for downloading updates for software installation", December 10, 2002.
[P24] WO 0190892, McCaleb, Jed, and Rive, Russell, Assignee: Everdream Inc., "Intelligent patch checker", November 29, 2001.

INVESTIGATING A SMART TECHNOLOGY

Kevin O'Sullivan, Karen Neville, and Ciara Heavin
Business Information Systems, University College Cork, Cork, Ireland

Abstract: Today's society is extremely apprehensive and cautious regarding security attacks with the result that identification and authentication have become a necessity. Sectors such as healthcare, education and transportation all require robust identification solutions and Smart-cards can deliver these solutions. The memory capacity and processing capabilities of the Smart-card make it vastly superior to competing technologies such as magnetic stripe cards, which are susceptible to such threats as 'skimming' and as a result are very insecure. Additionally, the data on the cards is often erased or corrupted by scratches or magnetic interferences. There are however many disadvantages to Smart-cards; such as the fact that both the cards and the infrastructure necessary can be costly. In order to be acknowledged as a standard and to enhance user acceptance of the cards, it requires a behavioural, on the part of the user, rather than technological change.

To date previous research studies have focused on Smart-card failures. However, this paper investigates the introduction of this Smart technology into an educational setting. Therefore the factors that affect its acceptance and use as well as the issues facing organizations and universities in adopting the technology are investigated. The paper provides a comprehensive analysis of the findings of the case through an illustration of the factors identified in relevant literature and those identified in the study (see Table 1) as well as unforeseen behavioral issues from the users such as a mass student protest against the use of the card.

Key words: Smart-card technology; innovation; user acceptance; security and education.

INTRODUCTION

As the need for trust, authenticity and security in digital communications becomes ever greater, the case for robust identification solutions grows stronger [Katz *et al.,* 2002]. This paper outlines how Smart-cards can deliver these solutions in an educational institution due to their inherent strengths focusing security among other factors. The benefits of the technology are discussed in the paper to explain why Smart-card technology is so an important for today's 'closed communities' and organizations. The advantages and disadvantages of Smart-cards are outlined to highlight the benefits that they can provide, as well as the disadvantages that may be hindering their acceptance and use. The reasons for the introduction of Smart-card technology are outlined and security will be argued as a reason why Smart-cards are utilized, by discussing the risks and issues involved and why security is so important and necessary for varied forms of operations; from accessing a building to conducting a financial transaction. Therefore, encryption and the levels used to combat security issues or threats are discussed to highlight the potential of the Smart-card to combat these threats. Additionally, the paper briefly explains the security risks that exist in conjunction with the Smart-card to illustrate that while the technology is an intrinsically secure device [Urien, 2000], it is not one hundred *percent* secure [McGraw *et al.*, 1999]. Innovation diffusion theory is discussed, as Smart-card technology is viewed as relatively new, and a model of some of the factors affecting the acceptance of an innovation is examined. The paper concludes that there is a need to research Smart-card technology and the factors necessary for its acceptance and use. It argues the validity of the technology as well as possible factors that may be slowing its acceptance.

1. THEORETICAL FOUNDATION

Moore (1994) believed that for an organization, innovation is any product, input, process, service or technology that the organization perceives as new. Truman *et al.*, (2003) claimed that Smart-card technology fits this description of an innovation as it is new to most individuals and organizations despite the fact that it has existed, albeit in various familiar forms such as telephone call cards. A popular model to explain and predict rates of IT innovation adoption is the diffusion of innovation theory (DOI) [Rogers, 1995], which aids new IT implementations. Rogers (1995) defines diffusion of innovations (DOI) as the process "*....by which an innovation is communicated through certain channels over time among the members of the social system*". The model identifies five essential characteristics that enhance the rate and effectiveness of diffusion as follows: (1) relative advantage, (2) compatibility, (3) complexity, (4) trialability and (5) observability. The first characteristic is the relative advantage of the innovation over the idea it replaces, including economic profitability, convenience and/or other benefits. The innovation is more likely to be accepted if it is perceived as providing advantages [Hebert & Benbasat, 1994]. The second characteristic is the compatibility of the innovation with the existing values, past experiences and needs of the adopters. People are more likely to adopt technology if it is functionally compatible to those previously adopted [Dearing *et al.*, 1994] and is consistent with the existing values, needs and past experiences of adopters [Rogers, 1995]. The third characteristic relates to the level of complexity or the ease with which an innovation can be understood. Finally, the fourth and fifth related characteristics are described as trial ability, or the degree to which adopters can implement an innovation, on an experimental basis and observability, or the extent to which results of an innovation are visible to others. Rogers's theory found that these *five* factors were dependent on the specific nature of the innovation but also on the specific characteristics of the adopting group. The people who do not trust technology, for example, are generally older, less educated and earn low salaries [Punishill & Shevlin, 2001]. Research has shown that the perceived characteristics of an innovation are closely linked to adoption [Rogers, 1995], more so than the personal characteristics of the adopting group [Tornatzky & Klein, 1982].

The value of innovative applications is dependent upon the adoption and acceptance by the relevant parties involved [Plouffe *et al.*, 2001] such as the party implementing it and the intended users because if one of the groups resisted, then it could threaten the introduction of the innovation. The benefits derived from increased usage of a technology, can be seen in the use of the telephone for example. If it was not used, then what would be the point of someone adopting it as the users would have no one to establish a connection with, but as more people used the technology, the benefits of adopting the technology (the Phone) continued to increase. Truman *et al.*, (2003) use this argument when explaining that Smart-cards technology is suffering from a similar fate as the benefits gained from Smart-cards will increase as more users adopt the card.

1.1 Smart-cards

A Smart-card is a "*...credit card sized conventional plastic card*", containing an embedded silicon computer chip (which can be non/programmable microprocessor) [Blakey & Saliba, 2000]. Di Giorgio (1998) describes it simply as a credit card with a '*brain*', which allows a large amount of information to be stored, accessed and processed either on or off line [Choi *et al.*, 1998]. Smart-cards are in fact differentiated by the type and size of integrated chip (IC) used by the manufacturer and the method of communication utilized to interact with Smart-card readers [Sorenson, 2001]. Smart-card technology has been in use since the early 1990s but it is still considered a relatively new technology by retailers, consumers and users [Truman *et al.*, 2003]. It has many technological advantages over rival technologies, such as the magnetic stripe card, which includes: *(1) security, (2) memory size, (3) portability, (4) convenience, (5) multiple applications, (6) cost savings* and *(7) micro-charging.*

(1) The *Security* component incorporated into the design of Smart-cards provides a secure means of physically carrying information as it protects against '*....the illegal use of lost or stolen cards, manufacture of counterfeit cards, the manipulation of data and fraudulent use of the card*' [Newing, 1998]. Carrying Smart-cards are extremely secure through the use of multiple factor authentications [Perkins, 2002] so that both the card and a personal identification number (PIN) are required. This two factor authentication that the Smart-card possesses can considerably reduce fraud, ensuring the integrity and security of transactions, therefore saving millions [Wallis, 2002] for financial institutions. It can also be applied to the Internet where the security threats faced means identification and authentication are very important for trust [Pohlmann, 2001]. However, when used as a wallet Smart-cards are like cash in that if they are lost the cash on the card is gone forever [McGraw, 1998]. The self-containment of the card makes them tamper resistant [Lett *et al.*, 2002]. Cryptographic algorithms can be stored locally in their internal circuitry, unlike the magnetic stripe cards, therefore protecting and retaining the users' *'secrets'* [M'Raihi & Yung, 2001].

(2) Smart-cards provide a greater *memory* capacity than magnetic stripe cards which have a total storage of 125 bytes while the microchip on the Smart-card can hold large amounts of data ranging from 1Kbps to 64Kbps [Kapoor, 2002]. One benefit of this is the ability to track customer spending records [Miller, 2002]. The card can also physically separate data into a multi-partition file system, so that many applications can be safely run on a single Smart-card [Rastogi & Das, 2002]. The extra memory can also allow them to utilize biometrics and encryption [Rastogi & Das, 2002].

(3) Smart-cards are *portable,* making the card and the credentials they carry, such as private keys, very manageable [Berney, 2000]. The extra layer of security that the card provides means that users are not limited

to a particular desktop computer [Coia, 2002]. However this user mobility is only possible if every machine that the user accesses has a Smart-card reader attached [Chadwick, 1999].

(4) Apart from the *convenience* added through their portability, smart-cards can also replace the various identification cards, notes and coins by combining them into a single card [Choi *et al*., 1998]. Smart-cards are ideal because of their convenience and ease-of-use [Lee *et al*., 2000] due to the use of a form (plastic card) that people are familiar with [Gemplus, 2003].

(5) The ability to handle *multiple applications* is one of the primary reasons for the cards growth. According to a study by Frost & Sullivan (2003), *'....smart-cards are the only token technology that provides multi-application capability coupled with a multi-function form factor that is virtually ubiquitous'*. Due to the processing power of smart-cards, the card is ideal to mix multiple functions, which can help organizations such as colleges or governments to manage and improve their operations at lower costs [Choi *et al*., 1998] and offer innovative services. The card allows companies to work with partners in other industries to provide complementary services and customers to enjoy more customised services that add convenience and ease of use. In fact, the interoperability or multi-application use is the way forward in terms of consumer acceptance [Alder, 2002].

(6) Smart-cards can have transaction *cost savings* over other stripe cards. When the card is read by an electronic reader the encryption devices validate and verify each other. The technology also allows transactions to be carried out off/online, eliminating the middleman as telephonic verification is no longer required for authorisation [Miller, 2002]. Smart-cards, unlike magnetic-stripe cards, can carry all necessary functions and information on the card and do not require access to remote databases at the time of the transaction [Coleman, 1998]. Smart-cards can also reduce labor costs by eliminating paper and therefore paper handling which is especially important in paper heavy industries such as healthcare [Choi *et al*., 1998] or education.

(7) Smart-cards are ideal for *micro-charging* or payments such as small Internet purchases because cheques and credit cards are too expensive [Karppinen, 2000]. There is also a growing demand for an alternative to credit cards because children and young adults will not be able to gain access to the smart-card e-purse which can be used for micro-payments [Lee *et al*., 2000].

Essentially the technology, as outlined, offers numerous benefits to the different types of users. However as with every technology the Smart-card is susceptible to issues that affect user acceptance.

1.2 Disadvantages of Smart-card Technology

Smart-cards, offer many incentives, however, the disadvantages arising from the technology must also be identified before its introduction into any environment. The following are some of the disadvantages of the technology: *(1) cost, (2) privacy, (3) standardization, (4) consumer acceptance* and *critical mass* and *(5) multiple application issues.* Each of the disadvantages identified are outlined in the next section:

(1) To avail of the technology, organizations need to deploy readers, which add to the *cost* of deployment and also limits the use of the cards to locations where the infrastructure is ready and available [Armstrong, 2001]. Currently, there is a lack of infrastructure to support Smart-cards. This is one of the greatest disadvantages for merchants due to the expensive cost of replacing former equipment with smart-card-compliant terminals as well as additional operating expenses and the cost of training employees [Manchester, 1997]. Increasing numbers of vendors and manufacturers are entering the Smart-cards market, which will force prices down [Christensen *et al*., 2001].

(2) One factor that is causing concern is *privacy*, especially as a single smart-card holds considerable information about its user and can create an audit trail of their transactions resulting in the loss of anonymity that existed with cash transactions [Beverly *et al.,* 2002]. The information it stores is usually already available in some format or another and the card merely makes that information portable, available and in the possession of the owner [Wood, 2002]. Credit card information, for example, already includes an enormous amount of customer data based on preferences and habits [Wood, 2002].

(3) *Standardization* is vital to the development and acceptability of Smart-card technology [Banerjee, 1997] because according to the emerging markets theories [Day & Fein, 2000] standard wars tend to slow down the diffusion of new technical innovations [Rogers, 1995]. Standardization and interoperability are crucial factors in achieving a critical mass of users [Papameletiou, 1999] and if they do not exist, it acts as deterrents to expanded Smart-card deployment [Frost & Sullivan, 2003]. Due to the amount of Smart-card systems entering the market, Smart-cards interoperability is important because people do not want to carry more cards and have separate incompatible ways to use them [Mäntylä, 2001]. It is also important for the Smart-card application developers so that they do not have to deal with a variety of different card terminals and operating system languages when developing their applications. Smart-card operating systems are extremely important because with open operating systems there is no dependence on a single manufacturer or application developer leading to a greater choice of manufacturers and

application developers [Chandak & Shah, 2001] cost reduction, processing capabilities and most importantly, interoperability [Moll, *et al.*, 2001] as multiple applications can reside on the same card.

(4) One of the biggest obstacles to the mass adoption of smart-cards is *customer education.* Most consumers do not know what they need or want until they actually have it [Wallis, 2002]. The use of a smart identification in organizations to provide access to both physical and digital resources will force employees to become accustomed to having their cards in their possession at all times. Education and advertising will be very important in changing people's habits and expectations of this new technology [Truman *et al.*, 2003].

(5) Smart-cards are flexible and therefore can be used for *different applications* [Pohlmann, 2001] but responsibility in the case of a problem (technical or legal) with a multifunctional card providing several applications from different services is a dilemma. The issue of control of the card and how it is managed will and does cause concern.

Today, Smart-cards exist in one form or another in many different sectors and are a part of everyday life in areas such as banking, transportation, access and mobile communications. Smart-cards offer almost unlimited application possibilities and realise their true value when a single card handles multiple applications. There is a move towards the multi-application smart-card with the maturity of operating systems such as Java and Multos, and falling prices. According to Briney (2002), the multi-application capability of the smart-card is the single principal driver of its growth. Hovenga Fancher (1997) claims that the smart-cards will be a tool for addressing the *'customer of one'* with customisable generic cards eventually becoming available allowing the customer to choose from a menu of applications. The primary market or use of the card are communities or *'closed systems'*, such as universities or the military. These communities generally tend to be successful [Truman *et al.*, 2003] as people are affiliated with them and there tend to be discounts or a lack of alternatives. This paper therefore investigates the adoption of the technology in an educational setting.

2. RESEARCH OBJECTIVE AND APPROACH

The objective of this research was to investigate the adoption of Smart-card technology in an educational environment considering the factors which affect its acceptance and use. The objective required the researchers to gain an in-depth understanding of Smart-card technology focusing on how the cards are deployed and utilized in an academic setting. Due to the qualitative and exploratory nature of this study, a single site case study was employed as the most appropriate research approach. Consequently, semi-structured interviews were conducted using a pre-constructed interview guide. The questions were prepared based on previous research in the area of Smart-card technology, the researchers found this approach to be adequately flexible, allowing the respondents to develop certain questions where necessary and to address areas that were not suggested in the guide but that they felt were pertinent to this research.

3. BACKGROUND TO THE CASE- WIT

Waterford Institute of Technology (WIT) is the sole provider of higher education in the South East region of Ireland, and has the highest number of third level students in the sector, with over 6,000 current full-time students and over 4,500 part-time students. The Auxiliary Services (AS) Committee at WIT controls all of the trading operations on campus with the aim of providing high quality non-academic services and facilities for the student population of WIT. Approximately seven and a half years ago, WIT made a decision to investigate the possibility of using Smart-cards for printing and photocopying due to the expense of paper handling. WIT initiated a research project where they researched the systems used in other colleges. For two years, WIT conducted onsite investigations and gathered research from other implementations in both American and European universities. WIT then created a final report with the best components from each University system that was suitable for an Irish environment. The college decided to employ their own team, and develop an in-house system. The photocopying and printing system was put in place two months later and the vending and point-of-sale over a period of two years. Currently, WIT has fifteen applications, running on their Smart-cards which the college developed in-house. Unfortunately there was not sufficient time to test the card initially as WIT were committed to introducing the card in September 1999, and also because the college felt it was very difficult to introduce it in a test situation primarily due to the fact that students would not take it seriously. Since then, any new application WIT introduces is accepted and implemented on a pilot basis. WIT succeeded in installing the entire project at no cost, sourcing finance and support from different sectors. A considerable benefit for the college was the introduction of the card for printing and photocopying as students had no other option but to use the card. When the college introduced vending and then point-of-sale in the restaurants, the students were already accustomed to the technology.

3.1 The WITCard

The WITCard is one of twenty-six different services that the committee provides. It was introduced in September 1999, by AS, and it is the official identification card for both staff and students. It is a multifunctional card which has replaced all of the other cards in use by integrating various applications into one single card, namely the following: the library, college identification, printing, photocopying, point-of-sale, vending, access control and voice mail. The card allows cashless purchasing on campus where the card is used at any point-of-sale on the campus, such as the restaurants and campus shops. A bar code on the card is still used in the library to allow users to borrow books and journals. In the event of a charge for late return of books, the electronic purse can be used to make the appropriate payment. There is also an Internet Card Management System (Internet CMS), recently developed by WITCard Services, which allows the card holder to check their card balance, view and print statements of all transactions, deactivate their card, and change their password.

3.2 Incentives for Use

The college conducted a joint survey with Irish and British banks on the cost of handling cash. The results of the survey concluded that the cost was somewhere between twelve and fifteen *percent*. If a student or staff member uses their card on campus to buy items such as food or stationary, they will get a ten *percent* discount due to the reduction in the costs of handling cash. Therefore, the benefits from the savings are passed onto the card user in the form of discounts. The college has also received other huge savings such as labor costs and safety. The WIT library is also a cashless environment; the restaurant will not accept cash, only a card, eliminating problems with floats, or cash. Prior to the introduction of the WITCard, the college did not have many security systems in place. The card used by the college was just an identification card with a barcode printed on it. Essentially, there was no security and for safety reasons, students have much more faith carrying e-cash as opposed to carrying cash. The PIN feature of the WITCard is not used except when security is required. Currently, the only place the PIN on the chip is used in the college is for access control to campus residences, to protect against thieves accessing those residences with stolen cards. Even when purchasing, at the tills there is no PIN as the manual entry of the PIN slows down the queue. While the facility is there for the PIN the college has not used it and they do not see the need to use it because they have not encountered any breach of security. Security has become an increasingly important issue for WIT and the college is using Smart-cards to deal with this issue. The Smart-cards is superior to the magnetic stripe in terms of security and makes students feel secure in the knowledge that user accounts will not be compromised and that students will not lose their money. Confidentiality, integrity, non-repudiation, and authentication are all key factors. At the moment WIT guarantee these factors as students are provided with back-office accounts. As EMV (a Europay, MasterCard, and Visa devised specification) develops and WIT incorporates an open electronic purse on the card and start using open payment systems such as Java cards, they will then have to utilize a very secure authentication system.

An additional advantage to the university is the increased productivity of their staff. For example, one simple benefit at the moment is modernising the 'clocking-in' systems. There was a 'Working Time Act', introduced in 1997, which obliged all employers by law to record the time and attendance of their employees. The act was implemented to stop claims by employees that their health had been damaged when they were forced to work more than the statutory forty-eight hours a week. In September 2003, all of WIT's non-lecturing staff, using their WITCard to access facilities, will have their time and attendance recorded and held on record for three years. For the students, the WITCard is extremely easy to use as well as portable, which means that they are not limited to any single location with the card. Students also have fewer cards to carry around as the WITCard is multifunctional and has replaced all of their other cards by integrating the various applications onto one single card. There is also the ten *percent* discount that the students get for using the card instead of cash. The college also promotes the WITCard as much as possible, and students can win prizes such as televisions and bicycles, by using the card at a particular time. This marketing strategy was very popular with both the students and staff, as every time they used the card they had a better chance of winning a prize.

3.3 Difficulties Encountered

The cost of the implementation was a very important factor for WIT, however once the college decided on a Smart-card system, they worked on ways of raising money to fund the project. The college selected a system, that was robust, that would actually handle magnetic stripe and allow migration of applications from the magnetic stripe to the chip. If WIT had not planned the migration from magnetic stripe to chip from the start of the project, the whole system would have had to be rebuilt. A lot of similar projects failed because they did not plan at the early stages for this change in technology two or three years later. As research has shown s*tandardization* is very important factor and WIT are currently working with colleges across Europe to develop standards for Universities and colleges so that there will be interoperability between them so that cards in one college should be able to work in another. The WITCard is compatible with standards such as common electronic purse specification (CEPS) and personal computer / Smart-cards (PC/SC) however these are not approved standards. There has to be an agreed standard under the International Standards Organization (ISO) which uses an accreditation system.

Training was part of the initial rollout and was provided and managed by AS. Courses were provided for the operators of the tills, as well as for students and staff. Students were even employed to tutor training courses and promote the card within the student population. AS also produced and provided promotional videos and pamphlets describing the card system. The college was expecting that in the second year of the introduction they would encounter *resistance* because in the first year the card was new and the students would view it as a novelty. At WIT, as their research had shown them, it was in the second year when the card actually started to take hold that the college experienced resistance from a group of the students for a period of about three months. More than 6,000 students organised by the students union, boycotted lectures at WIT for a day, in protest against the use of the new card system. The resistance centred on the fact that the card was expected to be insecure. Students also presumed that college management were reading the information stored in the back-office system, such as: where students were eating and what they purchasing, which, according to the college was not the case. When implementing change, there is always going to be resistance but it is important to target the core services that students require. The college succeeded in reducing the cost of printing so students experienced a massive reduction. The discounts were part of the strategy to increase acceptance but a lot of students felt that the college was discriminating against a core student body by giving a ten *percent* discount for card use. Another reason for the resistance was due to the fact that WIT was the first college to implement this type of card in Ireland. Other colleges considering implementing the Smart-card systems will be able to see the key benefits of the technology and they will be able to avoid the problems encountered by WIT. There is a sense of prestige or image for students of WIT to have this card because the WITCard was the first chip student card and is currently unique in comparison to other institutes. Some of the initial resistance was also caused by students who were angry that the majority of transactions on-campus were card-based, resulting in long queues for the few remaining cash tills. The benefits of mixed cash as opposed to a non cash system are not as high as there are still cash handling problems with the mixed system. Currently, the WIT has fifty *percent* of all their money on campus in electronic cash (e-cash), and fifty percent of it in cash. WIT is expecting that within the next few years it will increase to between seventy and seventy five *percent* e-cash. The driving factor for the card at the moment is the ten *percent* discount. Students will actually use the card if they get a ten *percent* discount and plus the fact that a lot of the college's operations at the moment, such as the sandwich bar, the new library, the campus bookshop, will not accept cash which means that every student or staff member at some stage has to use their card. The card is compulsory, in that it is a standard college identification (ID) card, therefore the card operates within a 'closed environment' effectively eliminating choice within the college and usability off-campus.

WIT has an acceptance agreement with all of their cardholders (both students and staff), that the college will not release any information that is stored on the cards or in the back-office account without the cardholder's written permission. The only exception to this is, if a student or staff member's health is at risk. Access will only be issued when there is clear evidence that the health of a student is at risk, for example if the student was missing and the police wanted to see where the student last used the card. Initially, the students were protesting because it was felt that the card was an intrusion on their privacy and that the college was monitoring the users spending habits and deducting library fines automatically from the user accounts (which was the case) during the Summer. Under the conditions of the privacy agreement formed with the student body, WIT can not, if there is a fine outstanding in the library, deduct funds from users it is currently the responsibility of the library to enforce the payment of fines, not the card office (see Table 1 for a summary of the findings).

Smart-Cards		*Educational Case: The WITCard*	
Advantages	*Disadvantages*	*Problems Encountered*	*Benefits Derived*
Security: Multiple factor authentication [Armstrong, 2001; Lewis, 2002] Processing capabilities Self containment Tamper resistant [Lett *et al.*, 2002],	**Privacy:** Loses anonymity of cash [Beverly, 2002].	**Cost:** The cost of the system was important early on but WIT wanted the best system they could buy– raised finance and support from different sectors.	**Security:** Fewer muggings of students. Less chance of robberies in college shops as there is no cash. Security is important and magnetic stripes

Access to memory controlled Lock-down [Lewis, 2002] Copy proof Gemplus, 2003] PKI [Bassett, 2001]		In house system. Planning was very important in saving later expenses such as migration costs.	can be *'skimmed'* too easily. Pin only used for access to campus residences as PIN's slow queues. Multiple applications only important where fraud is a problem.
Memory Size: Greater than magnetic stripes [Rastogi & Das, 2002] Allows multiple applications [Miller, 2002] Biometrics & Encryption	**Standardisation:** Standards not well developed [Husemann, 2001]. Standarisation and interoperability [Papameletiou, 1999].	**Standardisation:** WITCard is compatible with certain standards but there needs to be ISO accepted standards. Important to be EMV compliant. Modern chip obsolete by 2005.	**Cost savings**: Reduction in the cost of handling cash – 12 to 15%. Students get a 10% discount on all smart card purchases. Do not have to hire cash handling company.
Portability: Size of a credit card [Pikrammenos, 2002] Not limited to one location [Coia, 2002].	**Consumer acceptance:** Customer education Education and advertising [Truman *et al.*, 2003].	**Training:** Training courses for operators & staff. Promotion and marketing for students with pamphlets and videos.	**Convenience:** Replaced all other cards students had to carry around
Multiple Applications: Processing power Lower costs	**Multiple Applications:** Who manages the card? [Newman & Sutter, 2002].	**Resistance Usage:** Fears over security of money Privacy of information Tracking of student's use Length of queues Card was used for core services No choice	**Portability:** Students are not limited to one location with the card.
Convenience: Provides convenience	**Cost:** Deployment Readers	**Privacy:** WIT guaranteed privacy of	**Ease–of–Use:** Very easy to use for the students.

Ease-of-use Familiar method [Gemplus, 2003] Wallet size	Replacing former equipment Training	information on card.	
Cost Savings: No telephonic [Newcombe, 1999] Timesavings [Miller, 2002], Eliminates paper handling costs [Choi *et al.*, 1998] Cash handling [Kalakota & Whinston, 1996] More reliable and longer lasting [Chanson, 1998; Petri, 2002] Easily updated without reissuing [Gemplus, 2003]		**Initial Problems:** No major problems, some minor problems such as card not reading	**Productivity:** Makes job of college staff easier, for example, time and attendance.
Micro-charging: Ideal for small purchases [Karppinen, 2000].			**Transaction Times Reduced:** Special queues for students using smart cards, is faster as no change involved.

Table 1: **Case Findings**

4. DISCUSSION

Presently, WIT is using a 'Schlumberger Payflex' manufactured two kilobyte contact chip on their Smart-cards. The college was using magnetic stripe cards prior to the introduction of the WITcard as well as barcodes and felt that it was important not to implement change too quickly. For this reason, to date, all three methods have been retained on the card, which are used at different outlets. WIT's plan over the next two years is to transfer all of the applications onto the chip because *"...the chip is a much more secure system than the magnetic stripe"*. The college has never had a breach in the security with the card to date, which is very important as *"...you can never guarantee security*". WIT also plan to introduce a contactless technology using the 'Phillips MiFare Contactless' technology system, for access control and time and attendance. Contactless technology plays a significant part in Smart-card systems particularly in areas such as access control and transportation, resulting in benefits such as speed of transactions which is ideally suited to busy processes in WIT such as for example, taking the attendance of students. The weakness of contactless technology is that banks have yet to adopt it as a secure standard and it is really only suitable for low-level security applications like access control and transit where a large amount of money is not required. The college decided on a Linux based system with Oracle for the operating system because Microsoft was "*...a costly product due to licensing arrangements....*". The college also found Linux to be a very robust system, which worked very well. Originally, WIT would have bought an operating system from a vendor but there was nothing available in Ireland, the products available in the UK were very poor and the US systems were changed frequently so the college decided to just build their own. In addition, the college would also have had to learn the proprietary system, thus delaying the delivery of the system and making it harder to develop applications.

WIT is able to store their e-purse on the WITCard chip but the cards are in a closed environment. Currently, the purse is stored online in a back-office database. The college researchers identified a number of problems when students' downloaded money onto the chip as when the end users lost their card, they would automatically lose their money. Due to the back office account (saving the different transactions), the college can replace the card and replace the money instantly. It is possible for WIT to download money onto the chip. This functionality will be implemented in the future when management decides to extend the usability of the Smart-card to off campus, as a form of payment for public transport for example. This would involve the students downloading a small amount from their main back-office account onto the chip for use outside the campus.

5. CONCLUSION

Clearly, there are a number of lessons that may be learned from the WIT Smart-card implementation. Firstly, it is evident that in this current environment security issues are to the forefront of user's concern when utilizing Smart-card technology. Every application on the campus is currently online so there is no need to store money on the chip which ultimately provides greater security to the end-users, as the main money is in the back-office account. The WITCard is secure which is important because if a student does not feel the card is secure they will not use it. Although, the audit trail generated by such a card remains a limitation of the technology. Secondly, ease of use has become another key factor when considering the introduction of new technology to any environment. User's expectations have heightened over the last number of years as organizations strive to manage customer needs through the provision of products, services, information and most importantly ongoing support. Smart-card technology is no different, customers have come to expect the quickest and easiest means of doing business and for Smart-cards this means synthesizing a range of functionality into one single, portable, multipurpose card. Finally, it is evident from the WIT case that in order for user's to accept and effectively utilize the new technology, they must be provided with some kind of incentive to encourage them to do so. In this instance, students were offered a 10 percent discount on campus for using their cards. Considering the average demographic and income status of the student body, offering discounts was the key strategic move in promoting the widespread use of the WITCard. While the WIT Smart-card implementation experienced some problems, it seems that WIT is focused on a 'smart future' with plans for the card to store applications, *"...but you have to crawl before you walk and there is no point in going too far too quick"*.

REFERENCES

Alder, E., (2002), Smart Card Technology - Hong Kong: Legal Issues in Smart Card Technology,*Computer Law & Security Report*, Vol. 18, no. 2, Pg 120 – 123, 2002.

Armstrong, I., (2001), Smartcards: Still a Gamble?, SC Magazine, October 2001, Second Feature.

Banerjee, R., (1997), Smart Card Standards and Electronic Purse, A review paper, Card Dynamics Consultant to THE SMART CAMPUS project, May 1997

Berney, L., (2000), Smart Cards Begin to Arrive in B2B E-Commerce, E-Commerce World Magazine, 02/01/00.

Beverly, P. *et al.*, (2002), Secure Personal Identification Systems: Policy, Process and Technology Choices for a Privacy-Sensitive Solution, Smart Card Alliance White Paper, February 2002.

Blakey, E. & Saliba, C., (2000), Smart Cards Stack the E-Commerce Deck, E-Commerce Times, December 28th, 2000.

Briney, A., (2002), A Smart Card for Everyone?, Information Security Magazine, March 2002, www.infosecuritymag.com/2002/mar/cover.shtml

Chandak, A. & Shah, A., (2001), E-governance accelerates usage of smart cards in India, Express Computer Magazine.

Choi, S. & Whinston, A., (1998), Smart Cards: Enabling Smart Commerce in the Digital Age, CREC/KPMG White Paper, May 1998.

Coleman, A., (1998), The Future of Smart Cards: Java Card API, *Sun Journal*, Vol. 1, No. 4.

Day, G. & Fein, A., (2000), Shakeouts in the New Economy, Wharton Working Papers, 2001, hops.wharton.upenn.edu/people/faculty/day.html.

Dearing, J., Meyer, G. & Kazmierczak, J., (1994), Portraying the new: communication, *Science Communication*, 16, 11-42.

Gemplus, Inc., (2003), Smart Card Basics, http://www.gemplus.com/basics/what.html

Hebert, M. & Benbasat, I., (1994), Adopting Information Technology in Hospitals: The relationship between attitudes/expectations and behaviour, *Hospital and Health Services Administration*, 39(3), 369-383.

Hovenga Fancher, C., (1997), In your pocket: Smartcards, *IEEE Spectrum*, February 1997.

Kapoor, R., (2002), Enhancing customer value using smart cards, *Cards Worldwide*, 18/07/2002.

Karppinen, L., (2000), Attacks related to the smart card used in electronic payment and cash cards *Tik-110.501 Seminar on Network Security* http://www.tcm.hut.fi/Opinnot/Tik110.501/2000/papers/karppinen.pdf

Katz, *et al.,* (2002), Smart Cards and Biometrics in Privacy-Sensitive Secure Personal Identification Systems, A Smart Card Alliance, May 2002.

Lee, J., Walsh, E. & Gazala, M., (2000), Debit Cards Will Fuel Teen Online Spending, Consumer Technographics Brief, 2000, Forrester Research.

Lett, R., Brown, D. & Horrell, B., (2002), Smart Cards, *CS-590 Computer Security Planning & Engineering*, Spring 2002.

Mcelroy, D. & Turban, E. (1998), Using Smart Cards in E-Commerce, *International, Journal of Information Management*, 1998, Vol 18, No 1.

McGraw, G. & Felten, E., (1999), *Securing Java: Getting Down to Business with Mobile Code*, 2nd Edition, Published by John Wiley & Sons 1999

Manchester, D., (1997), Smart Cards: Key to Cashless Economy?, *The Futurist*, Jan/Feb., 1997, Pg 29-32.

Mäntylä, M., (2001), Smart card payment and risk scenarios, *T-110.501 Seminar On Network Security 2001*.

Miller, T., (2002), How Smart Are Smart Cards?, Entrepreneur.com, March 11, 2002

Moore, S., (1994), Understanding innovation in social science delivery systems, *Health Marketing Quarterly*, 11(4), 61 –74.

M'Raihi, D. & Yung, M., (2001), E-commerce applications of smart cards, *Computer Networks*, Vol 36, 2001, Pg 453 – 472.

Newing, R., (1998), Understanding Smart Cards, *PC Support Advisor*, Update 117, July 1998, Pg 7 – 12

Papameletiou, D., (1999), Study on Electronic Payment Systems for the Committee on Economic and Monetary Affairs and Industrial Policy of theEuropean Parliament, Vol I: Main Report, EUR 18753 EN.

Plouffe, C., Vandenbosch, M. & Hulland, J., (2001), Intermediating technologies and multi-groupadoption:a comparison of consumer and merchant adoption intentions toward a new electronic payment system, *Journal of Product Innovation Management*, Vol 18, Issue 2, March 2001, Pg 65-81.

Pohlmann, N., (2001), Smart Cards: The Authentication Solution for the E-business User, *Network Security*, Vol 2001, Issue 4, 1 April 2001, Pages 12-15.

Punishill, J. & Shevlin, R., (2001), Credit Card Issuers Need A New Approach To Online Security, TechStrategyBrief, July 2001, Forrester Research.

Rastogi, L., & Das, P., (2002), Re-Engineering Educational Institutions Through Smart Cards, SHTR Consulting Group.

Rogers, E., (1995), *Diffusion of Innovations*, 4th edition, New York: Free Press, 1995.

Sorenson, D., (2001), Smart-Card Devices and Applications, DELL White Paper, January 2001.

Tornatsky, L. & Klein, K., (1982), Innovation Characteristics and Innovation Adoption-Implementation: A Meta-Analysis of Findings, *IEEE Transactions on Engineering Management*, EM-29, 1, February, 28-45.

Truman, G., Sandoe, K. & Rifkin, T., (2003), An empirical study of smart card technology, *Information & Management*, Vol 40, Issue 6.

Urien, P., (2000), Internet card, a smart card as a true internet node, *Computer Communications*,Vol 23, pages 1655 – 1666.

Wallis, A., (2002), Interview with a smart card, Card Technology Magazine,25/09/2002,http://www.cardsworldwide.com/Tmpl/article.asp

Wood, C., (2002), Is That a Smart Card in Your Pocket?, PC Magazine, www.pcmag.com/article2/0,4149,1925,00.asp

PART TWO

IFIP TC11 WG 11.8 – INFORMATION SECURITY EDUCATION WORKSHOP

LABORATORY SUPPORT FOR INFORMATION SECURITY EDUCATION

Natalia Miloslavskaya, Alexander Tolstoy, Dmitriy Ushakov
Moscow Engineering Physics Institute (State University)
{milmur; ait; udv}@mephi.edu

Abstract: The Information Security Faculty of MEPhI has felt the necessity of designing educational environment for teaching information and network technologies and their security. MEPhI has already designed and implemented the Network Security Scientific and Research Laboratory. It consists of several logical segments: the Internet emulation segment, teams segments for mutual attacks and defense, control segment (a workplace of the administrator/instructor and entrance to the Internet), Distance Learning System and transport medium connecting all the segments. We defined traditional and distance educational courses utilizing the Laboratory, study objects and methods, preliminaries and resulting knowledge and skills, configuration of student/administrator working places, topology, methodical maintenance, scientific and research works, and technical support. Laboratory users carry out the following works: vulnerability and security testing and computer-aided testing facilities; familiarization with instruments used for ensuring system security; design of secure systems and subsystems. Several electronic tutorials for the different parts of the information security educational courses have been created.

Key words: security education, information security, network security, laboratory support, distance learning

1. INTRODUCTION

The Information Security Faculty of the Moscow Engineering Physics Institute (State University) (MEPhI) has felt the necessity of designing new educational environment for teaching information and network technologies. Higher education is undergoing structural changes in terms of not only student populations, but of learning paradigms and curricula. The student becomes an active participant in the classes. We need a testing area for student practices today more than ever, especially for the educational courses on computer and network security. This testing area should be "a real world in miniature" ready to different experiments on the network attacks and protection techniques that we cannot permit to our students in the real world of the University intranet or the global Internet. This is not surprising as it has pretty high theoretical foundation and at the same time has lacked any practical training. Of course, students were taught lectures, were recommended extra literature. Even various ways of implementing the obtained knowledge in everyday experience were described to them. Never the less we have to admit that all those activities are not sufficient nowadays. Applying for a job the person who has worked with the real equipment, who has designed and implemented even a small project, who is more or less familiar with the software in use, will undoubtedly have advantages over others. So, in fact, till now the students could oblige the knowledge and experience that they have got only to themselves, mainly because those knowledge and experience had been obtained with their own hands at the expense of aside activities during their free time.

MEPhI together with the Moscow's Microsoft representatives and some Russian commercial companies (such as STC Electron-service and CROC) has already opened the "Network Security" Scientific and Research Laboratory last year. Its main goal is to implement the "education-science-business" approach in practice. This, in turn, means:

1. new level of scientific and research activities of the MEPhI faculty;
2. increase of efficiency of specialist training in the group of "Information security" specialties and refreshing stuff training in the field of "security of information technologies";
3. adjustment of new educational technologies.

Having such a Laboratory, it is possible not only to continue the training of specialists in specialties "Complex protection of informatization objects", "Complex information security of computer-based systems" and "Computer security", but also increase its qualitative level. And having monthly personnel retraining courses for the Bank of Russia, Sberbank, Vnesheconombank, etc. on the basis of the faculty, it is possible to significantly increase the results of that training with the help of, for example, expansion of practical training or carrying out extra laboratory works.

Owing to such a considerable support we can use new educational technologies, for example, distance learning, distance progress testing (certification) and informational support of educational process.

Thus, there is evident increase of efficiency of specialist training and success in adjustment of new educational technologies. Students and even instructors themselves get real assistance in improvement of their theoretical and practical professional skill.

2. LABORATORY DESIGN

When only limited resources are available accurate planning and projection are a must for the most effective way of utilization those resources and high-quality implementation of the project. We defined the following stages of creation of the "Network Security" Scientific and Research Laboratory (further complex): preproject and projection stages, search for partners, project adjustment, assembling and start-and-adjustment work, presentation; operation testing and operation.

At the preproject stage the aforenamed Laboratory design premises were explored and the necessity of its creation was motivated. The project stage followed. It, in turn, included several stages at which the undermentioned points were defined:

- goals and tasks for the complex creation;
- educational courses utilizing the complex;
- objects and methods of Laboratory studies;
- preliminaries and resulting knowledge and skills;
- models of intruders, attack scenarios => necessary hardware configurations;
- configuration of working place of administrator and instructor;
- structure of complex;
- firmware requirements and specifications;
- teaching and methodical maintenance for laboratory, scientific and research works (textbooks, tutorials, policies, etc.);
- support of complex operation.

That is the projection stage related to compiling the logical project of the Laboratory and defining firmware requirements. At the same time after thorough analysis of the courses which will use the Laboratory the following main tasks for computer and network security education purposes were designated:

- research of the hardware, operating systems, data warehouses, software, and firmware and technical means of network protection;
- design of operational models of protected networks on the basis of new informational and network technologies on different platforms;
- adjustment of main methods and scenarios of distance learning and progress testing;
- creation of informational database of security technologies;

- education of users and students;
- detection of local and remote network attacks;
- analysis of mechanisms and means of attacks;
- discovery of channels of unauthorized information leaks from the system;
- definition of security policies and measures;
- elimination of the consequences of unauthorized intrusion into computer systems;
- evaluation of system's protectability;
- installation, configuration and administration of security equipment;
- development of new methods and systems for information protection;
- creation of "sandboxes" for temporary software and new technologies testing.

We know that "sandbox" laboratories for security education are not a new idea, however they are an excellent teaching and learning tool [for example 2, 3]. That is why we decided to implement it at the University.

To successfully carry out all those tasks the Laboratory should meet definite requirements. For example, when modeling secure networks it is essential to have sufficient flexibility of configuration and scalability, whereas when evaluating system's protectability and designing new methods of information protection – adaptability to new operational environment. Full list of project requirements was the following: maximum flexibility, simulation of various attacks, heterogeneity, low cost and availability.

The resulting logical structure of the complex satisfying all given requirements and able to carry out all listed tasks is depicted on the figure 1.

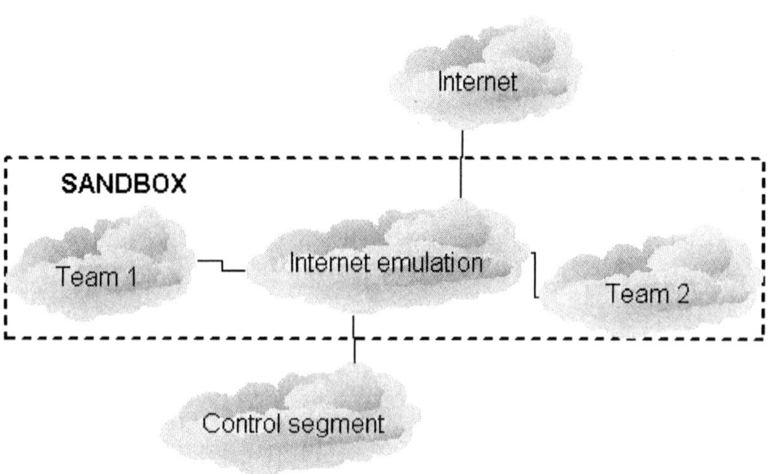

Fig.1: logical structure of the Laboratory.

Thus the Laboratory consists of several logical segments or areas performing different functions. This increases flexibility of the complex as a whole and allows its easy modification and/or expansion to fit new needs. The complex includes:

1. Internet emulation segment – a model of public data network.
2. "Team 1" and "Team 2" segments – for mutual attacks and defense.
3. Control segment – workplace of the administrator/instructor and glue to the Internet.
4. Transport medium, connecting all segments.

All segments include appropriate security equipment, the ultimate make-up being defined by the current solved problems.

Internet emulation segment plays the role of public data network and is the transit area, passing all the traffic of participating parties. That is why it is a proper location for various informational warehouses, "public" servers (DNS, proxy, Web, etc.) and a management system. The management system controls operations of the segment and executes the established security policy.

Team segments simulate different corporate subnets with typical for today set of work stations and network services. These segments play the roles of attacked networks, attacking networks or perform other functions (for example, serve as mini-sandboxes for temporary software testing). Accordingly team segments should contain the following widely used modern firmware:

- workstation software (OS on the most popular and probable platforms – Microsoft, Unix, Novell; as well as Web-browsers and other software necessary for the problem solution);
- communication facilities (may be absent if segment is being used as an "isolated" area);
- databases (Oracle, Informix, MS SQL, MySQL, etc. – the ultimate choice is defined by the problem being solved);
- e-mail facilities (servers and client software);
- different servers (application, Web-, file- and other, not yet defined);
- security subsystems and firmware security facilities;
- programming tools (for analysis of the existing and creation of own security facilities, for analysis of vulnerabilities and various technologies);
- adaptive network security and management tools, including systems for evaluation of protectability, for monitoring user activity, systems for traffic analysis and intrusion detection.

Control segment is the working place of the administrator (an instructor will play his role during the laboratory works) and controls access of participating subjects to external (relative to the complex) services (for example, the Internet). That is why this area should include adaptive network security and management tools, security subsystems and firmware security facilities, e-mail facilities and other servers.

All segments are linked into a single complex with the transport medium, which should be built with the most popular technologies used nowadays in private networks (intranet). In our case the transport medium is Ethernet because it is the most flexible, cheap, and scalable technology able to satisfy nearly all speed and QoS requirements.

Team segments (and the control segment) use various software varying from freeware, downloaded from the Internet for analysis, to licensed operating systems and security facilities (for example, network audit tools, software firewalls, antiviral software, etc.). Besides, organization of the unified database about all investigated vulnerabilities and methods of defense, about used firmware, as well as maintenance of centralized support server in the control segment are of special interest.

Implementation stage followed the project stage. But the faculty was unable to afford the self-dependent creation of the Laboratory because of limited resources. That is why executives addressed exterior organizations. They needed to open business relations and to attract investments. This was the search for partners' stage. The partners had to be interested in the creation of the Laboratory, maintaining it, at least because they could use it as a test-bed for their new ideas and shift their everyday routine research and testing activities to students' and post-graduate's shoulders. The partners were found (they are the Moscow's Microsoft representatives, the STC Electron-Service and the CROC company), but they made some modifications to the initial Laboratory topology so that it would be more flexible and more effective for solving various problems.

The final project of the complex compiled by the joint efforts is depicted on the figure 2.

All that was made by the students themselves. During the summer months the work was finished and the complex was ready for presentation and operation testing.

The Laboratory is divided in two main parts. One part of the Laboratory is designed for carrying out the following works within the complex's framework:

- examination of system vulnerabilities and analysis of unauthorized access to computers and networks;
- security testing and computer-aided testing facilities;
- extending students' knowledge of security concepts and principles;
- familiarization with instruments used for ensuring system security;
- design of secure systems and subsystems.

The second part of the Laboratory is intended for improvement of the basic techniques and scripts of distance learning and testing. Some new educational technologies based on multimedia computer systems and tools are widely used in many educational programs of various educational institutions from primary schools to universities. Their efficiency has already been proved in teaching foreign languages, in physical processes and phenomena simulation, and also as help-systems with a large amount of stored information. The application areas of computer learning systems along with many other fields of knowledge can become objects of study not only in classes but also during independent student's (or trainee's) work.

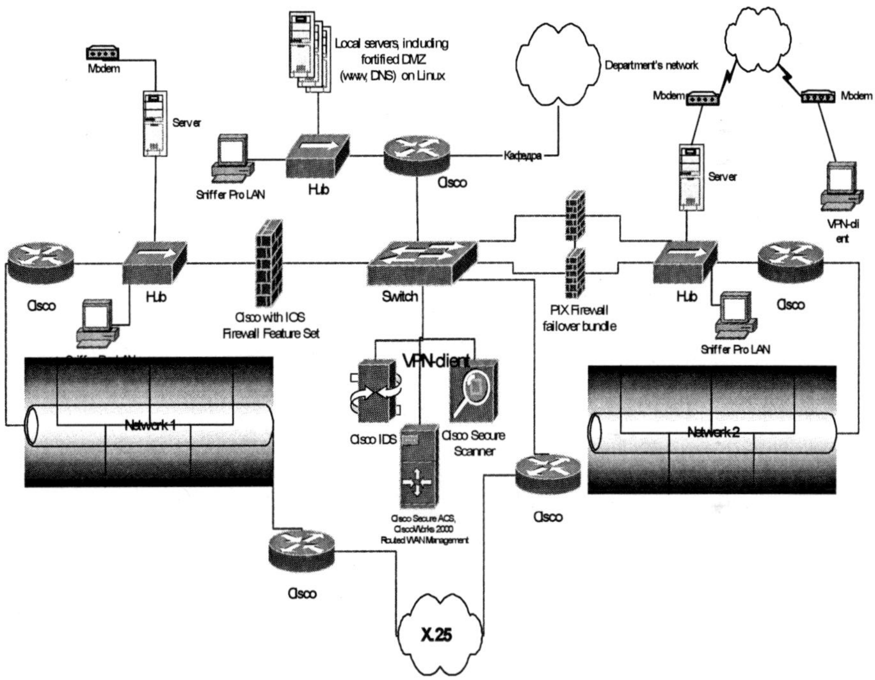

Fig.2: final Laboratory topology.

The basis of this part of the Laboratory is earlier developed at MEPhI's Distance Learning and Testing Systems (DLTS). It is a complex of software and methodical tools for distance learning and certification of the personnel based on the advanced Internet technologies and modern educational and testing techniques and accompanied by the specially trained personnel. Interactive DLTS Web site is constructed upon the Microsoft ASP technology. The Internet Information Server 5.0 provides the ASP support. VBScript language is used for the ASP scripts creation. The DLTS information environment consists of the educational material in the HTML format and the centralized database working under the Microsoft SQL Server 2000 control. The tools for new educational course development, the test creation tools and DLTS operation support tools are implemented as the Internet and Delphi applications. All DLTS's resources should be protected. That is why it is located in the Laboratory.

MEPhI's DLTS has more that 1500 tests on the different topics of the information and network security. We define test as a combination of interdependent or independent tasks of equal or different complexity, assigned "from simple to complicated", and allows adequately defining knowledge and other trainee characteristics important for the tutor (they are named in the brackets). The tests have the following aims:

- self-testing of trainees during the educational process on the information security programs,
- testing the level of preliminary training (so called pre-knowledge) before the laboratory works,
- testing comprehension of the studied theoretical material as addition to another forms of traditional progress testing during a term,
- testing student's ability to apply the newly acquired knowledge and skills for making own decisions and implement them as completed products and work out concepts, strategies, techniques etc.,
- certifying trainees and testing their competence as the final progress testing.

MEPhI's DLTS implements the following task types of different complexity: selection from a set, multiple selection, conformity, logical chain, term, object selection, situational task, symbol sequences input. We added one interesting point to that list – dialogue emulation. It is not trivial to implement it because all the possible actions of a trainee and emulated system process reactions should be determined in advance. We need to foresee all possible event development in artificially created situations. But that approach has positive features - trainee's practical experiments do not impact the real parameters of the network environment.

3. LABORATORY ACTIVITIES

Even now the Laboratory is used not only in "exterior" projects but also directly participates (or will participate in the nearest future) in student training in the following educational courses:

- "Information security basics",
- "Theoretical foundations of information security",
- "Operating system security",
- "Network security",

- "Database security",
- "Complex information security of computer-based systems",
- "Cryptographic tools of information protection",
- "Technical methods and tools of information security",
- "Firmware methods and tools of information security",
- "Legal aspects of information security",
- "Organization of information security" and
- "Building secure computer-based systems".

Besides there are plans to introduce the following new courses: "Secure network technologies", "Monitoring of network security", "VPN management", "Informational and mail systems", "Information security administrators", "Building data networks" and "Network management tools".

But the most important are, probably, the knowledge that trainees could learn in the Laboratory. For example, it allows to obtain knowledge in the undermentioned areas:

- reveal unauthorized computer access;
- reveal network attacks;
- analyze the procedures and means for performing attacks;
- discover threats to informational computer systems;
- discover vulnerabilities and bugs in systems, services and network protocols through which adversary's intrusion can be expected;
- discover channels of unauthorized information leaks from the system;
- perform the network security monitoring;
- operate the access isolation systems providing a controlled access to informational and network resources;
- design secure informational systems;
- elaborate the system's security policy;
- define measures and procedures of accident prevention;
- eliminate the consequences of unauthorized intrusion into a system;
- evaluate the system protectability;
- define the purpose, basic functions and place of information security standards in the system; usage peculiarities of the specific standard;
- evaluate the functional capabilities of the existing security equipment and determine the applicability of firmware in network architectures;
- configure the security facilities built into many systems;
- ensure the secure operation of system applications;
- administer security equipment;
- develop methods of defense;
- implement new systems and means of information protection;
- know the basic legal documents and standards in information security;
- prepare documentation for new security equipment for further state level certification.

This is not a comprehensive enumeration. But even it should not be understood literally because every student will choose his own specialization and questions that he will thoroughly study. It is just impossible to be a specialist in every field. Never the less all students will obtain the necessary minimum of knowledge in the aforementioned problems to continue independent studies and research.

But to make the most of working in the Laboratory, without distracting attention to “secondary” questions when solving definite problems, there is a list of prerequisites: TCP/IP stack, network services, basic principles of network security and technologies of security, network operating systems (Unix, Windows 98/2000, NT, Netware...), database management systems, computer viruses (malware) and programming technologies and languages.

The following works are going to be carried out within the complex’s framework:

- examination of system vulnerabilities and analysis of unauthorized access to computers and networks;
- security testing and computer-aided testing facilities;
- extending students’ knowledge of security concepts and principles;
- familiarization with instruments used for ensuring system security;
- design of secure systems and subsystems.

Titles of the possible works are very different. For example, the work with the title "Buffer overflow attacks" is designed for the "Programming technologies" course. For the "Computer hardware" course functioning of packet filters, channel encryption devices and other hardware should be studied in the Laboratory. Revealing of leakage paths is a good illustration for the "Communication networks and systems" course. Analysis of OS’s protectability and setup of configuration files corresponds to the "Operating systems" course. Specific DBMS threats and built-in protection capabilities are the main topics for the "Database management systems" course. Network attacks and methods of their detection best of all suits the "Computational networks" course. The "Management basics" course should imply designing of security policies and studying of the main administrator’s responsibilities etc.

At that objects of Laboratory studies are network hardware & software, protocols & services, standards, legal and normative documents, standalone computers or groups of computers in the internal and external networks with specific hardware platform and installed software — primary (for example, OS) and applied (network), with the Internet access. As for protection hardware & software students should study means designed for intrusion detection, security monitoring and audit, protection means (such as firewalls, encryption tools), access control implementation, security policy development and, of course, document base, regulating actions in the field of information security. This is achieved with the following methods of research:

- emulating intruder's activities;
- discovery of system vulnerabilities by scanning and probing;
- experiments with security facilities and means of unauthorized access detection to determine their functional capabilities and to elaborate recommendations for their installation and improvement;
- control of network information flows through traffic analysis;
- assessment of protection of computers, networks, services, protocols, hardware and software in accordance with fixed procedures and in compliance with Russian standards and guidelines;
- testing of security policies and new procedures of protection in order to determine their comprehensiveness and validity;
- analysis of documents, regulating information security.

With reference to learning network security this means:

- examination of standard attacks described in different publications;
- intrusion detection and elimination of their consequences;
- discovery of software and hardware vulnerabilities of standalone computers or network as a whole;
- operation of access control systems with respect to informational and network resources;
- elaboration of system security policy and definition of means of its achievement;
- evaluation of functioning systems' protectability and elaboration of recommendations for its enhancement;
- design, installation, configuration, and administration of security facilities and patches for present software and hardware.

On the basis of those typical basic tasks as well as on the basis of personal experience of complex design the following immediate problems were prepared for students. All of them are the titles of the practical assignments for one laboratory work.

1. Emulation of network protocols.
2. Emulation of secure network protocols.
3. Emulation of specific attacks.
4. Creation of interfaces emulating operation of security facilities.
5. Research of dependence between network topology and attacks.
6. Research of dependence between transport medium in use (Ethernet, FastEthernet, FDDI, ATM…) and attacks.
7. Research of peculiarities of telephone channel attacks.
8. Research of peculiarities of fiber-optic attacks.
9. Research of peculiarities of attacks from the Internet.
10. Research of attacks on network hardware.

11. Research of vulnerabilities and protection of Web-servers and applications.
12. Research of vulnerabilities of network services and commands.
13. Research of attacks on electronic document interchange.
14. Crypto protection. Digital signature. Public key infrastructure.
15. Research of attacks on firewalls.
16. Research of attacks on proxies and their detection.
17. Research of vulnerabilities of client/server architecture.
18. Research of vulnerabilities of databases and database management systems.
19. Research of basic means of network protection – protection against an unauthorized access.
20. Research of basic means of network protection – firewalls.
21. Research of basic means of network protection – adaptive network security.
22. Research of basic means of network protection – anti-viruses.
23. Research of basic means of network protection – virtual private networks.
24. Research of basic means of network protection – security policy development and management.
25. Research of means for file and session encryption.
26. Research of network-based intrusion detection systems.
27. Research of host-based intrusion detection systems.
28. Research of attacks on intrusion detection systems.
29. Research of system security scanners.
30. Research of network security scanners.
31. Research of security services: intrusion tests.
32. Research of application-level attacks and application protection.
33. Research of trusted operating systems.
34. Vulnerabilities and protection of workstations.
35. Design of own means and methods of defense.

4. ELECTRONIC TUTORIALS FOR INFORMATION SECURITY EDUCATION

Let's allocate main objectives of creating the electronic tutorials for information security educational process. They are the following:

- to help teachers to present their professional knowledge in a new, most effective — electronic — way that would give them necessary modern level and high quality of stated material;

- to apply teaching based on automated and involving extensive information resources of the Internet approaches to educational schedule exposition to students;
- to place students in such an environment, where they can creatively use this technology as a part of their daily exercises within the framework of self-education; students can actively construct their own knowledge setting their individual style of training and mastering of new information in this environment;
- to give state-of-the-art information on the theme at the expense of usage of hypertext references to Web-sites with the newest documents, demos of the latest software information protection tools for networks, and descriptions of functionality of hardware protection tools.

In 2003 several electronic tutorials used to study network security at the laboratory have been developed and tested on the under- and post-graduate students. Their themes are the following: "Secure network protocols", "Remote network attacks", "Firewalls", "Intrusion detection systems" and "Scanners". "Virtual private networks" tutorial is under construction now.

On an example of the first named tutorial we would like to show main features of the others. The product named ZSPs (from the Russian abbreviator of Secure Network Protocols) is used both to learn theory of the protocols and to get initial practice in their configuring (during laboratory works). To achieve the goal the emulation of the basic dialogs is performed. The main purpose of it is to make the education persistent and to exclude the gap between the theory and the practice. ZSPs gives the possibility to put through persistent educational process – students get the knowledge and use it in practical tasks immediately - and thereby increase the quality of education.

The ET is meant for those familiar with network technologies foundations, system and security managers. ZSPs is intended to be used by the students of the Information Security and Network Security specialties.

ZSPs is directed to study secure network protocols, tightly integrated in different network environments. It realizes some elements of client-server configuring of the basic network protocols such as creating PPTP and L2TP tunnels and IP Security connections. Windows 2000 Advanced Server has been chosen as the basic system, because it's one of the most widely used Microsoft OS for creating powerful and convenient network environments. The product aids in solving the following tasks in the common concept of learning: giving the basic knowledge in the protocols functioning, methods of their application and so giving skills in configuring network connections to use security services of them.

The configuring of protocols inside ZSPs does not impact the real parameters of the OS. The following reasons have chosen such kind of realization:

As the inexperienced students use the application, there is the possibility of incorrect configuring the protocols, and thereby breaking the functioning of the whole complex.

As the product does not change the OS parameters, it can be used in any Windows system, and not only Windows 2000 Advanced Server.

ZSPs, emulating work of the basic network protocols, has the following characteristic features:

- Granting of an opportunity to receive both knowledge and practical skills.
- Independence from concrete OS and opportunity to be used in any Windows environment.
- Exclusion of the probability to infringe the OS under which the application is used.
- User-friendly interface.
- Realization of theory as HTML documents that allows the teacher to modify and supplement the material easily without a threat to the application.
- Help system, including instructions for tutors and trainees.
- Implementing the system of user registration, logging and reporting.
- Realization of a test system to examine trainees.

Subjects of teaching, as well as everything concerned with the modern networks, the Internet and intranets, are very dynamical: literally each day malefactors develop new methods of system breaking and crashing; in return the market of protection tools responds with releasing appropriate products for intrusion detection and defense. For the reason the dynamic principle should be incorporated into the basis of the approach to creating electronic tutorials on the given area of knowledge.

5. CONCLUSION

Thus, the "Network Security" Scientific and Research Laboratory allows not only to significantly improve student training in existing group of information security specialties, but also to bring the educational and research activities of the faculty up to a new standard. This results in both increased efficiency of training and retraining courses in old and new educational programs and participation in federal special programs. Besides, availability of the complex allows online exchanges of experience with foreign partners and to carry out joint investigation and research. Moreover, having mutual agreement it is possible to participate even in joint laboratory works when, for example, Russian and foreign students from Australia [2] or

Italy [3] compete with each other for better knowledge of network protocols, technologies, and network security tools. Several electronic tutorials for the different parts of the information security educational courses have been created.

REFERENCES

[1] Miloslavskaya N., Tolstoy A. "Network Security" Scientific and Research Laboratory" Proceeding of the IFIP TC11 WG11.8 Third World Conference on Information Security Education. 26-28 June 2003, Monterey, USA. Pp. 231-242.
[2] Armstrong C.J., Armstrong H.L. The Virtual Campus. Proceeding of the IFIP TC11 WG11.8 Second World Conference on Information Security Education. 12-14 July 2001, Perth, Australia. Pp. 161-168.
[3] Vigna.G. Teaching Network Security Through Live Exercises. Proceedings of the IFIP TC 11 WG 11.8 Third World Conference on Information Security Education, June 2003, Monterey, USA. Pp. 3-18.

AN HOLISTIC APPROACH TO AN INTERNATIONAL DOCTORAL PROGRAM

Louise Yngström
Department of Computer and Systems Sciences, Stockholm University& The Royal Institute of Technology, The IT university in Kista, Sweden.
louise@dsv.su.se

Abstract: The paper discusses forms and structures for an international doctoral program with specialization in information security and information assurance based on an analysis of international educational efforts in the area 1995-2003. The presentation underlines the need for holistic approaches to the IT security area and presents, as an example, the Systemic-Holistic Approach, SHA.

Key words: Systemic-Holistic, Information Security, and PhD Education

1. INTRODUCTION

Many problems within information security are multidisciplinary in nature – there are needs for knowledge from natural sciences as well as law, social sciences and humanities. This becomes problematic in research (as well as in practice) since each science has its own defined knowledge field and well established research methodologies. Basically two world views clash – the formal/hard and the informal/soft. To bridge the gap inter-, multi- and cross disciplinary methods are often used successfully but they demand each participant to have detailed knowledge in each involved discipline. Holism takes the meta-approach where an actual problem is investigated from some generalized system-concept; this may emanate from any area of science but is initially scrutinized as one whole. The result of the systemic analysis will further direct the course of research and actions. This way knowledge from soft and hard sciences is bridged. This paper discusses how to use an holistic approach to a PhD program in information security and information assurance.

The paper is organized as follows: The international doctoral program with a bias towards a holistic approach is discussed. The WISE1-3 conferences are revisited to conclude about holistic and interdisciplinary demands within the area, and to underline the international developments within academic teaching 1995-2003. Finally there is a section on the Systemic-Holistic Approach, developed and used by the author.

2. DISCUSSING THE INTERNATIONAL DOCTORAL PROGRAM

Following the Systemic-Holistic Approach, SHA, (see section 4), the content of any holistic oriented research needs a description of the field of study. Thus the core curriculum of such a PhD program needs to be specified in terms of what courseware in IT security is needed in addition to courseware in science, including scientific and research methodology. I will use the SHA approach for sketching and discussing the international doctoral program with specialization in information security and information assurance; doctorate by research and a professional doctorate; different sectors including academic, military and armed forces, law enforcement, government and private industry. The approach includes in short: delimit the system of study from the environment, define the existing environment, define the system through its inflow, through-flow and outflow, and structure the in-built control system to deal with inner and outer variety

2.1 The system of study

The system itself is the education with its processes, the students including their learning processes, the main advisors including their preferences and knowledge, the department (subject) and university, eventually also the nation, where the PhD candidate is enrolled. I will assume that a professional doctorate candidate will have some home-department apart from his/her company (equivalent).

2.2 The environment

The most important environment will include all the other international departments and universities which are part of this "international federation of doctoral consortium". Each one is viewed as a system of its own. Defining it this way, each department and university can use their own internal as well as external rules.[1] The environment also encompasses the companies/organizations and many of the problems which will be involved in the research. Particularly in research, there will also be international organizations of various kinds which are either interested in the research, conduct or fund research themselves, are involved in actions which interacts with /parts of/ research, etc.

2.3 The system; its inflow, through-flow and outflow

I will assume that a doctorate will take 3 years of full-time research, and that the candidate will have a bachelor and a master degree (app. 3+2years) prior to entering the PhD education. In an ideal case the candidate will already have studied security in relation to IT on the undergraduate or graduate level. The minimum knowledge in information security (equiv) ought to be somewhere similar to programs described in Proceedings of the WISE conferences (see section 3 of this paper) of an extent to about 1,5 years of full time studies. In addition I would wish the candidate to have studied general science, scientific methodology, research methodology and scientific communications (oral, procedural, and writing including an /under/graduate thesis or project) to the equivalence of approximately 1 year. The candidate entering the PhD program should be a mature person with an urge to learn – and in the ideal case – also have a problem area of interest. Scrutinizing this problem area together with an advisor should result in a provisional and individual research plan. This plan may include courses or specification for courses, and projects. All specifications should be guided by the goal of the PhD, which initially will be rather hazy, but gradually materialize into a clearly defined specification. This implies that I do not favour course-work per se within the PhD education except when the knowledge is identified as a need. This also implies the existence of a present, knowledgeable and interested advisor. Initially the advisor will "point will full hand" towards the goal and its content, but gradually the PhD candidate should take over full responsibilities for his/her research. I really see no principal differences between a professional doctorate and a doctorate by research, except for maybe the scope. Still, both doctorates will need to

[1] Experiences within similar curricula development (Erasmus/Socrates) show that each country has its own regulations and it takes long time to harmonize university educations. Even if Europe is in a process of harmonizing its system of higher education (the Bologna process) it will still take time to implement it. An international program probably takes even longer.

show how to use sound scientific methods even though the balances between practical and theoretical work may be different.[2]

This implies that the best way of cooperating internationally is to be able to offer the courses we do give to the international forum, thus for the international doctorate program I suggest IFIP 11.8 members to put up a course catalogue on the web site for this purpose as a start.

When it comes to the "holistic" doctorate, I view the approach as a scientific research methodology that may be used for inter-, multi- or crossdisciplinary problems. This usually implies incorporating knowledge from related fields such as management, economics, law and culture, but may also be used to incorporate aspects of software engineering and information systems. I believe a course on holistic approaches, as indicated in section 4 could be part of the scientific methodology.

2.4 Structure the in-built control system to deal with inner and outer variety

Since I suggest each department and university partaking in the international activities of a PhD program in information security as a system of its own, each department will be left with their own rules. International agreements, such as the Bologna process for European higher education may change this gradually.

3. WISES REVISITED

International Federation for Information Processing, IFIP, has through its working group 11.8 conducted workshops and conferences since 1995 within the wide area of education in information security and information assurance. For the purpose of this paper, the author went through all the proceedings to bring the WG up-to-date with our findings. The analysis shows that the area has matured; the academic international education is converging towards consensus of core knowledge, and there are many detailed examples given of courses, contents, extent and laboratory work. Driving forces seem to have been the ERASMUS/SOCTARES program in Europe and the National Colloquium for Information Systems Security Education in the US - many universities have contributed their knowledge to

[2] This actually implies that I believe a MSc or a MBA towards security should be the preferred professional degrees for people working practically with security outside the academies. A professional PhD could still imply research, but maybe then more directed towards problems of a specific organization.

the success. In 2001 bodies outside the traditional universities, such as police and armed forces joined with their plans and experiences. In 2003 we note reports strongly arguing for holistic, inter- and multidisciplinary approaches to information security particularly for business-oriented education. Didactic questions are starting to appear, in particular distance-education and forms for assessment of programs. Along come also reports from developing countries, changes in profiles of infosec professionals, training approaches for SMEs, teaching PETs, etc. Apart from one paper on forensics and one on IPR, problematisations from legal points of view on information security education on any level is lacking, as is value-oriented questions and extensive comments on educational programs targeting trade&industry. Each of the conferences is characterized through listing of given titles and themes.

3.1 Pre-WISE work

IFIP's working group within the Technical Committee on Security and Protection in Information Processing systems (TC11) number 11.8 Information Security Education, was established in 1991. In 1995 a series of workshops intending to build a critical mass of active international members named *Information Security Education – Current and Future Needs, Problems and Prospects* were initiated to run in parallel with the annual SEC95-98 conferences. Major themes in Cape town, South Africa 1995 were European academic IT security education, Information security education in the business administration environment and Demands for ethical curricula in the information age. The following year, 1996, on Samos, Greece themes were Awareness models, Teaching and learning models and Needs for standard curricula for different groups and levels, in addition to papers on Privacy, Laboratories and Holistics. In Copenhagen, Denmark 1997 themes were extended towards reporting on practical approaches and experiments with a much wider international appearance also including teachers, pupils, data protection officials – and post graduate level. Finally, the forth workshop on a boat on the Danube between Vienna, Austria and Budapest, Hungary in 1998 presented detailed educational programs, mainly academic, from the international scene.

By 1999 the time was ripe to start dedicated international conferences on themes around the teaching and learning of information security. They were named WISE particularly to underline that the teaching and learning about security in IT systems calls for reflections and analyses of what these systems – once made secure in some sense – will be able to accomplish in the real world. "Will they provide for trust in information systems, will they lead to a more secure world, for whom, will they perhaps change existing balances and power structures, will they tend to control individuals, etc.?

The creation of awareness and understanding of the demands for security in IT systems has proven necessary; lacking acceptance with the users will result in inadequately functioning IT security. Also lacking awareness and understanding with the computer scientists and technicians of the demands for security in IT systems from business and user perspectives cause deficient IT security. This is what WISE is about – to present, analyse and discuss what, how, and whom to teach about information systems' and information technologies' security." (Yngström, 1999, p v). The acronym stands for World conference on Information Security Education, suggested by our late 11.8 member Peter Fillery after the 1996 workshop. Hopefully the WISEs will be vehicles not only for how-to-do-reports – even if they are extremely helpful for the international audience – but also for exhibiting and discussing specific research problems incorporated within the teaching of and learning about IT security and information assurance.

3.2 WISE1

Looking back at WISE1 in 1999, themes were introvert and reported in depth on what today would have been called traditional academic IT security education. There were only a few non-academic target groups added and the focus on teaching IT security to trade and industry was almost negligent. Very few research problems were discussed. Titles talk for themselves: Academic Curricula and Curricula Developments in Europe – The ERASMUS/ SOCRATES Approach, Incorporating Security Issues Throughout the Computer Science Curriculum, The Reference Monitor Concept as a Unifying Principle in Computer Security Education, Personnel Training for Information Security Maintenance in Russia, IT Related Ethics Education in Southern Africa, Data Protection in Healthcare and Welfare, A MixDemonstrator for teaching Security in the Virtual University, On the Experiment of Creating the Electronic Tutorial "Vulnerability and Protection Methods in the Global Internet Networking" in Moscow State Engineering Physics for Education of IT Security Professionals, Information Security Best Practice Dissemination: The ISA-EUNET Approach, Amplifying Security Education in the Laboratory, IT Security Research and Education in Synergy, Developing an Undergraduate Lab for Information Warfare and Computer Security, Internet Groupware Use in A Policy-Oriented Computer Security Course, Teaching Computer Security – the Art of Practical Application, Some Aspects of Cryptology Teaching, Explaining cryptosystems for the general public, Approaching the concept of IT security for young users, Introducing IT security Awareness in Schools; The Greek Case, Making information security awareness and training more effective, The Value and Assessment of Information Security Education and Training,

The Manual is the Message – an Experiment with Paper based and Web based IT security manuals. (Yngström&Fischer-Hubner, 1999).

3.3 WISE2

In WISE2 the scope had widened, nationally as well as internationally. There were reports on international curricula, important educational problems and impacts also outside established academic institutions such as the police and armed forces, the cyber environment, small enterprises, distance education and societal issues. The inter- or multidisciplinary issue was raised by many authors.

Titles were: Global Impacts, Future Challenges and Current Issues in Training within the Police Computer Crime Unit, Information Warfare and Cyber Warefare: More Than Just Software Tools, Information Security; International Curriculum Projects, The Russian Experience – Information Security Education, Updates on the SOCRATES/ERASMUS Program, Teaching Cyberwarefare Tactics and Strategy, e-Education Frameworks: Applying Generalized Development Strategies to IT Security Courses, An Information Security Education Program in Finland, Information Security Education, Teaching Security Engineering Principles, Core Curriculum in Security Science, Problems in Designing Secure Distance Learning Systems, The Virtual Campus, Action learning in practice, Progress Testing in Distance Learning, A Security Training Approach for UK Small and Medium Sized Enterprises, IFIP World Computer Congress/SEC 2000 Revisited, Teaching Privacy-Enhancing Technologies, Game-Based learning within IT security Education, Human Aspects of Information Security, Awareness and views on Intellectual Property Rights concerning the Internet, Analysis of Teaching GNY-Based Security protocol, Information Security Aspects in the Expert Training Program on Physical Protection of the Objects, Reaching for the Stars – a practical case study in securing computer facilities.(Armstrong&Yngström, 2001).

3.4 WISE3

At the time of WISE3 the area had matured profoundly. There are many detailed curricula reports, including laboratory experiments with different flavours, extensions, levels, depths, widths and target audiences; excellent aids for new-comers. The developed west-oriented world dominates, but also smaller and less developed countries report progress. There are more quests and suggestions for interdisciplinarity, in particular marrying IT security education with education in business administration and intelligence. Computer forensics and information assurance are emergent concepts for education and existing definitions and focuses are problematized. Evaluation appears as a separate subject and the concept of education is widened to include re-training and the activating of alumnae and other external groups. A natural extension of the curricula towards the postgraduate level is present and there are suggested research areas and themes. Titles are: Cyber Security as an Emergent Infrastructure, Teaching Network Security Through Live Exercises, Information Warefare in the Trenches, Changes in the Profile of Security Managers, A Tutoring System for IT Security, Design of a Laboratory for Information Security Education, Integrating Information security and Intelligence Courses, Internet Security Management, Information Security Fundamentals, Australia's Agenda for e-Security Education and Research, Is Security a Great Principle of Computing, IT Security Readiness in Developing Countries, A Program for Education in Certification and Accreditation, Mastering Computer Forensics, Assembling Competitive Intelligence Using Classroom Scenarios, Teaching Undergraduate Information Assurance, Out-come based Assessment as an Assurance Education Tool, Evaluation Theory and Practice as Applied to Security Education, Ten Years of Information Security Masters Programmes, Network Security Scientific and Research Laboratory, A Comprehensive Undergraduate Information Assurance Program, Training the Cyber Warrior, Security Education for Times of Netwar and Peace, Improving Security Awareness Through Computer-based Training, Identification and Integration of Information Security Topics, A Dedicated Undergraduate Track in Computer Security Education (Irvine&Armstrong 2003).

4. AN HOLISTIC APPROACH TO INFORMATION SECURITY AND INFORMATION ASSURANCE

When I first started to study – and later – to teach about information security from a holistic - later called systemic-holistic – base, I did not understand fully that it was a difficult (and to some extent even until today unsolved) scientific problem. My department was one of the first ones to consider computer science and information systems together – to our notion computers process data which in some sort of intelligent process (often involving humans) may be transformed to information. And viewing the IT security problems (initially of privacy) from the point of view of a generalized system, made it easy to state/understand the security problems as problems of integrity. To my understanding no system, not even 'privacy' could be totally without an environment with which is has relations; thus it boils down to some sort of control problem. Cybernetic systems are controlled through feed-back; and in theory they apply 'control from within' (Wiener 1948, Beer 1964, 1968). They appear in various forms. Thus security to me could be viewed from the point of view of building /a/ control system/s/.

The third central part of the holistic approach was General Systems Theory, GST. The purpose of GST(von Bertalanffy 1956,1968) was to further the development of theoretical systems applicable to more than one of the traditional disciplines into a meta-theory. This way analogies and isomorphies can be used from one known area to another. GST rests on five postulates and ten hallmarks, which in essence view the world from formally provable realities where general laws and structures may be transferred from one level to another, from one area to another provided there are strong similarities. Thus assessed research methods could be applied in new fields.

In the theoretical building of the systemic-holistic approach also the Theory of General Living Systems (Miller 1978) took part. Miller delimits his theory to deal with concrete, open, homeostasis aiming complex systems, composed by 19 critical subsystems. Miller himself notes (1978, p 42): "My analyses of living systems uses concepts of thermodynamics, information theory, cybernetics, and systems engineering, as well as the classical concepts appropriate to each level. The purpose is to produce a description of living structure and process in terms of input and output, flows through systems, steady state, and feedback, which will clarify and unify the facts of life".

With the aid of system theories and cybernetics the systemic-holistic approach was structured to facilitate understanding IT security problems as how to construct robust and survivable structures. Now, this was not the way most IT security people viewed their task: I spent time researching how and why people saw the world they did as compared to mine – and what the results were of the different world views. At the time (Yngström 1996) I outlined and discussed some areas as an illustration to why it was/is problematic to understand security in relation to IT:

- A language problem – English is the language used in most scientific communications, whereas many other languages understand 'security' much wider.
- Is cryptography the same as security? Cryptographic functionalities are based on secrecy but used in quite different ways.
- Whose point of view is security for? Most often the view is to protect assets of the firm and not of the individual.
- How is the environment considered? The environment if often implicit – to the developers. It is not necessary the same as understood by the users.
- Information or data security? The two concepts are often used interchangeably giving an unsolid ground for decisions.

- CIA as the main definition/description. As technology and use of IT extends, definitions are not good enough; even these three include contradictions.
- Problems of specifying IT security criteria. We live with that all the time, and I still favour Abrams' (1994) comments that there is not one good model to cover all aspects, despite CC.
- Measurements of security. Today security metrics seem to be a large field for research.

Presented issues contain gleanings from often discussed matters. Certainly they could have been headlined or related differently - this is the whole point with an SHA approach. Many perceive the issues as a mesh of opinions or ideas built on specific knowledge, and somehow – which is not obvious - connected to each other. This is where a generalised concept of a system may be used as a basic model for understanding and structuring matters; expressed by the following steps:

1. Understanding and conceptualisations,
2. Demarcations: delimit the system of study from its environment including defining the relevant environment,
3. Definitions: specify inflows, throughflows and outflows, and
4. Measurements of control: structure controls to deal with relevant varieties.

Following this, the problematic issues mainly dealt with:

1. Understanding and conceptualisations: Language and Cryptology,
2. Demarcations: Whose point of view to take, and Taking account of the environment,
3. Definitions: Information or data, IT security criteria, and Confidentiality, integrity, and availability, and
4. Measurements of control: Measurements of security.

However, few of the issues are unequivocal and someone else might want to classify them as:

1. Understanding and conceptualisations: Confidentiality, integrity, and availability, Whose point of view to take, and Taking account of the environment,
2. Demarcations: Measurements of security, and Information or data,
3. Definitions: Language, and
4. Measurements of control: IT security criteria.

This illustrates exactly why the issues are problematic: they cannot with any kind of certainty be allocated into one model easily understood and agreed upon even amongst involved professionals. Still, the generalised concept of a system can be used differently - to form a base for a *subjective* appreciation of the area which also is objectively communicative to others.

4.1 The Systemic-Holistic Approach spelled out

General Systems Theory had its origin in observations of similar phenomena existing in many different sciences. To study these interdisciplinary, Bertalanffy chose the concept of 'system'. He used 'system' as an epistemological device to describe organisms as wholes, and showed that it could be generalised and applied to wholes of any kind. Checkland developed this further [Checkland 1988] in discussions on the confusion between what exists (the ontological entity) and what is an abstraction (the epistemological entity).

Checkland´s view is that humans can only perceive reality through a methodology which uses abstract concepts. While perceiving /a part of/ reality, humans are able to reflect on their findings - and in doing so, they will test and change their concepts in order to fit them better to the perceived reality. In this actual process of testing and changing, there is a multi-creating relationship between the perceived reality and the intellectual concepts which in fact constitutes a learning process.

In efforts to control, humans may choose to assume that the reality *is* a system rather than could be looked upon *as* a system through the learning process. The control method used in the first case Checkland labels engineering or hard systems thinking, the second one systemic or soft systems thinking. The main underlined differences between the methods are, that in hard systems thinking perceived realities are treated as existing systems (the ontological entity) and their problems solved by systematic methods, while in soft systems thinking perceived realities are treated as problems (the epistemological entity) and solved by systemic methods. Through soft systems thinking, humans can learn how the concept of a system *reflects* the real world, and may represent one - and possibly changing - understanding of the world. Checkland does not refrain from hard systems thinking and engineering, rather he underlines that soft systems and hard systems thinking are complementary to each other. But the decision when to change from one to the other is a human subjective one.

The confusion between "what seems to exists" and "what exists" has been labelled by Checkland as "the confusion between the images of the systems and the systems image" [Checkland 1988, p. 40]. By Laufer [Laufer 1985] it is described as the confusion between the science of nature and the science of culture; what is neither nature nor culture is artificial. And the science of the artificial is the science of systems, i.e. cybernetics.

Laufer offers one more explanation of importance to the security area: the main reason for the confusion between what is nature and what is culture is that the ultimate locus of control is undecided. This generates an on-going crisis with two distinct states. Either the problem is very simplistic and implies a great number of similar events; in that case a manager can predict future states of the system and is confronted with the relatively safe risk of controlling the probable. Or - and more often - assumptions cannot be made about the similarity of future events or about their independence, and management is confronted with the problem of controlling the improbable. The results of trying to control and cope with the improbable is to control it symbolically; for instance through laws that authorise, commissions to deal with abuses or prevention, ad hoc commissions to deal with any new emerging problems, security norms produced by suitably composed commissions, or public opinion through opinion polls [Laufer 1990].

Checkland and Laufer, following Bertalanffy and General Systems Theory, thus gives grounds for studying the concept of 'system' as an epistemology for viewing and understanding perceived realities. The actual choice of when to change over to hard systems thinking *becomes subjective, but is done consciously*, and becomes a part of the conceptual model and the pedagogics.

General Living Systems Theory forms the third building block to the concept of systems, since it deals with systems that really exist - the ontological entity. It offers a concrete understanding of how physical realities restrict theoretical models, so frequently used within IT security that we tend to believe that the models are the reality.

General Living Systems Theory [Miller 1978] deals with living, concrete, open, homeostas aiming, systems composed of matter and energy and controlled by information. Matter and energy are considered in their physical form, and information is defined as physical markers carrying information. Thus a living system is composed of physical entities. Moreover, living systems exist on seven levels: cell, organ, organism, group, organisation, nation, and supranation; each level needing nineteen critical subsystems for its survival. Each subsystem is described through its structure and process and through measurable representative variables. The model is recursive on each level. General Living Systems Theory offers knowledge and insights on how to link reality to theoretical models; through understanding of physical realities, restrictions of the domains of different theories can be understood.

Sequentially - because we know no other way of presenting material - the Systemic-Holistic Approach starts with General Systems Theory and Cybernetics which presents the foundations of the epistemology, the way to understand and learn. It is interleaved with adequate, contemporary IT security examples.

It is further developed along General Living Systems Theory, exemplifying for instance the following citation from [Hofstadter 1979, p. 686] elaborating on the issue "Do words and thought follow formal rules?":

"... the ultimate answer is Yes - provided that you go down to the lowest level - the hardware - to find the rules ... neurons run in the same simple way the whole time. You can't "think" your neurons into running some non neural way, although you can make your mind change style or subject of thoughts ... Software rules on various levels can change; hardware cannot - in fact, to their rigidity is due the software's flexibility!".

It also sheds some lights into some obvious reasons to IT security problems [Hoffman 1992, p. 4]:

"The traditional and widespread von Neumann architecture is inappropriate for systems shared by a large number of users, not all of whom trust each other ... The technical communities will have to produce changes in the basic architecture of personal computers to avoid the threat of expensive product liability suits".

General Systems Theory makes it possible to define and investigate systems and their phenomena free from any biases than that of the concept itself. This way paradigms, values, and other related entities can be explicitly defined and discussed in context.

None of the presented theories give absolute criteria as when to change from an epistemological to an ontological treatment to reach security - rather, this is directed to be performed in interaction with the phenomena themselves. It becomes a /subjective/ assessment based on a specific domain of action, a context. But together they indicate how to organise conceptualisations for establishing continuous learning processes in IT security: always to question if "facts" really can be considered as such, and always try to confront facts with context, even different contexts. This may also be a suitable mode governing the design, operation, management, and evaluation of secure IT structures.

The conceptual model, called the Systemic-Holistic Model, is very simple; it consists of a three dimensional framework and a Systemic Module as shown in Figures 1.

The framework describes the areas of interest while the Systemic Module acts as an epistemological device for "facts" in the framework. The framework is organised into three dimensions: Content/subject areas, Levels of abstraction, and Context orientation. The Systemic Module presents foundations of General Systems Theory and Cybernetics, Soft System Methodology and General Living Systems Theory. Through these, security as the concept of control and communication, can be defined, investigated, and explained on a level free from any other biases than the system concept itself. This meta knowledge may then be applied at any level of the dimensions of the framework; each practical interpretation may thus be viewed as an instance of subject area, level of abstraction and context.

The Systemic Module and the framework is viewed as a system with the potential to be viable in the sense of [Beer 1979]: in order to establish a control system that will grant viability to a system, three levels need to be analysed: the system itself (system in focus), its environment (the meta system) and the level below the system in focus. Together the three dimensions may be referred to as Beer's three levels of analysis, and the analysis is eventually also applicable recursively in the dimensions separately.

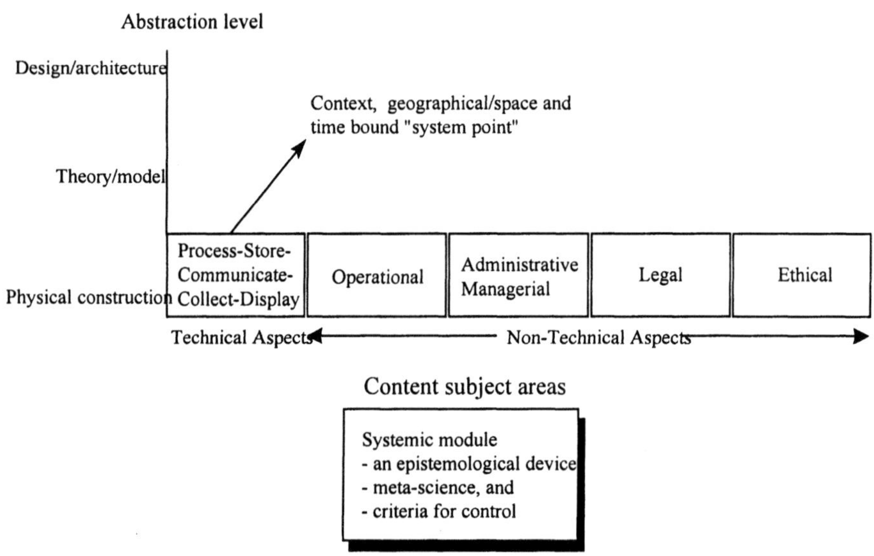

Figure 1. Details of the framework and the methodology for Security Informatics - the Systemic-Holistic Model

4.2 Some critique of the SHA for researching IT security

The most fundamental critique lays with the subjectivity; when a physical person has to decide to change from epistemology to ontology, from systemic/problematic to systematic/hard science. But this, to my understanding, is connected with what efforts we want to make: if we can deal only with one side of the problem, we can use scientific methods proved for these problems, if we want to deal with realities including systems, applications, people, etc in various roles we need a bridging science, such as the SHA approach. Other authors, for instance Fillery-James (1999) Siponen (2003) and Truex et al (1999) have presented similar approaches. The

(2003) and Truex et al (1999) have presented similar approaches. The approach as such may very well be further developed, there are indications that a totally new scientific base, which can bridge the areas of both hard- och soft sciences based on second order cybernetics is under way (Kjellman 2003,2001).The particular approach is called the Subject-oriented Approach to Knowledge, SOA, and has many resemblances with the SHA.

5. REFERENCES

(Abrams, 1994): Abrams, Marshall D., Symbiosis Among IT Security Standatds, policies, and Criteria, in Seizer, R., Yngström, L., Kaspersen, H. and Fisher-Hubner, S. (eds) Security and Control of Information Technology in Society, IFIP Transactions A-34, North-Holland, 1994, pp.145-159

(Armstron&Yngström 2001) Armstrong, H., Yngström, L.,(eds) Linking government, industry and academia to raise information security awareness, education and training in an age of cybercrime, Proceedings of IFIP TC11/WG11.8 Second World Conference on Information Security Education, 12-14 July, 2001, Perth, Australi, Edith Cowan University and IFIP 2001, ISBN 0-7298-0498-4

(Beer 1964) Beer, S., Cybernetics and Management, John Wiley & Sons, 1964.

(Beer 1968) Beer, Stafford, Cybernetics and Management, Science Edition, John Wiley, New York, 1968.

(Beer 1979) Beer, S., The heart of the enterprise, John Wiley & Sons, 1979.

(Checkland 1988) Checkland, P.B., Images of Systems and the Systems Image, Presidential address to ISGSR, June 1987, Journal of Applied Systems Analysis, Vol 15, 1988, pp. 37-42.

(Fillery-James 1999) Armstrong H., (Fillery-James H.L.) A Soft Approach to Management of information Security, PhD thesis, School of Public Health, Curtin university of Technology, Australia, 1999

(Hoffman 1992) Hoffman, Lance J., Reducing Society's Vulnerability as Computers and Networks Proliferate, The George Washington University, Institute for Information Science and Technology GWU-IIST-92-19, 1992.

(Hofstadter 1979) Hofstadter, Douglas R., Gödel, Escher, Bach: an eternal golden braid. A Metaphorical fugue on minds and machines in the spirit of Lewis Carroll, Penguin Books, Harvester Press Ltd, 1979.

(Irvine&Armstrong 2003) Irvine, C.,Armstrong, H., (eds) Security Education and Critical Infrastructure, Proceedings of IFIP TC11/WG11.8 Third Annual World Conference on Information Security Education (WISE3), June 26-28, 2003, Monterey, California, USA, Kluwer Academic Publishers, 2003

(Kjellman 2001) Kjellman A., Sociocybernetics – the path to a science of becoming, presented at the 3rd Int. Conf. On Sociocybernetics in Leon, Mexico, June 2001

(Kjellman 2003) Kjellman, A., Constructive Systems Science – the only remaining alternative?, PhD thesis, Department of Computer and Systems Sciences, Stockholm University, 2003, DSV report serie 03.014

(Laufer 1985) Laufer, R. : Cybernetics, Legitimacy and Society, in Yngström, L., Sizer, R., Berleur, J., Laufer, R., eds., Can Information Technology result in Benevolent Bureaucracies? Proceedings of the IFIP TC9/WG9.2 Working Conference, Namur, Belgum, 3-6 January, 1985, North-Holland, 1985, pp. 29-42.

(Laufer 1990) Laufer, Romain, The Question of the Legimitacy of the Computer: An Epistemological Point of view, in Berleur, J., Clement, A., Sizer, R., Whitehouse, D., eds., The Information Society: Evolving Landscapes, Springer Verlag & Captus University Publications, 1990, pp. 31-61.

(Miller 1978) Miller, James G., Living Systems, McGraw Hill, 1978.

(Siponen 2002) Siponen, M., Designing Secure Information Systems and Software. Critical evaluation of the existing approaches and a new paradigm, PhD Theisi, Faculty of Science, University of Oulu, Finland, ISBN 951-42-6789-3

(Truex et.al.1999) Truex, D, Baskerville, R., Travis, J., Amethodical Systems Development: The Deferred Meaning of Systems Development Methods, pre-copy to be printed in Accounting, Management and Information Technologies, 1999.

(von Bertalanffy 1956) von Bertalanffy, L., Main Currents in Modern Thoughts, in Yearbook of the Society for General Systems Research, Vol 1, 1956.

(von Bertalanffy 1968) von Bertalanffy, L., General Systems Theory, Braziller, 1968.

(Wiener 1948) Wiener, N., Cybernetics or Control and Communication in the Animal and Machine, John Wiley & Sons, 1948.

(Yngström 1996) Yngström, L., A Systemic Holistic Approach to Academic programmes in IT Security, PhD thesis, Department of Computer and Systems Sciences, Stockholm University, DSV report serie 96-021, 1996 (CC).

(Yngström 1999) Yngström, L.Preface in Yngström, L., Fischer-Hubner, S., (eds) WISE1 Proceedings of IFIP TC11 WG11.8 First World Conference on Information Security Education, 17-19 June 1999, Kista, Sweden. DSV and IFIP ISBN 91-7153-910-7, pp. v-vii

(Yngström&Fischer-Hubner 1999) Yngström, L., Fischer-Hubner, S., (eds) WISE1 Proceedings of IFIP TC11 WG11.8 First World Conference on Information Security Education, 17-19 June 1999, Kista, Sweden. DSV and IFIP ISBN 91-7153-910-7

A NEW PARADIGM FOR INFORMATION SECURITY EDUCATION AT DOCTORAL LEVEL

Nimal Jayaratna
Curtin University of Technology, GPO Box U1987, Perth, Western Australia,6845 Australia

Abstract: The Information Security is one of the fastest growing research areas in the field of Computer science and Information Technology/Systems. However, if research into security is to be successful, then researchers' mindsets have to match and exceed those who engage in intrusive, unlawful and unethical activities in the field of Information Systems and Technology. Security Professionals and for that matter those engaged in research and security product/service development need to be able to 'think like the criminals but not act like them'. Such a task is extremely difficult because unlike criminals/terrorists, Security Professionals thinking is highly conditioned by regulations, law, rules, procedures, documentation, policies, values ethics, and concern for the consequences of undesirable action on those affected. There is of course the danger that if you follow the criminal ways of thinking then you may become tempted to follow their behavior eventually. So, how can the mindsets be trained to enable Security Professionals to think freely without necessarily having to go through experience based learning! How can we develop doctoral programs that specifically target the development of the conceptual mindsets of the researchers! What specific sets of concepts will be useful for addressing these issues! These are questions that will be addressed in this paper.

Key words: IT security education, doctoral programs.

1. INTRODUCTION

Criminals and Terrorists' mindsets are guided by misplaced creativity and innovation. That creativity comes naturally to them as they consciously or unconsciously decide to take no regard for procedures policies, regulations, rules, the law or concerns for others while those who abide by those behavioral guidelines are constrained in their thinking. This creates a huge disadvantage for Security Personnel as they are forever engaged in detection and recovery as their primary mode of learning. Some alternative ways of thinking have to be encouraged among Security Professionals. Doctoral programs that plan to develop Security Professionals skills need to deliberate target the development of their conceptual mindsets if they are to prepare them for the difficult tasks of preventing, detecting and recovering aspects of socially valued legal activities. This is a task that has been undertaken by the use of 'Systems' philosophy and concepts (Ackoff 1971) for many years.

'Systems' are simply an holistic way of understanding real world phenomena. Systems concepts help to focus people's minds on the interconnections of parts before the study of the individual parts. In essence, systems concepts help us to understand the nature of the interconnections required to achieve the outcome and behavior of an entity (Ackoff 1972). Systems concepts and philosophy have been around for thousands of years. For example the systems phrase 'A whole is greater than the sum of its parts' has been attributed to Aristotle. These concepts were revived in the 60s to help address the much required integrative aspects of knowledge, skills, and the design/development of objects, products and services (Katz and Khan 1966). If so what new paradigmatic shift is necessary for those engaged in doctoral research into information security issues?

Systems concepts that are discussed in the literature and applied in practice since the 60s take what Checkland (1999) defines as a 'hard' systems view (Katz and Rosenzwig 1970). That is those who use 'systems' in this sense take the world to contain 'systems' i.e. 'taken-as-given' systems – see Checkland for a rich account of the shift from Science to Systems way of thinking in problem solving. In this way researchers and practitioners have been able to take a much wider and holistic view of the situations than before and develop better and more effective solutions that focus on integration to produce the desirable results. The use of systems notions in this way of thinking is to describe the world in systems terms e.g. education systems, transport systems, security systems. We name this as the use of 'systems' in ontological mode meaning that knowledge about systems are not subject to question.

The paradigmatic shift that is advocated in this paper is one of mode rather than the nature of the concepts. We name this new paradigm shift as 'systems epistemology'. In this mode Checkland (1999) considers the enquiry of the world to be assisted by 'systems' notions rather than consider the world itself as consisting of systems. He classifies this as 'soft' systems thinking. In arguing for this richer and a more powerful mode of enquiry, Checkland (1999, A11) conceives the enquirer's role as one of 'I spy complexity and confusion; but I can organize exploration of it as a learning system'. Churchman (1971) in his famous book on 'The Design of Enquiring Systems' also illustrated similar mode of enquiry of the world using different philosophical notions each of which yields a different perception of reality. Vickers (1968) called this mode of thinking as 'Appreciative Systems'. These are schemata formed within the mindsets that help to make sense of some part of reality but not others.

> '*Whatever the mind can represent to itself, from a cow to a contract, from a law of nature to a legal principle, is recognized by applying schemata – "readiness to see" which are themselves developed or restricted, confirmed or confused, elaborated or simplified, by further use…….This circular process, which contains the real answer to all conundrums of "hen-and–egg" type, is ubiquitous through the whole range of learning. It is the commonest fact of life – and the first foundation for a scientific epistemology*' (Vickers 1968, p193-194).

All three authors have been trying to shift enquirers' attention away from things-out-there in the world to thinking about the ways of conceptualizing meaning of the things-out-there and discuss the nature of the frames of references for use in that structuring processes.

Let's contrast these two different modes of using the same 'systemic' concepts in order to appreciate the power of the paradigm shift for doctoral education.

Ontological Mode	Epistemological Mode
Attention is to discover the 'system' out there in the world to be modeled and changed. Systems have existence without us and can therefore be named and observed.	Attention is to question 'Why I should consider the chosen set of observed phenomena as a 'system'? Systems don't have no existence without an observer.
The process of boundary construction is implicit or unconscious. Because of this any changes that are undertaken to boundary position tends to be either defended as a challenge to personal status or position or accepted as part of political process of accommodation.	The process of boundary construction is explicit or conscious. Questions to the boundary position is encouraged and pursued. The wish is to ensure that the boundary position is relevant and useful and the interest is to discover the rationale for the views.
Select phenomena in the world to match the 'systems' characteristics that are carried in the mind set.	Evaluate the phenomena in the world for their potential for inclusion in the modeling using 'systems' ideas.
Locked into the 'systems' boundary. The boundary separates the system and its environment and therefore the enquirer's attention is on those inputs and outputs that cross the boundary.	Since the boundary is an artificial construct, a system and its environment construction are subjective. The inputs and outputs will depend on the boundary position.
Focus is on the re-arrangement and the modification of the systems' **content**. The boundary is not open to question.	Focus is on the relevance of the chosen boundary and its systems' **context**. Question is whether relevant elements have been included.

Ontological Mode continued	**Epistemological Mode** continued
In general, the mapping of 'systems' is a one-off activity. This is confirmed by the phrases 'I found **the** system', '**the** system is', 'the problem with **the** system', 'I designed **the** system', etc.	In general, the mapping is a continuous set of activities. There is never **the** system as it is an artificial selection of a set of related phenomena for exploration.
Since the system is established, any subsequent questions that challenge the boundary of the system are rejected. Questions are seen as a challenge to authority, status and position. The reactions are expressed by emotional rejection or as political denial.	Since the relevance and validity of a system is never established, there is continuous seeking of information to confirm the status of its relevance. Neither emotions nor politics have a part to play in this mode of logical analysis.
Skills used are for the transformation of the content of the system. Enquirers are pre-occupied with re-design or construction.	Skills used are for the examination of the context of the chosen 'system'. Enquirers are interested in establishing the justification for the design.

2. EPISTEMOLOGICAL AND ONTOLOGICAL MODES OF THINKING AND SECURITY

In the epistemological mode of thinking, there are no absolute 'systems' in the world. What may exist is a selected sets of perceptions about the world which we may justify as 'systems' using a set of systemic characteristics as the basis for making that selection. In that sense, the choice of 'systems' is a deliberate and a conscious intellectual activity (Jayaratna 1994). This means that 'systems' has no existence outside the observer/enquirer. Since 'systems' do not exist without an enquirer then it makes sense to concentrate more on the role of 'systems' on the mindset of the Security Personnel than on the technology, objects or physical aspects of security issues. This is the same philosophy that has been used for underpinning the design of the

Masters Program in Internet Security Management curriculum (Armstrong and Jayaratna 2002).

As discussed earlier, criminals naturally think outside the box while we, through our childhood training, secondary and university education and work experience together with other conditioning factors such as values, procedures, policies, law, regulations, values, ethics and our concern for others of our actions tend to think within strong boundaries. These boundaries constrain our ability to become creative and innovative. Since it is difficult and also raises ethical and value issues for learning to think like a criminal, we have to find other ways of freeing the minds of the Security personnel. We believe that the same level and ways of learning to think can be achieved through the use of epistemological notions of 'systems' as discussed in Checkland (1981), Churchman (1971) and Vickers (1968). This way of conceptualizing security breaches across boundaries, free the researchers to think of security boundaries as artificially constructed devices that could be placed anywhere, not necessarily at the level physical layout of buildings, hardware networks, groups etc. Equally the freedom, to construct 'systems' in their mindsets, enables doctoral students to be more creative and innovative in their research. They are better able to organize the knowledge thus gained. As Checkland humorously puts it 'A cat can be considered as part of a mouse eliminating system'. Indeed it can also be considered as part of: a home entertainment system; a friendship network system; affectionate generating system; or a child substitution system. Pursued in this way, doctoral students are able to pursue their methods of enquiry and solutions in many novel ways.

The conceptual closure of a 'system' from its environment does not necessarily insulate us from the observed or non-observed phenomena in the world. The boundary is artificial and therefore is permeable and that is the reason why the enquirer needs to become open on a continuous basis for external feed back and information that help them to adjust or shift those boundaries. This ability to conceptualise and re-conceptualise systems boundaries is critical for Security Personnel thinking processes as they have to continuously match or anticipate the actions of the criminals/terrorists.

For example, the ontological mode of systems thinking makes the Security Personnel focus on inputs and outputs at fixed points e.g. entry to the building, network access, while the epistemological mode of 'systems' thinking enables them to draw boundaries anywhere and at any level. Each re-drawing will highlight a different set of security related inputs and outputs.

Doctoral programs that are intended to generate knowledge for industry use therefore need to include the preparation of the intellectual mindset of their students to a very high and deep level. Students need to be exposed to many different philosophical ways of understanding phenomena. Most essentially, they need to develop ways of conceptualizing and re-conceptualizing. Epistemological mode of 'systems' thinking help such a development to take place in a very effective way.

3. CONCLUSION

Criminals and terrorists have very creative and innovative mindsets. It is their actions that are highly misplaced. Security Personnel who have to match or anticipate such actions need to have equally deep levels of creativity and innovation but currently they are constrained in their thinking because of the rules, regulations, laws, policies, procedures, documentation, values, ethics and concern for others. If Security Personnel have to be effective then they need to 'think like a criminal but not act like one'. Doctoral programs that are targeted at the reasoning processes of Security Personnel need to raise the conceptual abilities and capacity of their students. This paper discussed the new paradigm shift that has to be achieved using 'epistemological mode of 'systems' that can achieve the shift.

4. REFERENCES

Ackoff, R.L., 1971, Towards a System of Systems concepts, management science, Vol. 17, No. 11

Ackoff, R.L., Emery, E., 1972, On Purposeful Systems, Tavistock Institute, London

Armstrong, H., Jayaratna, N., 2002, Internet Security Management: A Joint Postgraduate Curriculum Design, Journal of IS Education, JISE, Fall Issue, Vol. no. 13, No. 3, 2002

Checkland, P.B., 1981, Systems thinking, Systems Practice, Wiley and Sons, UK

Checkland, P. B., Scholes, J., 1990, 'Soft' Systems Methodology in Action, Wiley and Sons, UK

Churchman, W., 1971, The Design of Enquiring systems, New Basic Books, USA

Jayaratna, Nimal, 1994, Understanding and evaluating Methodologies, McGraw-Hill, UK

Katz, D., Khan, R. L., 1966, Common Characteristics of Open Systems, Wiley and Sons, UK

Katz, D., Rosenzwig, J. E., 1970, Organisation and Management: A Systems Approach, McGraw-Hill, USA

Vickers, G., 1968, Value systems and Social Processes, Pelican, UK

HIGHLY QUALIFIED INFORMATION SECURITY PERSONNEL TRAINING IN RUSSIA

V.Gorbatov, A.Maluk, N.Miloslavskaya, A.Tolstoy
Moscow Engineering Physics Institute (State University)
{milmur; ait}@mephi.edu

Abstract: Highly qualified personnel training is one of the priority national tasks in the field of education, which is aimed at supporting the specified level of the personnel potential for fulfilling scientific research and teaching in the system of higher education. Extensive experience in that field has been accumulated in Russia. The general organizational requirements of the existing Russian system as a whole, as well as intensional peculiarities of candidate and doctor of sciences in scientific specialties' related to information protection and information security training are posed in this report.

Key words: highly qualified personnel training, security education, information security, thesis requirements, Russia

1. THE SYSTEM OF HIGHLY QUALIFIED PERSONNEL TRAINING IN RUSSIA

The process of highly qualified personnel training is carried out in large research institutions, leading universities and other institutions of higher education. The basis of training is formed by the system of state certification which is organized by the social-state authority, namely Higher certification committee of the Russian Federation (HCC of Russia), operating at the Ministry of Education of the Russian Federation. The HCC of Russia issues normative documents regulating activities in the considered field of educational services, creates social boards carrying out the main certification procedures, and adopts final decisions on giving the corresponding qualification to candidates.

Russian system of certification is based on the two-stage technology of giving qualifications by results of successful defense of scientific-qualification grace papers (theses): "candidate of science" (the first stage) or "doctor of science" (the second stage). To pass the second stage it is obligatory to defend the candidate of science grace thesis first.

According to the HCC of Russia a candidate's thesis should either include a solution of an essential problem in the given area of knowledge or state scientifically founded technical, economical or technological innovations having vital importance for the country's economy.

Doctor thesis should include either results of scientific research a collection of which could be qualified as a new scientific achievement, or solution of a big scientific problem having significant social-cultural or economic significance, or state scientifically founded technical, economical or technological solutions whose implementation would bring an important contribution to country's economy development.

An obligatory condition of presenting a candidate of science grace thesis is successful sitting for at least the following three examinations: scientific specialty, philosophy, and foreign language.

As a rule, highly qualified personnel training, involving realization of specific scientific-research work, education, and sitting for disciplinary examinations similar to the candidate level, is carried out by including candidates in post-graduate studies founded at leading scientific institutions, universities and other educational-scientific centers. Duration of post-graduate studies is three years internally and four years without isolation from the main job (by correspondence course). State budget form of training at the expense of state financial support and contract form of training at the expense of candidate's funds are distinguished depending on the method of payment. Carrying out post-graduate student training, being one of the forms of educational services, requires obtaining a license from the Ministry of Education of Russia.

Each thesis is implemented within a definite scientific field whose list totals 25 titles. For example, in the field of information security it could be physico-mathematical sciences, technical sciences, and legal sciences. These titles are accordingly added to the scientific degree (e.g. candidate of technical sciences, doctor of physico-mathematical sciences).

2. THESIS REQUIREMENTS

The HCC of Russia determined that a person competing for a candidate or doctor scientific degree should hand in his thesis to the corresponding board in the form of a specially prepared typescript or a published monograph.

The thesis should be written by the author himself, include a collection of new scientific results and statements proposed by the candidate for the public defense, have inner uniformity and be evidence of the author's personal contribution to science.

The new proposed by the author solutions should be consistently argued and critically evaluated in comparison with other known solutions.

A thesis having applied significance should include information about practical use of scientific results obtained by the author, whereas in a thesis having theoretical significance – recommendations for use of scientific conclusions.

The main scientific results of a thesis should be published in scientific editions recommended by the HCC of Russia.

3. HIGHLY QUALIFIED PERSONNEL TRAINING IN THE FIELD OF INFORMATION SECURITY

There is only one specialty related to information security in the list of scientific specialties approved at the level of public administration authorities: "Methods and systems of information protection, information security". That specialty requirements are formulated in the so called "specialty passport". That document approved by the HCC of Russia establishes the list of problems which should be solved by the candidate in his scientific research corresponding to this specialty, determines the role (significance) of the specialty, indicates the fields of science to which belongs the specialty, and defines its place among other specialties.

Scientific research dealing with the problems of analysis, development, use and perfection of methods and means of information protection in the process of its gathering, storage, processing, transfer, and distribution as well as technical, organizational, and legal support of state, community and personality information security relate to the considered specialty "Methods and systems of information protection, information security".

Scientific research within that specialty should be important for solving methodical, scientific-technical and organizational-legal problems on the basis of design of new and development of existing methods and means of information protection to ensure information security of technical, social-economical, biological and other systems of any kind and different areas of application, to perfect and develop the corresponding legal regulation as well as forms and methods of confrontation with violations in the informational realm.

Here is a list of fields of research which may be carried out within the concerned specialty:

- analysis of fundamental problems of information security in the process of formation of modern informational society, providing the balance of personal, social and governmental interests in the informational area;
- methods, models and means research and development for detection, identification and classification of threats of information security violation of objects of different kinds and classes;
- analysis and scientific reasoning of public and local authorities' main lines of activities in providing the information security of the Russian Federation, including development and perfection of monitoring system of the Russian Federation's information security status;
- study and prediction of consequences of modern information technologies incorporation and wide proliferation, including development of personality and society informational-psychological security methods and models;
- scientific reasoning and development of organizational-legal mechanisms for securing constitutional rights and freedoms of citizens in the informational area, with these rights and freedoms regulating creation and use of informational resources, means of information protection, assessment, standardization, information and informational resources quality certification and control, high-technology area crimes prevention and investigation, federal, subjects' of the Russian Federation and local authorities cooperation in the informational area, countries' cooperation for providing collective information security;
- protectability analysis of information circulating in the various existing systems of documents circulation. Development of methods and means of information protection in the systems of electronic documents circulation including cases of use of digital signatures and other cryptographic methods and means for providing electronic payment and electronic commerce systems' information integrity;
- design of measures and mechanisms for information security policy formation and support for objects of all hierarchy levels of different control systems;
- development of general theory of information security and information protection with various technical, organizational and legal methods and means including foundations and project solutions (technical, mathematical, organizational, legal, etc.) for prospective means of information protection and information security creation;
- analysis and risk management, evaluation of possible damage as a result of information security breach, and vulnerabilities of systems of any kind and field of application including models and methods of evaluation of

information protectability and information security of objects of various classes, information security systems' and complexes' efficiency;
- development of theory of conflict functioning of informational-telecommunicational systems (ITCS) of any kind and field of application;
- research of new physical processes and effects allowing to increase the ITCS security;
- development of technologies of ITCS users' and subjects' identification and authentication, access control, antivirus and ITCS destructive software influence protection;
- creation of computational systems, models, methods and means of providing stability and protection for data object, database and metadata creation at various stages of their lifecycle. Research and development of methods and means for protecting ITCS data and knowledge bases;
- synthesis of integrated ITCS information security systems including means of automated design targeted at their security increase;
- research and development of models, methods and means (complexes) of passive and active information counteraction to information security threats in networks, including such open networks as the Internet, providing inner audit and monitoring of status of ITCS being under the influence of information security threats, ITCS information security management;
- research and creation of models of technical covert channels, design of the corresponding counteraction means. Development of methodology of technical information protection for objects of any kind and field of application;
- design of methods and systems of technical information protection including the necessary algorithmic support, analysis and synthesis of analogous and digital signal processing means for the sake of objects' information security;
- creation of quantitative methods and models of legal and normative base analysis and evaluation. Research of offense dynamics, development of forms and methods of crime control in the field of information security and information protection.

4. HIGHLY QUALIFIED PERSONNEL TRAINING EXPERIENCE IN MEPHI

Highly qualified personnel training in the field of information security has been launched in the Moscow Engineering Physics Institute (State University) (MEPhI). Post graduate courses in specialty "Methods and systems of information protection, information security" and a board for candidate and doctoral thesis protection in two fields of science – technical and legal – are available in the university. In future it is planned to broaden the board privileges by adding the physico-mathematical sciences branch. The post graduate studies are attended by graduate students of the MEPhI's Information Security Faculty, who successfully finished the full educational course and obtained the higher education in the specialty "Complex maintenance of automated system information security" or "Jurisprudence".

Other theses prepared in different scientific and educational centers lacking dissertation boards are also accepted for defense.

A list of several theses' topics defended recently is given as an example in the conclusion:

1. Research and development of algorithms of secure information access in data storage networks.
2. Research of information protection means' trustworthiness in automated systems of depository services.
3. Development of algorithms for software cryptographic transforms' modeling and analysis.
4. Research and development of design methods of complex object security systems.

DOCTOR OF PHILOSOPHY: IT SECURITY

Jill Slay
University of South Australia, School of Computer and Information Science, Mawson Lakes Campus, Mawson Lakes, SA 5095, Australia
{Gerald.Quirchmayr; Jill.Slay}@UniSA.edu.au

Abstract: This paper compares and contrasts the curricula of a PhD and a Doctor of IT programs in IT Security offered by the School of Computer and Information Science of the University of South Australia

Key words: IT Security; Doctorate; Curriculum

1. RELATIONSHIP BETWEEN TITLE AND NATURE OF OUR DOCTORAL PROGRAMS

In the Australian government university system, titles of doctoral programs are very specific. In a technical program in IT Security, the choice of a Doctor of Philosophy (PhD) which is a research doctorate and a Doctor of IT (DIT) which is a Professional doctorate which would need to contain one-third coursework and two-thirds research are available

2. TYPES OF PROGRAM

Currently offer both the PhD and DIT are offered. The PhD is a long-established research program in a wide range of computer science and IT sub-fields. The DIT is a new program, designed in conjunction with our own local defence-focussed industries and the first students are yet to be enrolled

3. OBJECTIVES OF THE PROGRAMS - COMPARISON

The DIT is a structured research degree. The DIT degree is differentiated from the Ph.D. by the following features:

- The structured program of research induction and, most notably, the focus on applied research which differs from the structured program currently operating within the Divisional Ph.D. induction, in its theory and focus on methodology. It is designed to cater to the needs of a graduate student cohort configured as mainly, although not totally, part time, and with a study focus that complements their work.
- The provision of opportunities for professionals to update their academic knowledge in the latest theory and methodologies within their fields. The research induction focuses on applied Information Technology Security research, attending to how current industry issues can be conceptualised and examined from within the most recent theoretical concepts and methodological practices arising in our discipline, and then applied to our current IT Security practice.
- The provision of an extended study semester, to meet the needs of working professionals. The program will be delivered through a mix of intensive summer and winter schools, and face-to-face and online seminar groups and supervision sessions, over a 6 month rather than a 3 month semester. This will enable students to work at a depth and at a pace which will accommodate the demands of their working lives.

4. DURATION WHEN UNDERTAKEN AS A FULL-TIME PROGRAM

Both the DIT and PhD are 3 year full-time programs but the DIT is designed to be studied part-time by practicing professionals.

5. ENTRANCE REQUIREMENTS

Both the DIT and PhD require a student to possess at least an upper second class honours degree (characterised by at least one semester of research) or an equivalent masters degree. The DIT also requires five years of appropriate industry experience. The undergraduate qualification is expected to be in Computer Science, Computer Systems Engineering and possibly in Information Systems. Undergraduate studies would not have necessarily included any coursework focussing primarily on IT or IS security

6. PROGRAM STRUCTURE

The PhD consists solely of three years of research. The research question and research agenda are determined by the Principal Supervisor and the student. While some learning support is available in research methods and thesis writing, primary, and sometimes total, input comes from the supervisor and, possibly, his or her research group

The DIT has the following structure

FIRST YEAR	SECOND YEAR	THIRD YEAR
Semester 1 Research Practice Professional Seminar 1 Elective Elective Semester 2 Professional Seminar 2 Elective Elective Elective	Semester 1 Information Technology Thesis 1 Semester 2 Information Technology Thesis 2	Semester 1 Information Technology Thesis 1 Semester 2 Information Technology Thesis 2

The only core modules are the Professional seminar and Research Practice

The Electives will be developed out of the Supervisor and research lab directors' current research interest and direction. In our case Electives will be taken from:

- Security Architectures
- E-Commerce Security
- Ad-hoc wireless network security
- Forensic Computing

- Information warfare

Also other electives could be taken (eg in advanced databases) if some correlation between that and the student's potential thesis could be established

7. RECOGNITION OF PRIOR LEARNING

The PhD program does not allow for any recognition of prior learning but the DIT program permits credit for prior learning in exceptional cases when the applicant is able to demonstrate that the prior learning is the equivalent to the core courses in the program. However, exemption will not be granted for the thesis component or for research seminars.

8. REQUIRED SIZE AND NATURE OF RESEARCH PROJECT

A PhD thesis is typically 100,000 words whereas a DIT thesis can be between 30 and 50, 00 words. The PhD project focuses on creating new knowledge while a DIT thesis may be of a more applied nature and directed primarily at an industry focussed applied research issue.

9. INTERNATIONAL STANDARDS TO BE CONSIDERED

As with other universities in Australia, the University of South Australia tends to focus primarily on ACM and IEEE for international benchmarking

10. POTENTIAL FUNDING SOURCES, INDUSTRY PARTNERS AND SCHOLARSHIPS FOR RESEARCH PROJECTS

Our government supplies scholarships for most Australian citizens with 1st class honours degrees or equivalent coursework masters degrees. Government funded cooperative research centres can also supply "top-up" funding for students and some hardware, software and "in-kind" support.

Our local situation with respect to industry collaboration and co-operation is good and projects are supplied by software and hardware companies such as Motorola and Tenix, by our State and Federal Police Departments and by the Defence Science and Technology Organisation, as well as smaller players.

11. POSSIBLE AREAS OF CURRICULUM SPECIALIZATION YOUR ORGANIZATION/INSTITUTION MAY BE ABLE TO PROVIDE AS A PARTICIPATING PARTNER

The University of South Australia would be able to contribute in areas of:

- Information Security Management- especially cultural issues
- Security Architectures
- Ad-hoc wireless network security
- Forensic Computing
- Information Warfare

12. ANY OTHER INFORMATION RELEVANT TO THE PROGRAM

The university has a holistic focus and tends now to want to develop an integrated skill set in researchers. University documentation states a research student

1. *has an understanding of current research-based knowledge in the field, its methodologies for creating new knowledge, and can create, critique, and appraise new and significant knowledge.*

2. *is prepared for lifelong learning in pursuit of ongoing personal development and excellence in research within and beyond a discipline or professional area.*

3. *is an effective problem solver, capable of applying logical, critical and creative thinking to a range of research problems.*

4. *can work both autonomously and collaboratively as a researcher within a particular discipline or professional area and within wider but related areas.*

5. *is committed to ethical action and social responsibility as a researcher in a discipline or professional area and as a leading citizen.*

6. *communicates effectively as a researcher in a discipline or professional area and as a leading member of the community.*

7. *demonstrates international perspectives in research in a discipline or professional area and as a leading citizen.*

Research supervisors, in taking on the supervision take are acknowledging that they "guarantee to the academic and professional sectors that our research degree postgraduates have already engaged in original research in order to solve significant problems, that in doing so they have learned how to work autonomously and collaboratively, that they have set up lifelong learning patterns and networks, that they have been effectively able to communicate their research findings, that they have performed research in an ethical manner and they have introduced international perspectives into their research." [1]

They are required to assess my postgraduate students against this generic framework and this might be adapted to the IT Security context to give us a set of criteria against which to measure the effectiveness of an IT Security postgraduate, and potential long-term researcher.

REFERENCE

[1] Crotty, R 2003, *Towards a Quality Research Environment at UniSA*, Research Supervisor Resources, viewed 2 March 2003 <http://www.unisa.edu.au/resources>

DOCTORAL PROGRAMME ON ICS SECURITY AT THE UNIVERSITY OF THE AEGEAN

Sokratis K. Katsikas
Laboratory of Information & Communication Systems Security, Dept. of Information & Communication Systems Engineering, University of the Aegean, Karlovassi GR-83200, Greece
ska@aegean.gr

Abstract: The paper presents the doctoral programme of study on information and communication systems security at the University of the Aegean, in Samos, Greece.

Key words: Doctoral Programme, Information & Communication Systems Security Education

1. INTRODUCTION

The purpose of this paper is to present the doctoral programme of study on information and communication systems security at the University of the Aegean, in Samos, Greece, in order to contribute to the discussion within IFIP WG 11.8 towards the definition of an international doctorate programme in the field.

The doctoral programme of study on information and communication systems security at the University of the Aegean is a research doctorate programme, which has been offered since the initial operation of the Department in 1998 and is still being offered.

2. PROGRAMME AIMS AND OBJECTIVES

The main objectives of the doctoral programme are:

- To give all interested students the opportunity to take advantage of the results of the joint effort of several Universities worldwide to develop a modular - but integrated - doctoral Programme in the areas of Information and Communication Systems Security.
- To further support the establishment of a wide, international network of experts who teach, consult and conduct research in the fields of information and communication systems security, as well as the closely related fields of dependability and safety.
- To support, enhance, stimulate and utilise the mobility of University students, researchers and teaching staff among different European Union Member States.
- To provide interested industrial and governmental institutions and bodies with a unique point of contact and co-operation with several centers of excellence in research on information and communication systems security, with a real European flavour.

3. DURATION, ADMISSION AND DEGREE REQUIREMENTS

The duration of the program, when undertaken as a full-time program varies with several factors, such as, for example, the entrance actual qualifications, the student's actual research capabilities etc.; the duration can vary between a minimum of 3 years and a maximum of 6 years.

For admission to the programme, an M.Sc. in Information Systems, Communications, Informatics, Engineering, Sciences or Business Administration is required. An M.Sc. in Information and Communication Systems Security is highly desirable.

Formally, the sole doctoral degree requirement is the successful defense of the doctoral thesis before the jury. There is no formal requirement for having completed a specific number of course credits, nor for having undertaken any coursework, as in all Greek Universities. However, doctoral students that do not hold an M.Sc. in Information and Communication Systems Security are strongly advised to attend as many M.Sc. courses as possible, during the course of their doctoral study.

4. COURSES

The following courses are offered in the winter semester (in parentheses the subjects covered): *Cryptography I* (Introduction; Mathematical background: Probability theory, Information theory, Complexity theory, Number theory, Algebra, Finite fields; Crypto services; User authentication; Data authentication; Data integrity; Data origin authentication; Non-repudiation of origin; Data confidentiality; Basic cryptographic principles; Cryptography; Symmetric and asymmetric systems; Principles of authentication; One-way functions and hash functions; Message authentication codes; Digital signatures; Crypto protocols; User authentication protocols; Key management protocols), *Network Security I* (The necessity for network security; Attack types; Basic network security concepts; Technologies and services offered by Certification Service Providers and PKI; Case studies; Security architecture in the ISO/OSI model; Threats; Services and mechanisms; The Internet security architecture; Security protocols at the Internet layer; Security protocols at the transport layer; Security protocols at the application layer; Security protocols above the application layer; Applications, Firewalls; Censorship and context-dependent access control technologies; Privacy enhancing technologies: Anonymous Browsing, Anonymous Publishing), *Database Systems Security* (Database systems architecture; Database models; confidentiality and integrity; security services; authorization; access control, auditing; database security examples; security in SQL environments, secure multilayer databases; privacy protection in databases; logical inferencing; security in object-oriented databases; security in distributed databases; security in federated databases; security in data mining systems; Medical database security; case studies: Oracle RDBMS etc.), *Crypto algorithms implementation techniques* (Implementing crypto algorithms in software and in hardware; Secure systems design; Java security and Java crypto extensions; Security token technology: Smartcards; Case studies). The following courses are offered in the spring semester: *Cryptography II* (Modular arithmetic; discrete logarithms; prime factoring; P, NP, NP-complete problems; probabilistic polynomial time algorithms; next-bit checks, random cryptography; zero-knowledge protocols; obvious transfer. LFSRs: shift registers, m-sequences, linear equivalence, Berlekamp-Masey; Shannon Theory: Entropy, probability, random ciphers, perfect secrecy; Combinatorics: authentication, thresholds schemes, secret sharing schemes, key distribution; Design criteria: Non-linearity, correlation properties, Boolean functions, discrete Fourier transform; crypto algorithms evaluation; identification, authentication and digital signature schemes), *Network Security II* (Generalised application layer security systems; Distrib authentication systems: Kerberos, SESAME; Network management security: Network management services in OSI networks and in the Internet model: SNMP, CMIP/TMN, JMX; Mobile code security models: Java, ActiveX, SafeTcl; Intrusion Detection Systems; Digital Rights Protection Technologies; Middleware security models; Financial transaction systems security: Electronic Cash Systems, Electronic Checks, Electronic Credit Card Payments, Micropayment Systems; Electronic voting systems security; Wireless network security: Wireless LAN and 802.11, wireless Ad hoc Networks and Bluetooth, wireless Handheld Devices and PDA, Smartphone; Crypto protocols and formal analysis and design methods: The AAPA2 tool), *Standardisation – Certification – Evaluation* (Access control: ISO/IEC 10181-3, ISO/IEC 10181-n; Security mechanism standards: Encipherment algorithm register (ISO/IEC 9979), block cipher mode (ISO/IEC 10116), cryptographic check function (ISO/IEC 9797), digital signatures (ISO/IEC 9796), hash functions (ISO/IEC 10118), key management (ISO/IEC 11770), security management (ISO 17799); Evaluation criteria: TCSEC (Orange Book), ITSEC, US Federal Criteria, Common Criteria, Canadian CTSPEC; Security evaluation: ITSEM, industry standards: ECMA, Posix; Quality standards: ISO 9000; National and international standards in banking: key management, hash functions, digital signatures, data integrity mechanisms, PIN management etc.), *Social and ethical issues* (Computers and society: IT as a revolution and an evolution, the future with IT, knowledge and machines: AI, VR, user interfaces, usability and IT, issues related to the new work environment, change management; privacy and security oriented systems design; ethical issues: wotk monitoring, surveillance, social control, creativity issues, work transformations, quality of work and life, the new capitalism model; new technologies and economic development; using IT in politics and in elections; deontology and ethical codes; case studies: ACM, BCS, IEEE, IFIP; ethical issues related to hacking; IT security social impact; scientific, research and professional liability; Computer crime; Computing Forensics).

5. THESIS

The doctoral thesis must reflect original research work, undertaken by the candidate him/herself, that promotes scientific knowledge in the field. There is no formal requirement on the actual size of the thesis itself, but the average size is approximately 200 A4, single spaced, 12 font pages.

6. POTENTIAL FUNDING SOURCES

The best potential source of funding for qualified students is the European Union, through its numerous funded research framework programmes. Some possibilities also may arise within national programs of funded research. Potential non-academic partners include the European industry as well as the national industry. Finally, some scholarships are offered, but these are limited to Greek nationals only.

7. CONCLUSIONS

The doctoral programme of study on information and communication systems security at the University of the Aegean, in Samos, Greece has been presented, with a view towards contributing to the discussion for the definition of a, international similar programme in the field. The Department would be very keen to cooperate with institutions of a similar standing towards the definition, as well as the implementation of the international doctorate. To this end, some possible areas of curriculum specialization that the Department could contribute to a possible international partnership include Security management, network security, legal – social – ethical issues.

AN INTERNATIONAL SECURITY EDUCATION PERSPECTIVE

Gerald Quirchmayr
Universität Wien, Fakultät für Informatik, Liebiggasse 4/4-6, A-1010 Wien, Austria and University of South Australia, School of Computer and Information Science, Mawson Lakes, SA-5095, Australia

Abstract: The intended contribution of this paper is to motivate the need for an internationalization of IT security education. Starting from the existing situation and a look at selected existing concepts, the paper then presents an idea for international security education cooperation at a doctoral level

Key words: IT security education, international cooperation, doctoral programs.

1. INTRODUCTION AND BACKGROUND

There is an obvious need to introduce minimal standards in the field of IT security. Today, the situation is very unfortunate in that no internationally accepted minimal standard for IT security knowledge exists. There however are national attempts, mostly following the "core body knowledge" principle in several countries. Curricula suggestions of ACM, IEEE, ACS and many other computer societies clearly recommend a minimal security education for all IT and IS students. With these organizations and advanced universities driving the development, a reasonable standard could be established in the leading universities of the industrialized world. The problem of very few tertiary educational institutions offering a specialization in IT security however still remains to be solved. Ambitious groups and institutions around the world, which the US National Information Assurance Training and Education Center (NIATEC) the European Erasmus/Socrates partnerships of universities carrying out research-oriented education in IT security (Katsikas & Gritzalis 2000) and the nascent cooperation in this field between universities who are partners in the Australian Technology Network (www.atn.edu.au) indicate that the need of educational cooperation on the national and international is beginning to be met. The primary motivation behind this cooperation is easy to explain. It is becoming more and more difficult to cover the whole area of IT security as single educational institution. There are a few examples of universities that can sustain post-graduate programs in IT security on their own, but this is rather exceptional.

2. WHAT ARE THE NEEDS, WHERE ARE THE MODELS TO FOLLOW?

As mentioned in the introduction there are very few attempts towards the internationalization of IT security education, the most promising perhaps being the activities being developed inside the European Union. The scale of the projects and their resources might be considerably smaller than national programs, but their conception is truly international. Successful cooperation on curriculum design, joint development of course content, development of a credit transfer system that works across several countries, and the exchange of staff and students have amply demonstrated that this cooperation is possible. When comparing these initiatives with work that is planned or already carried out on the national level in the US and Australia, it becomes obvious that the intentions of these activities are very similar.

The major motivation is to as quickly as possible spread new knowledge and develop the next generation of IT security experts, which, due to the developing threats, must be far larger than the comparatively small group we have today (see the efforts of the IPICS programs). With probably the only exception being defense, all sectors are coping very badly with the effects of attacks and the need to rethink their approach to systems design, implementation and operation. Government agencies and some selected civilian industry sectors, namely banking and finance, are starting to develop and implement the right responses.

The experience of the past decade has clearly shown that while undergraduate education can be provided, a truly research-oriented education that produces the experts needed for developing tomorrow's solutions, can, like in all other fields of science, only be provided in an international setting. That is why the few existing large-scale networks in the US and on the European level will determine most of the future research outcome. It is very specific to IT security that the success of research education is also closely linked to national interests. That is why truly international cooperation will always be somewhat limited and why currently the only tight cooperation model being followed in practice is the one being applied inside the European Union.

3. DEVELOPING A COMMON RESARCH AGENDA BACKED BY DOCTORAL LEVBEL EDUCATION

Whatever different views on IT security the involved core players (governments, industry, and education) might have, the need for closer research and educational cooperation becomes evident when looking at the many different aspects of IT security. Probably no single institution can claim to have top experts in fields being as disparate as law, sociology, psychology, and business at one end and cryptography and operating system, network and database security at the other. That is why, especially in universities in the European Union, a more realistic approach was developed. It does admittedly add to the cost of running programs to move students and staff around the continent, but given the urgent need of networking the present and future generations of IT security experts and building expert teams, the return on the investment made can be expected to be very high. Pooling knowledge and human resources is the only way of meeting the future requirements. In spite of attack patterns becoming more and more advanced, the number of successful attacks in relation to the number of attacks launched has dropped steeply. This trend justifies the sometimes quite heavy investments made in the past and gives IT security experts at least some of the much needed time to breathe.

It is a t this stage important to identify possible future threats and to start developing respective answers. Crime trend analysis and crime development forecasts, as used by criminologist for many decades, seem to be an appropriate paradigm to work from. Combined with the monitoring of technology trends, this gives an indication of the sort of problems we will be exposed to in the coming years. A research agenda can clearly be developed from such a scenario, but such a scenario-based analysis can also be used to dcfinc thc cducational nccds. Mccting thcsc cducational nccds will in turn produce the experts and researchers needed to master the future challenges.

4. MOVING TOWARDS AN INERNATIOANL RESEARCH EDUCATION PROGRAM

As the arguments discussed in the previous sections have shown, the need for an international cooperation at the upper end of research-oriented education clearly exists.

Given that a not too small number of bureaucratic obstacles will occur and that acts of political will like the EU's Bologna Declaration (Hackl 2001) will not quickly be repeated on a worldwide level, harmonization of content rather than the regulation of programs is the obvious answer.

We basically have to consider four interesting types of programs, the traditional research-oriented Master and PhD programs and the recently more and more popular professional Master and Doctoral programs. Cooperation in the traditional research programs is most easily established by appointing international colleagues as supervisors or co-supervisors and by allowing students to spend one term or one academic year in the middle of their studies at a partner institution (sandwich approach). Provided that there are mutual benefits and that the exchange is no one way system, this type of cooperation is rather easy to handle.

The real challenge is to establish a collaboration model suitable for professional programs that are to a substantial extent based on coursework. The challenges will range from the agreement on the content of courses and their accreditation to their required number and the duration of the program. The experience with cooperating at the level of Master programs across several disciplines in the European Union has shown that, unless two institutions have very similar academic structures and programs, the cross-accreditation of modules or individual courses is the only sustainable alternative.

5. WHAT CAN WE BUILD ON?

Luckily enough academics around the globe can in our field build on having successfully cooperated in the past, be it in the organization of conferences, joint research projects, or staff exchange programs. As essential as this personal basis is, it cannot replace more institutionalized approaches. When left to single institutions the resulting number of different models of cooperation might easily lead to a chaotic situation. Building on existing national (NIATEC, ATN) and international networks (IFIP) therefore is the most promising way of moving towards an organized form of cooperation. Pioneering models like the Erasmus/Socrates one, which is now applied in approximately 30 European countries, can serve as base to start from.

In a first step it is however essential to identify relevant national and international models for academic cooperation and accreditation that already exist and are suitable.

6. CONCLUSION

National as well as international cooperation in the field of IT security research education is still in its infancy, but successful pioneering efforts made in the US, Europe and Australia are indicating that especially universities at the cutting edge of technology are driving towards establishing the necessary environment. It is only a matter of time for these advanced groups to join forces and establish mutually accredited research and professional education frameworks. With the increasing need for national and international cooperation in the area of cyber crime prevention it is definitely not a minute too early to start thinking about establishing educational standards to assure that experts participating in joint efforts can count on their partners having the right level of expertise. It is obviously research and development projects that will benefit first, but the positive impact on industry and government cannot be denied, e.g. in cyber crime prevention and IT forensics.

7. RECOMMENDED RESOURCES

NIATEC:http://cob.isu.edu/schou/niatec.htm
NCISSE: http://www.ncisse.org
ATN: http://www.atn.edu.au
IPICS: http://www.tol.oulu.fi/kurssit/811327A/IPICS2004.htm

(Hackl 2001) Elsa Hackl, Towards a European Area of Higher Education: Change and Convergence in European Higher Education. EUI Working Papers, Rsc. No. 2001/09. European University Institute, Badia Fiesolana, I-50016 San Domenico (FI), Italy.

(Katsikas & Gritzalis 2000) Katsikas S., Gritzalis D. (Eds.), A proposal for a postgraduate programme on information and communication systems security, European Commission, SOCRATES & Youth TAO, Report IS-CD-4b, Athens, January 2000.

DO MILITARY FORCES NEED PH.D.'S?

Major Ronald C Dodge, JR.
Department of Electrical Engineering and Computer Science,
United States Military Academy, West Point, New York, 10996

Abstract: The rate of technological advancement and the relative disparity of military power amongst many countries have fueled an oncoming revolution in warfare. To prepare to defend against the new emerging technology threats, forces must invest time and resources to develop a corps of soldiers capable of using and defending against advanced technology.

Key words: Military, Higher Education, Technological Warfare Revolution

1. INTRODUCTION

Military forces are in a state of technological transition where advances in robotics, artificial intelligence, high performance computing, and communications are setting the stage for a potential revolution in the conduct of war. Some might argue that the revolution has begun. Developing core competencies in the areas of information technology in the military services is critical to the establishment of policies and procedures to usher in new paradigms in warfare. This is increasingly important as rapidly advancing technologies are fueling the deployment of force multiplying tools without clear policy or soldier training. A revolution in warfare is described as[1]:

---

1 Tom McKendree, The Revolution in Military Affairs—Issues, Trends, and Questions for the Future, paper presented at 64th MORS Conference, Fort Leavenworth, Kansas, June 1996

> "a military technical revolution combining [technical advances in] surveillance, C3I [command, control, communications, and intelligence] and precision munitions [with new] operational concepts, including information warfare, continuous and rapid joint operations (faster than the adversary), and holding the entire theater at risk (i.e., no sanctuary for the enemy, even deep in his own battlespace). "

The existence of a cyber threat is now universally accepted. Clearly the conditions exist for a new pattern in war fighting and military forces must leverage the new technologies or become a victim of their use. Potential actors include hackers, hactivists, industrial spies, organized crime groups, terrorists and national governments. The most serious threat comes from nation states. The PLA Daily reported in January 2003[2] that the Chinese government was taking "new steps in the Air Force Engineering University to train high-quality military talents targeting on the academic leading edge. " Additionally, development of a Chinese "Cyber Corps" has been reported as early as 2001. Other countries have responded to this threat: Taiwan established an Information Warfare force, in 2001, to counter potential Chinese cyber-attacks.[3] The force will eventually be about battalion sized and be independent of any military service.[4] The South Korean government is planning on establishing specialist units for cyber warfare.[5] The Japanese Defense Agency is also rumored to be establishing a cyber-warfare organization.

The need for a growing and evolving knowledge base in information security as part of the transition to technological warfare should be clear, as well as the need to continue to engage in understanding and developing new technologies. To affect the leveraging of these emerging technologies, members of the military must understand the technologies and be directly involved in the research and development process.

---

2 Ren Peilin and Meng Feng http://english.pladaily.com.cn/english/pladaily/2004/01/06/20040106001028_ChinaMilitaryNews.html, January 6, PLA Daily

3 Jane's Defence, Jane's Sentinel Security Assessment, Armed Forces – Taiwan, 9 April 2002.

4 Jane's Defence, Jane's Sentinel Security Assessment, China and Northeast Asia, 8 March 2001.

5 Jane's Defence, Jane's Sentinel Security Assessment, China and Northeast Asia, 9 April 2002.

2. EXISTING DEPARTMENT OF DEFENSE SUPPORTED PHD PROGRAMS

The United States Military has long recognized the necessity to have service members educated and involved in the various technologies being employed. Currently the services have thousands of soldiers enrolled in advanced degree programs for the purpose of bringing technology back to the individual service. The programs attended by the soldiers have no definitive restriction on where the advanced degree it attained. Currently, Department of Defense personnel attend programs from United States public and private colleges and universities to programs in foreign countries. The diversity, both in focus and location of the programs attended by soldiers is critically important to the continued growth of not only academically qualified but also culturally diverse educated soldiers. A brief history of the quest for educated soldiers in the United States is[6]:

- 1802 – President Thomas Jefferson signed legislation authorizing the creation of the United States military Academy, the first engineering school in the United States
- 19th century – Most large engineering projects completed in the United States benefited directly fro the involvement of West point graduates.
- 1925 – The Army sent Jimmy Doolittle to the Massachusetts Institute of Technology to earn a doctorate in aeronautical engineering.
- WWII – Numerous scientists in uniform served the nation and the Army.
- 1947 – MAJ GEN Henry S Aurand, director of research and development, general staff at the war department, tried to create a corps of scientist-officers.
- 1984 – Lt. Gen. Maxwell Thurman, Army deputy chief of staff for Personnel, directed the establishment of the Army's Technology Enhancement Program (TEP); sending officers to masters and doctoral programs.
- 1985 – Brig Gen. Hines, deputy commanding General of the Army Personnel Command, created a new officer branch to manage officers in the TEP – the Science and Technology Corps.
- 1990 – Gen William Tuttle, commanding General of the Army Material Command, offered 140 positions for a Uniformed Army Scientist program.

---

[6] Barry Shoop and Kenneth Alford, Army Transformation: Uniformed Army Scientists and Engineers Dec 2002 Issue Cross talk , the Journal of defense software engineering

- 2002 – Gen Eric Shinseki, Army Chief of Staff, approved in principle the establishment of a formal Uniformed Army Scientist program.
- 2004 – First officers selected for the Uniformed Army Scientist program.

In 1996, a report issued by the Army Science Board stated[7]

"... the Army's reliance on modern weapon systems and technology has been growing, its cadre of technology- literate line officers and science, math, and engineering (SM&E)-educated officers has been reduced. " Six years later in 2002, the formal Uniformed Army Scientist program was defined to address this shortfall.

Focusing more specifically on information assurance, the United States Department of Defense has established an Information Assurance Scholarship Program. This program consists of three Department of Defense Centers of Academic Excellence in Information Assurance that sponsors graduate programs in information assurance. These three institutions are the Information Resources Management College (IRMC) of the National Defense University (NDU), the Naval Postgraduate School (NPS), and the Air Force Institute of Technology (AFIT). Partner schools include: George Mason University, James Madison University, Mississippi State University, Syracuse University, University of Dallas, University of Maryland Baltimore County, University of Maryland University College, University of North Carolina Charlotte, and the University of Tulsa.

3. MILITARY NEEDS

The needs of the Department of Defense differ in some important ways from other market sectors. The non-Department of Defense markets receiving students graduating with advanced degrees tend to pick the most qualified from the set of graduates. If a student does not complete the program nor does anything to set him or her apart from the other graduates, the only loss is to the student. In Department of Defense programs, officers typically will return to the service regardless of their performance in the degree program. Additionally, in the past, the pursuit of advanced degrees has not been seen as a promotion enhancing activity. This greatly reduced

[7] U.S. Army. "The Science and Engineering Requirements for Military Officers and Civilian Personnel in the High Tech Army of Today and Tomorrow." Army Science Board Study, Feb. 1996

the set of qualified officers seeking to enroll in masters or doctoral programs.

3.1 Unique Need for Rapid Return to the Force

The framework for programs designed to support the Department of Defense need to focus on a seemingly competing set of goals; the need to produce highly educated officers, skilled in information assurance and the need to have those highly educated officers out of degree programs as rapidly as possible to ensure maximum productivity while in the service. A normal career in the United States military is 20 years. Currently officers are not identified for a doctoral degree program until he or she has been in the service for ten or twelve years. Even at that point several must still complete a masters program. This places the service and the soldier in difficult situation if there are any delays in completing the academic program.

3.2 Skill Sets

Another area that differs from other markets is the focus on a more hands on experience in the designated domain. As indicated previously, the longevity of many officers after completing a doctoral program is somewhat limited. The ability for an officer to learn the necessary skills in a specific domain is crucial to the ability of the officer to contribute.

The skill sets attained while in pursuit of a doctoral degree are most beneficial when they are tied to a specific problem that the officer will tend to when leaving the school environment. This is difficult to implement in practice given the widely varying interests and foci of sponsoring faculty at the different degree granting institutions and the classification level of some research.

3.3 Advantages To A Multi-University / Multinational Program

The mission of the armed forces for the United States is entirely outward focused. In fact, the United States constitution has specific clauses prohibiting the use of active duty members of the armed services from operating (other than training) in the United States. This presents the Department of Defense with a unique goal of producing culturally diverse officers capable of interfacing with other nationalities. One might argue that a service member with a doctoral degree would no longer be considered in the collection of officers with an outward focus, however at the most basi level, every soldier regardless of specialty must be able to function in the basic mission. A program designed to place the officer in programs in countries other than the United States is the most direct way of achieving this diversity and understanding while at the same time moving toward our educational goal.

A second advantage to service members completing all or part of their degree in an institution outside the United States is the different academic foci. As more collaboration is conducted amongst geographically close schools, the research content and methodology of the institutions naturally begins to homogenize. Much like the cultural diversity goal of the Department of Defense, a diverse approach to formulating and solving problems should be a heavily weighted consideration.

3.4 Disadvantages To A Multi-University / Multinational Program

The primary disadvantage to conducting a multi-institution program of study is the coordination of research goals and practices. As important as it is for the Department of Defense to have diverse officers, the integration of differing processes, which can in some cases be fundamental in nature, make collaboration difficult, if not impossible. Additionally we must consider the goal of conducting directly relevant research and the timely completion of the doctoral research.

The nature of Department of Defense sponsored research adds a further layer of complexity to research area development where security classifications are a problem. This however can be mitigated and does not present an insurmountable hurdle.

The third area of concern is the time is takes to complete the program. Like the research process, inserting disruption in the dissertation process has the potential of disrupting the successful completion of the research. An officer typically must complete a masters program in two years and a Ph.D. in three years. If not complete in the three year window, the officer may continue the dissertation for an additional two years, but must do so in addition to normal military duty. Completing a Ph.D. under the umbrella of a two year extension is very difficult and the challenge is compounded as travel to the institution (New York to Sydney for example) adds complexity.

4. CONCLUSION

The goals of a Military PhD program must be formulated with the focus of advancing the ability for the service to fight and win wars. Today, the militaries of the world are on the verge of a revolution in waging war. The advancement of technology will impact the way we fight on many fronts. As an example, depending on the sophistication of the enemy, significant disruption, aimed at an enemy's center of gravity, can be attained through cyber attacks. The ability of a force to capitalize on technological advances before an enemy will be a defining factor in victory. In the late 1800's, Sir William Francis Butler, withstanding the specific technology, recognized the necessity of education:

> "The nation that will insist on drawing a broad line of demarcation between its fighting man and the thinking man is liable to have its fighting done by fools and its thinking done by cowards."

The Department of Defense goals of diversity, timely completion, and rapidly transferable experience need to be balanced with establishing a productive framework within which a successful doctoral program can be completed.

A DOCTORAL PROGRAM WITH SPECIALIZATION IN INFORMATION SECURITY

A High Assurance Constructive Security Approach

Cynthia E. Irvine and Timothy E. Levin
Department of Computer Science, Naval Postgraduate School, Monterey, California

Abstract: A doctoral program in computer science with a specialization in information security is described. The focus of the program is constructive security. Key elements of the program are the strong computer science core upon which it builds, coursework on the theory and principles of information assurance, and a unifying research project. The doctoral candidate is a member of the project team, whose research contributes to the goals of the project and to fundamental advancements in high assurance security.

Key words: Information assurance, education, doctoral program

1. INTRODUCTION

As computing platforms become smaller, increasingly pervasive, and highly networked, the rampant exploitation of system vulnerabilities represents a threat to our ability to safely use information technology. Those who choose to wreak havoc on our systems do so with impunity. Fear that flawed systems may invite problems ranging from the annoyances of spam, identity theft, and loss of productivity, to catastrophic damage to critical information is turning computing from an enabling to a disabling technology. We are faced with the prospect that Gresham's Law will once again hold: the bad will drive out the good.

To address these problems in a military context, the Center for Information Systems Security Studies and Research (CISR) at the Naval Postgraduate School (NPS) has developed a program in Information

Assurance and Security education that addresses a broad range of information security issues through education and research. An important element of that program is the nurture of doctoral students.

1.1 Computer Science Ph.D. Program Overview

To conduct doctoral research in information security at NPS, one must look to the Computer Science Department. NPS started its Computer Science program in the mid 1970s and has offered Ph.D. degrees, i.e. research doctorates, for over two decades. The majority of students at the Naval Postgraduate School are engaged in a terminal Master's Degree program, while a smaller number are involved in the doctoral program. The Ph.D. program meets several objectives by providing educators to military universities, research-level personnel to oversee a wide range of technical projects in the military and government, and researchers in government laboratories.

The duration of the Computer Science Ph.D. program is three years for full time students. This may seem short relative to the four to five years usually required for doctoral students at other U.S. institutions, however NPS students are atypical with respect to the benefits afforded them. First, their tuition is paid for in its entirety by a sponsoring entity such as one of the military services or the U.S. Government. Second, each student continues to receive a pre-student salary from the sponsoring organization. Thus, the students have the freedom to pursue their studies without the distraction caused by attempting to offset their educational costs through external employment. Their work is also accelerated because NPS is on a year-round calendar with four full quarters of teaching and research per year.

In general, applicants to the Ph.D. program in Computer Science at NPS must have a Master's Degree in Computer Science or closely related field. Admission to NPS requires the submission of certified transcripts of all courses taken at the university level, both undergraduate and graduate. Graduate Record Examination scores are required for applicants not currently at NPS. It is expected that all grades and scores will be above average. Supporting material, such as Masters thesis, research reports, or published papers, that demonstrates the candidate's ability to conduct research is also encouraged. International students and non-native English speakers are required to score well on the TOEFL examination as a requirement for admission to the NPS Ph.D. program.

A Master's degree in Computer Science is an expected prerequisite. In some fields, the Master's degree is considered a "consolation prize" for students failing to pass certain examinations for the doctoral degree. This means that these programs often admit students with the intent of taking them directly to the doctorate without stopping for a Master's degree. In contrast, a Master's degree in Computer Science is deemed a valuable terminal degree and is a generally expected milestone.

The funding model for Ph.D. programs at NPS is quite different from that of most other U.S. universities. Military and government civilian students are sponsored by a military service or agency. Thus, all of tuition and salary (at the pre-student income level) is paid for by external sources and does not have to be sought by the faculty Ph.D. supervisor. Some doctoral students are existing employees who have been involved in ongoing research projects. In such cases, the dissertation advisor is obliged to seek continued research support for the dissertation research through scholarships or research grants from a variety of funding agencies such as the National Science Foundation, the Office of Naval Research, the Defense Advanced Projects Research Agency, etc.

Support is also possible through industry as several of our ongoing research projects in cyber security involve industry partners. Usually these partnerships revolve around the use of specialized equipment or software, but they occasionally include financial support. We discourage doctoral students from engaging in proprietary or classified research, since the results would have restricted distribution and therefore not be considered a contribution to the overall body of knowledge in Computer Science, a requirement for a successful dissertation.

Each doctoral candidate is required to demonstrate knowledge of core computer science by passing a written qualifying examination. In addition, students must meet requirements in a minor subject and must pass an oral qualifying examination, the latter before commencing dissertation research. Upon completion of the dissertation, the candidate must defend the work in an oral examination.

1.2 Information Assurance and Security Specialization

Over the past decade, the thirteen quarter-long information security courses listed in Table 1 have been developed and are offered by the Computer Science Department. Many prerequisites are cumulative, i.e. Operating Systems requires Discrete Mathematics, Data Structures, Computer Architecture, and an appreciation of programming fundamentals.

Table 1. Information Assurance and Security Courses with their Prerequisites

Course	Course Title	Prerequisites	Students	
			MS	Ph.D.
CS3600	Introduction to Information Assurance	Computer Architecture	✓	✓
CS3640	Analysis of DoD Critical Infrastructure Protection	CS3600	✓	✗

Course	Course Title	Prerequisites	Students	
			MS	Ph.D.
CS3670	Secure Management of Systems	CS3600	✓	✗
CS3675	Network Vulnerability Assessment	CS3600	✓	✗
CS3690	Network Security	CS3600, Networking	✓	✗
CS4600	Secure Systems	CS3600, Networking, Operating Systems	✓	✓
CS4603	Database Security	CS3600, Databases, Operating Systems	✓	✗
CS4605	Security Policies, Models and Formal Methods	Discrete Mathematics, CS3600, Algorithms	✓	✓
CS4610	Information Ethics	none	✓	✗
CS4614	Advanced Topics in Computer Security	CS3600, CS4600, CS4605	✓	✓
CS4677	Computer Forensics	CS3600, CS3670, Computer Architecture	✓	✗
CS4680	Introduction to Certification and Accreditation	CS3600, CS3670, CS3690	✓	✗
CS4685	System Certification Case Studies	CS3600, CS3670, CS4680	✓	✗

Masters students may enroll in all of the courses listed in Table 1, while doctoral students enroll in selected (checked) courses intended to prepare them for dissertation research. Candidates in the Information Assurance and Security specialization generally meet their minor requirements by enrolling in courses in Mathematics or Electrical and Computer Engineering. A more concrete binding to the minor is achieved by having the non-Computer Science Dissertation Committee member come from one of those departments.

Dissertation research consumes the vast majority of a doctoral candidate's time. While prior experience and learning may shorten the duration of a candidate's research program, there is currently no formal recognition of those achievements. For example, a candidate with significant experience in the use of formal methods for high assurance development would have a head start when embarking on a program of related research.

Research for a Ph.D. requires that each student conduct dissertation research on an original topic that results in a new contribution to the field of computer science and, in this case, information security. The size of the dissertation is of less importance than its quality and contribution. (Louis de Broglie (1923) provides an example of high quality brevity.)

2. UNIFYING HIGH ASSURANCE RESEARCH PROJECT

Doctoral research is generally centered around a unifying research project being conducted by a member of the faculty. Currently CISR has embarked on the *Trusted Computing Exemplar* (TCX) Project (Irvine et al. 2004b), which provides a context for Masters theses and Ph.D. dissertation research. A brief motivation for and description of this effort follows.

2.1 Motivation

Much of the global critical infrastructure has now been constructed using commodity systems and depends upon "layered defenses" for which there is no well-founded protection model (Schell 2001). Through a process of constructive security engineering it is possible to describe security architectures for which there is a concrete protection model (Irvine 2003). These architectures can combine both commodity elements and components at selected junctures that provide high assurance of correct policy enforcement as well as evidence that they have not been subverted (Irvine 2004a). The TCX project is motivated by a recognition that construction of high assurance systems has not been a priority in the commercial sector. Even during the 1970s and 1980s, only a few score people contributed to the construction of high assurance systems and information was insufficiently detailed at best (Gasser 1988, Schell et al. 1973). To exacerbate the esoteric nature of these systems, those that were successfully developed were classified or proprietary. Market-driven academic institutions have not invested in course materials that teach the concepts of high assurance secure systems development in a coherent manner. Thus, we lack the availability of high assurance trusted systems, developers who can create these systems, as well as public domain worked examples upon which new projects could be modeled.

2.2 Trusted Computing Exemplar Project

The *Trusted Computing Exemplar Project* is intended to provide an openly distributed ***worked example*** of how high assurance trusted computing components can be built. It encompasses four related activities: creation of a prototype framework for rapid high assurance system development, development of a reference-implementation trusted computing component, evaluation of the component for high assurance, and open dissemination of results related to the first three activities. Each of these is discussed in greater detail below.

2.2.1 Rapid high assurance system development framework

A prototype *high assurance development framework* is being created, and used to design and develop a reference implementation *trusted computing component,* the *TCX Separation Kernel*. High assurance methodologies and techniques are applied during the entire lifecycle. The TCX project is using openly available tools for the development framework; these tools are selected on the basis that they do not impose restrictive licensing requirements upon the results of the effort. The prototype framework for rapid high assurance development is intended to provide a set of interoperable tools and define a set of efficient, repeatable procedures for constructing trusted computing systems and components.

2.2.2 Reference-implementation trusted computing component

We are developing a high assurance, embedded micro-kernel, and trusted application, as a reference implementation exemplar for trusted computing. The TCX Separation Kernel will enforce process and data-domain separation, while providing primitive operating system services sufficient to support simple applications.

2.2.3 High assurance Evaluation

Under sponsorship from the National Security Agency, we are the lead writers of a Separation Kernel Protection Profile. This effort will result in an official NSA protection profile, which will be used for the evaluation not only of our Exemplar Separation Kernel, but also of a wide range of trusted separation kernels. This work is a key first step toward evaluation.

2.2.4 Open dissemination of results

To provide materials to other educators who want to learn about and teach the techniques of high assurance design, development and engineering, we will make all of the results of our activities available. The documentation, source code, development framework and other evidence for a third-party evaluation will be made *openly available* as they are produced, providing previously unavailable examples of "how-to" for high assurance trusted computing. This will include not only the code and evaluation documentation, but descriptions of the analysis and decisions that took place in our efforts.

A wide range of research topics has emerged from the TCX activities. Examples include surveys and applications of formal methods; modeling; hardware analysis; protocol analysis; development of materials related to Common Criteria evaluations; and tools design and implementation. The TCX project has already provided thesis areas for two graduated Masters students and, currently, the effort provides research topics for six Masters students and two doctoral candidates. The breadth and depth of the project will continue to accommodate future students.

An advantage of the overarching project is the involvement of the student as part of a larger team tackling a wide range of project-related research and development. In choosing a model for a unifying research project, Multics (Corbato 1965) was viewed as a highly successful example. Even though the student may concentrate his or her thesis or dissertation research on a small, highly focused research topic, the exposure to the work of others and the appreciation of the challenges associated with high assurance secure technology contributes to a broader perspective. Often, the research projects benefit from the insights drawn from the operational experiences of the students.

3. CONCLUSION

A research doctoral program has been described. It is based upon a core in computer science and provides both classes and research in computer and network security. A theme underlying all coursework and research is that of improving cyber security through constructive security engineering. Through a unifying research project doctoral research is given a context. The team approach provides a stimulating learning environment.

REFERENCES

de Broglie, M. L., 1923, Ondes et quanta, *Comptes rendus*, Vol. 177, pp. 507-510.

Corbato, F.J. and Vyssotsky, V.A. 1965. Introduction and Overview of the Multics System, *Proceedings of AFIPS Federal Joint Computer Conference*, pp. 619-628.

Irvine, C.E., 2003, Teaching Constructive Security. *IEEE Security and Privacy*, 1(6):59–61, November.

Irvine, C.E., Levin, T.E., Nguyen, T.D., Shifflett, D., Khosalim, J., Clark, P. C., Wong, A., Afinidad, F., Bibighaus, D. and Sears, J., 2004a, Overview of a High Assurance Architecture for Distributed Multilevel Security. To appear in *Proceedings of of the 5th IEEE Information Assurance Workshop*, West Point, NY, June.

Irvine, C.E., Levin, T.E., Nguyen, T.D., and Dinolt, G.W., 2004b, The Trusted Computing Exemplar Project, To appear in *Proceedings of the 5th IEEE Information Assurance Workshop*, West Point, NY, June.

M. Gasser, M, 1988, *Building a Secure Computer System*, Van Nostrand Reinhold, NY, NY.

Schell, R. R. 2001. Information Security: Science, Pseduoscience. *Proceedings of the 17th Annual Computer Security Applications Conference*, pp. 205–216, New Orleans, LA, December.

Schell, R.R., Downey, P.J., and G. J. Popek, G.J., 1973,, Preliminary Notes on the Design of Secure Military Computer Systems. Technical Report MCI-73-1, Electronic Systems Division, Air Force Systems Command, Hanscom AFB, Bedford, MA, 73.

PART THREE

I-NETSEC04 3RD WORKING CONFERENCE ON PRIVACY AND ANONYMITY IN NETWORKED AND DISTRIBUTED SYSTEMS

A SECURITY MODEL FOR ANONYMOUS CREDENTIAL SYSTEMS

Andreas Pashalidis* and Chris J. Mitchell
Information Security Group, Royal Holloway, University of London
{A.Pashalidis,C.Mitchell}@rhul.ac.uk

Abstract This paper proposes a formal model of the Bellare-Rogaway type [Bellare and Rogaway, 1994] that enables one to prove the security of an anonymous credential system in a complexity theoretic framework. The model abstracts away from *how* a specific instance of anonymous credential system achieves its goals; instead it defines *what* these goals are. The notions of credential unforgeability, non-transferability, pseudonym unlinkability and pseudonym owner protection are formally defined and the relationships between them are explored. The model is a step towards a formal treatment of the level of privacy protection that anonymous credential systems can and should achieve, both in terms of pseudonym unlinkability and user anonymity.

Keywords: anonymous credential systems, pseudonym systems, privacy, anonymity, unlinkability, provable security

1. INTRODUCTION

1.1 Background and motivation

Anonymous credential or 'pseudonym' systems allow users to interact with organisations using distinct and unlinkable pseudonyms. In particular, a user can obtain a credential (a statement of a designated type that attests to one or more of the user's attributes) from one organisation and then 'show' it to another, such that the two organisations cannot link the issuing and showing acts; this renders the user's transactions unlinkable. Of course this unlinkability is limited; if only one credential is ever issued with a particular set of attributes, then clearly all credential showings containing this set of attributes can be linked

*The author is sponsored by the State Scholarship Foundation of Greece.

to each other and to the unique issued credential. Pseudonym systems must prevent users from showing credentials that have not been issued (i.e. they must guarantee 'credential unforgeability'), and prevent users from pooling their credentials (for example, to collectively obtain a new credential that each user individually would not be able to). This latter property is usually referred to as 'credential non-transferability'.

Security models of pseudonym systems, and proofs (where given), do not usually allow reasoning about the resulting degrees of user anonymity and pseudonym unlinkability. This paper, following the ideas first set out by Bellare and Rogaway in [Bellare and Rogaway, 1994], proposes a model that is based on complexity theoretic arguments and which potentially leads to information theoretic anonymity metrics. It abstracts away from the particulars of *how* specific pseudonym system instances achieve their goals; instead it focuses on *what* these goals are. The model captures security properties for both organisations (credential unforgeability and non-transferability), and users, both in terms of 'traditional' security (pseudonym owner protection) and privacy (pseudonym unlinkability and user anonymity). The model makes a clear distinction between the different notions and allows the relationships between them to be analysed.

1.2 Related work

Pseudonym systems were first introduced by Chaum in the 1980s [Chaum, 1985]. Since then, numerous pseudonym systems have been proposed, each with its own particular set of entities, underlying problems, assumptions and properties. Some examples are given in [Brands, 2000; Camenisch and Lysyanskaya, 2001; Chaum and Evertse, 1987; Damgard, 1990]. The most relevant work to this paper is probably the formal treatment of the anonymous credential system in [Camenisch and Lysyanskaya, 2001]. There, security is defined based on the indistinguishability between the transcripts of protocols that occur in an 'ideal' world (where a universally trusted party guarantees security), and the 'real world' (where such a party does not exist). In that model, transactions between users and organisations correspond to well-defined events, and the adversary acts like an event scheduler; he can arbitrarily trigger events of his choice. In the model of [Camenisch and Lysyanskaya, 2001], however, the relationship between the different security notions that a pseudonym system should satisfy is somewhat hidden by the fact that the universally trusted party takes care of them. Also, in that model, the adversary is not allowed to corrupt players in an adaptive fashion. While our model retains the property that the adversary gets to specify the order of events in the system, he can also adaptively corrupt players. Further, the model allows a relatively easy analysis of the relationships between different notions. This is due to the fact that we abstract away from properties that do not lie at the same level of abstraction as that at which a pseudonym system operates.

1.3 What we *don't* do

Our model does not capture 'traditional' communications security properties, such as entity authentication. This is not an omission; these issues are outside the scope of the model (other well-established security models can be used to reason about such issues). Of course, if users do not authenticate organisations, and if the integrity and confidentiality of communications in the system are not guaranteed at the session level, then there cannot be any security. However, the way these services are provided lies at a different level of abstraction. We therefore assume that they are provided by the infrastructure that allows users and organisations to communicate. We also assume that, within this infrastructure, users remain anonymous to organisations (i.e. we assume an anonymous channel).

The remainder of the paper is organised as follows. The next section describes the formal model of pseudonym systems. Section 2.2 establishes the notions of pseudonym owner protection, credential unforgeability and credential non-transferability, which together capture the notions of soundness for a scheme. Further, section 2.3 provides a brief discussion of the notions and explains the relationships between them. Section 2.4 establishes the notion of pseudonym unlinkability which is discussed in section 2.5. Further, section 2.6 establishes the notion of pseudonym indistinguishability and shows it is a necessary condition for unlinkability. Finally, section 2.7 addresses the issue of anonymity in pseudonym systems, while section 3 concludes the paper and gives directions for further research.

2. SECURITY OF PSEUDONYM SYSTEMS

In this section we describe our model of a pseudonym system. We regard a pseudonym system as being comprised of the players in the system and the procedures through which they interact. The players, in particular, are divided into users, issuing organisations and verifying organisations. Since users are known to each organisation under a different pseudonym, indeed possibly under multiple pseudonyms, a procedure must be in place according to which a user and an organisation establish a new pseudonym; we call this the 'pseudonym establishment protocol'. Procedures must also be in place that allow users to obtain credentials (on the pseudonym that was established with the issuer) and to show them (on the pseudonym that was established with the verifier). We call the former the 'credential issuing protocol' and the latter the 'credential showing protocol'.

In our model, credential types are in one-to-one correspondence with (combinations of) user attributes; in other words, each combination of attributes defines a credential type. An organisation, for example, that issues demographic credentials containing the fields `sex` and `age group`, with possible values of {`male`,`female`} and {`18-`,`18-30`,`30-50`,`50+`} respectively, in our model may actually issue up to 8 different credential types (one for each combination of values).

2.1 The model

A protocol `prot` is assumed to be a tuple of interactive Turing machines; an execution of `prot` is said to be successful if and only if all machines accept. The set of all non-zero polynomial functions in the natural number k is denoted by $\mathtt{poly}(k)$. A real-valued function $\epsilon : \mathbb{N} \rightarrow \mathbb{R}$, is said to be negligible in k if and only if $0 \leq \epsilon(k) < 1/|q(k)|$ for any $q \in \mathtt{poly}(k)$ and for all sufficiently large k.

REMARK 1 *We are concerned in this paper with situations where two functions f and g satisfy $f(k) > g(k) + \epsilon(k)$ for any negligible function ϵ and for all sufficiently large k. To simplify the discussion we abuse our notation slightly and simply say that f is greater than $g + \epsilon(k)$, i.e. we omit explicit references to k, and we also omit the rider 'for all sufficiently large k'.*

DEFINITION 1 *A pseudonym system is a tuple*

$$(k, \mathtt{init}, U, I, V, P, T, \mathtt{peprot}, \mathtt{ciprot}, \mathtt{csprot})$$

whose elements are as follows.

- *k (a natural number) is the system security parameter.*
- *`init` is the initialisation algorithm; on input k, it outputs the elements of the sets U, I, V and descriptions of the sets P, T. Hence, U, I, V (and also P and T) are (implicitly) regarded as functions of k.*
- *U is the set of users, $|U| \in \mathtt{poly}(k)$.*
- *I is the set of credential issuing organisations ('issuers' in short), $|I| \in \mathtt{poly}(k)$.*

- *V is the set of credential verifying organisations ('verifiers' in short), $|V| \in$* $\texttt{poly}(k)$.
- *P is the set of pseudonyms.*
- *T is the set of credential types.*
- `peprot` *is the* pseudonym establishment protocol*: any user/organisation pair $(u, o) \in U \times (I \cup V)$ may execute* `peprot`*; if the protocol succeeds, u and o will have established a pseudonym $p \in P$ and we write* $\texttt{peprot}_{u,o,p}$*. (The user u is called the* owner *of p and will typically also possess some private output associated with p as necessary to engage in* `ciprot` *and* `csprot`*.)*
- `ciprot` *is the* credential issuing protocol*: any user/issuer pair $(u, i) \in U \times I$ may execute* `ciprot` *with respect to a pseudonym $p \in P$ associated with u and i (established using* `peprot`*) and for a particular credential type $t \in T$. If successful, we say that i has issued a credential of type t on pseudonym p to u, and we write* $\texttt{ciprot}_{i,p,t}$.
- `csprot` *is the* credential showing protocol*: any user/verifier pair $(u, v) \in U \times V$ may execute* `csprot` *with respect to a pseudonym $p \in P$ associated with u and v (established using* `peprot`*) and for a particular credential type $t \in T$; if the protocol succeeds we say that u has shown a credential of type t on pseudonym p to s and we write* $\texttt{csprot}_{v,p,t}$.

Each issuer $i \in I$ defines a set $T_i \subseteq T$ of credential types that it intends to issue in the future[1]. It is required that, for all distinct $i, i' \in I$, $T_i \cap T_{i'} = \emptyset$[2]. We denote the set of active credential types in the system by $T^* \stackrel{def}{=} \bigcup_{i \in I} T_i$. It holds that $|T^*| \in \texttt{poly}(k)$.

2.2 The games and soundness

In order to formalise our notions of security for a pseudonym system, we define a series of games between two Turing machines: a Challenger and an Adversary. Each game captures a specific property of the pseudonym system. In this section we define Game 1, which captures 'pseudonym owner protection', Game 2, which captures 'credential unforgeability', and Game 3, which captures 'credential non-transferability'. In sections 2.4 and 2.6 below we define Game 4 and Game 5, which capture 'unlinkability' and 'indistinguishability' of pseudonyms, respectively.

At the beginning of all games, the Challenger sets up the system by running `init`. At this point, the Challenger controls all users, issuers and verifiers of the system. He defines the sets T_i for each issuer. The Adversary, which is assumed to be a probabilistic polynomial time (and space) algorithm and is denoted by $\mathcal{A}$, then receives as input the sets U, I, V, and T_i, descriptions of the sets P and T, and the system's public information. As explained above, it is assumed that the underlying communication infrastructure provides authentication of issuers and verifiers to users, that it protects the integrity and confidentiality of their communications, and that it binds each protocol execution to exactly one session between the involved parties. Thus, $\mathcal{A}$ models a passive adversary that faithfully transmits messages between parties.

Each of the games consists of two distinct and successive phases. During the first phase of each game, $\mathcal{A}$ may issue (oracle type) queries to the Challenger; during the second phase he may not. During the first phase of Game 1, 2 and 3, $\mathcal{A}$ may issue the following types of query to the Challenger.

`runpeprot`(u, o): $\mathcal{A}$ may arbitrarily select a user/organisation pair $(u, o) \in U \times (I \cup V)$ and issue this query. When this happens, the Challenger makes u and o execute $\texttt{peprot}_{u,o,p}$. The Challenger replies `true` if the protocol execution is successful and `false` otherwise. (If the execution is successful, u and o will have established a new pseudonym $p \in P$; $\mathcal{A}$, however, does not learn its value.)

`runciprot`(u, i, t): $\mathcal{A}$ may arbitrarily select a user/issuer pair $(u, i) \in U \times I$ and a credential type $t \in T_i$ and issue this query. When this happens, the Challenger selects a pseudonym p from set of pseudonyms that u and i have established[3] and makes u and i execute $\texttt{ciprot}_{i,p,t}$. He replies `true` if the protocol execution is successful and `false` otherwise (including the case where u and i have not established any pseudonym). Note that $\mathcal{A}$ does not learn the value of p.

`runcsprot`(u, v, t): $\mathcal{A}$ may arbitrarily select a user/verifier pair $(u, v) \in U \times V$ and a credential type $t \in T$ and issue this query. When this happens, the Challenger selects a pseudonym p from the set of pseudonyms that u and v have established and makes u and v execute $\texttt{csprot}_{v,p,t}$. He replies `true` if the protocol execution is successful and `false` otherwise (including the case where u and v have not established any pseudonym). Note that $\mathcal{A}$ does not learn the value of p.

`corruptUser`(u): $\mathcal{A}$ may arbitrarily select a user $u \in U$ and issue this query. When this happens, the Challenger hands all the private information of u to $\mathcal{A}$. This includes u's pseudonyms, credentials and all his past protocol views. From that point on, the control of u is passed from the Challenger to $\mathcal{A}$.

`corruptIssuer`(i): $\mathcal{A}$ may arbitrarily select an issuer $i \in I$ and issue this query. When this happens, the Challenger hands all the private information of i to $\mathcal{A}$. This includes the set of pseudonyms i has established and all its past protocol views. From that point on, the control of i is passed from the Challenger to $\mathcal{A}$.

`corruptVerifier`(v): $\mathcal{A}$ may arbitrarily select a verifier $v \in V$ and issue this query. When this happens, the Challenger hands all the private information of v to $\mathcal{A}$. This includes the set of pseudonyms v has established and all its past protocol views. From that point on, the control of v is passed from the Challenger to $\mathcal{A}$.

In all games, a global and monotonically increasing variable τ counts $\mathcal{A}$'s queries. We say that the query is issued at the time indicated by τ. At some point in time, $\mathcal{A}$ exits the first phase and enters the second phase. The value of τ at that point is denoted by $\tau_{\mathtt{max}}$. In the second phase $\mathcal{A}$ may no longer issue any queries; what happens is specific to each game and is described below.

To describe the games we require some additional notation. In the following, $P_{u,o} \subseteq P$ denotes the set of pseudonyms the user $u \in U$ has established with the organisation $o \in (I \cup V)$ at time $\tau_{\mathtt{max}}$ (via $\mathcal{A}$'s `peprot` queries), i.e. $P_{u,o} \stackrel{def}{=} \{p \in P \mid \text{a successful } \mathtt{peprot}_{u,o,p} \text{ occurred at a time } \tau \leq \tau_{\mathtt{max}}\}$. The set of pseudonyms belonging to u is defined as $P_u \stackrel{def}{=} \bigcup_{o \in (I \cup V)} P_{u,o}$ and the set of pseudonyms that o has established is defined as $P_o \stackrel{def}{=} \bigcup_{u \in U} P_{u,o}$. (Since $\mathcal{A}$ does not learn the value of pseudonyms during their establishment, only u knows P_u and only o knows P_o.) The set of active pseudonyms in the system is defined as $P^* \stackrel{def}{=} \bigcup_{u \in U} P_u$, or, equivalently, $P^* \stackrel{def}{=} \bigcup_{o \in (I \cup V)} P_o$. Since $\mathcal{A}$ is polynomially bounded in k, it holds that $|P^*| \in \mathtt{poly}(k)$. It is required that, for all distinct $u, u' \in U$, $P_u \cap P_{u'} = \emptyset$[4]. The function $f : P^* \rightarrow U$ maps pseudonyms to their owners, which is well-defined by the assumption that $P_u \cap P_{u'} = \emptyset$.

Let $\hat{U} \subseteq U$, $\hat{I} \subseteq I$ and $\hat{V} \subseteq V$ denote the subsets of users, issuers and verifiers respectively that $\mathcal{A}$ corrupted during the first phase. Further, let $P_{u,t}(x) \subseteq P_u$ denote the subset of pseudonyms belonging to user $u \in U$ on which a credential of type $t \in T^*$ has been issued prior to time x, i.e. $P_{u,t}(x) \stackrel{def}{=} \{p \in P_u \mid \text{a successful } \mathtt{ciprot}_{\cdot,p,t} \text{ occurred at time } \tau \leq x\}$.

We now describe the second phase of Games 1, 2 and 3. As mentioned above, $\mathcal{A}$ may no longer issue queries to the Challenger in this phase. He may, however, engage in $\mathtt{ciprot}_{p,i,t}$ and $\mathtt{csprot}_{p,v,t}$ executions directly with organisations (while pretending to be the user $f(p)$).

GAME 1 *(pseudonym owner protection): $\mathcal{A}$ selects a pseudonym/verifier/type triple $(p, v, t) \in P^* \times (V - \hat{V}) \times T$ such that $f(p) \in (U - \hat{U})$. We say that $\mathcal{A}$ wins the game iff he can make v accept in a $\texttt{csprot}_{p,v,t}$ execution with probability greater than any negligible function in k.*

GAME 2 *(credential unforgeability): $\mathcal{A}$ selects a pseudonym/verifier/type triple $(p, v, t) \in P^* \times (V - \hat{V}) \times (T - \bigcup_{i \in \hat{I}} T_i)$ such that $P_{f(p),t}(\tau_{\max}) = \emptyset$ and $\bigcup_{u \in \hat{U}} P_{u,t}(\tau_{\max}) = \emptyset$. We say that $\mathcal{A}$ wins the game iff he can make v accept in a $\texttt{csprot}_{p,v,t}$ execution with probability greater than any negligible function in k.*

GAME 3 *(credential non-transferability): $\mathcal{A}$ selects a pseudonym/verifier/type triple $(p, v, t) \in P^* \times (V - \hat{V}) \times (T - \bigcup_{i \in \hat{I}} T_i)$ such that $P_{f(p),t}(\tau_{\max}) = \emptyset$. We say that $\mathcal{A}$ wins the game iff he can make v accept in a $\texttt{csprot}_{v,p,t}$ execution with probability greater than any negligible function in k.*

DEFINITION 2 *A pseudonym system is said to offer pseudonym owner protection, credential unforgeability or credential non-transferability if and only if no adversary $\mathcal{A}$ can win Game 1, 2 or 3, respectively.*

2.3 Discussion

Game 1, ‘pseudonym owner protection’, captures security for users; nobody — even when colluding with users, issuers and verifiers — should be able to successfully show a credential on a pseudonym of which he is not the owner (i.e. on a pseudonym which was not established by himself). The property is typically achieved by having the pseudonym establishment protocol generate some private output for the user. This output is then treated as a secret that enables the user to authenticate himself as the pseudonym owner during the execution of the credential issuing and showing protocols.

Games 2 and 3 capture security for organisations. In particular, Game 2 captures what is usually perceived as ‘credential unforgeability’. If a (dishonest) user can construct a credential by himself (i.e. without obtaining it legitimately from an issuing organisation), if, in other words, the user can *forge* the credential, then the system clearly does not offer credential unforgeability. Game 2 captures unforgeability in this sense. There is, however, a simplistic way for a user to ‘forge’ a credential: by ‘borrowing’ it from another user with whom he colludes (and who legitimately obtained the credential from an issuing organisation). This type of ‘forgery’ is not captured by Game 2. In some applications credential sharing is not a concern while forgery is.

Game 3, credential non-transferability, captures the case of credential sharing between users. In a system that offers credential non-transferability, no user can successfully show a credential of a type he himself was never issued. This holds even in the case he colludes with other users that have been issued credentials of that type.

It is interesting to observe the relationship between the notions of unforgeability and non-transferability: the latter, being stronger, implies the former. Clearly, if a dishonest user can construct credentials by himself, there is no need for him to collude with other users in order to forge one. In the model, this is simply reflected by the fact that the adversary is more restricted in his choice of the credential type in the (second phase of the) second game than he is in the (second phase of the) third. A system that offers non-transferability also offers unforgeability.

This relationship between unforgeability and non-transferability motivates the following definition of a sound pseudonym system.

DEFINITION 3 *A pseudonym system is said to be sound if it offers pseudonym owner protection and credential non-transferability.*

As a side comment, note that non-transferability of credentials is probably the most challenging property for a pseudonym system to achieve. How can colluding users be prevented from sharing their credentials? Certainly, if two users share all their secrets, then they can act as each other in all circumstances. Thus, one will always have to assume that users will not share *all* their secrets, either because they will be prevented by some means, e.g. by the use of tamper-resistant hardware, or because they will be given a sufficiently strong incentive not to. Examples of schemes that follow the latter strategy include the ones in [Lysyanskaya et al., 2000], where sharing credentials implies sharing a highly valued key (this is called 'PKI-assured non-transferability'), and [Camenisch and Lysyanskaya, 2001], where sharing one credential implies sharing all credentials (this is called 'all-or-nothing non-transferability').

2.4 Unlinkability of pseudonyms

We now define Game 4 in order to capture the first privacy property required of pseudonym systems, i.e. the property of pseudonym unlinkability. A second (weaker) privacy property is defined in section 2.6.

In the first phase of the Game 4, $\mathcal{A}$ is allowed to issue queries from the following set of query types, which are similar but not identical to the first three query types of section 2.2.

`runpeprot`(o): $\mathcal{A}$ may arbitrarily select an organisation $o \in (I \cup V)$ and issue this query. When this happens, the Challenger selects a user u according to a probability distribution $\mathcal{D}$ from U and makes u and o execute $\texttt{peprot}_{u,o,p}$. He replies `true` if the protocol execution is successful and `false` otherwise. (If the execution is successful, $\mathcal{A}$ knows that u and o have established a new pseudonym $p \in P$ but learns neither p nor the identity of its owner.)

`runciprot`(p, i, t): $\mathcal{A}$ may arbitrarily select a pseudonym/issuer pair $(p, i) \in P \times I$ and a credential type $t \in T_i$ and issue this query. When this happens, the Challenger selects the owner of p and makes him execute $\texttt{ciprot}_{i,p,t}$ with i. He replies `true` if the protocol execution is successful and `false` otherwise (including the case where p has no owner). Note that $\mathcal{A}$ does not learn who the owner of p is.

`runcsprot`(p, v, t): $\mathcal{A}$ may arbitrarily select a pseudonym/verifier pair $(p, v) \in P \times V$ and a credential type $t \in T$ and issue this query. When this happens, the Challenger selects the owner of p and makes him execute $\texttt{csprot}_{v,p,t}$ with v. He replies `true` if the protocol execution is successful and `false` otherwise (including the case where p has no owner). Note that $\mathcal{A}$ does not learn who the owner of p is.

`corruptUser`(u): As in section 2.2.

`corruptIssuer`(i): As in section 2.2.

`corruptVerifier`(u): As in section 2.2.

We now describe the second phase of the Game 4. We denote the set of pseudonyms that belong to uncorrupted users by $P^{**} \stackrel{def}{=} P^* - \bigcup_{u \in \hat{U}} P_u$.

GAME 4 *(pseudonym unlinkability): $\mathcal{A}$ outputs two distinct pseudonyms $p_1, p_2 \in P^{**}$. We say that $\mathcal{A}$ wins the game iff $f(p_1) = f(p_2)$.*

$\mathcal{A}$ may apply a variety of strategies in his effort to correlate pseudonyms. We now consider what is probably the most naive strategy and arrive at the following simple result.

LEMMA 1 *If the Challenger, during* `runpeprot`(o) *queries of an instance of Game 4, selects users uniformly at random (i.e. $\mathcal{D}$ is the uniform distribution), and two pseudonyms, p_1, p_2 say, are chosen at random from P^{**}, then the probability that $f(p_1) = f(p_2)$ is $1/|U - \hat{U}|$.*

Proof Suppose $f(p_1) = u \in (U - \hat{U})$. Then the probability that $f(p_2) = u$ is $1/|U - \hat{U}|$, since the pseudonyms are allocated uniformly at random to users, and hence also to uncorrupted users. The result follows. □

Thus it is tempting to define a pseudonym system that offers unlinkability of pseudonyms as a system where $\mathcal{A}$ cannot win the Game 4 with probability greater than $1/|U - \hat{U}| + \epsilon(k)$ for any negligible function ϵ. However, this is only a reasonable definition of unlinkability if

$\mathcal{D}$ is the uniform distribution and if no credentials are shown during the first phase of the game, i.e. there are no instances of `runcsprot`. Any instance of `runcsprot` potentially provides the adversary with information about possible links between pseudonyms, and hence potentially increases the adversary's probability of success in linking pseudonyms. Thus, the definition of pseudonym unlinkability needs to take this additional information into account.

Assuming a sound pseudonym system, there are two types of deduction that can be made.

- Suppose a `runcsprot` invocation, say `runcsprot`(p, v, t) for some p, v and t, issued at time τ, returns `true`. Then $\mathcal{A}$ can deduce that there exists some $p' \in \bigcup_{u \in U} P_{u,t}(\tau)$ such that $f(p) = f(p')$.
- Suppose a `runcsprot` invocation, say `runcsprot`(p, v, t) for some p, v and t, issued at time τ, returns `false`. Then $\mathcal{A}$ can deduce that $f(p) \neq f(p')$ for all $p' \in \bigcup_{u \in U} P_{u,t}(\tau)$.

In any instance of Game 4, which in its first phase will involve a series of queries, $\mathcal{A}$ will be able to make a series of deductions about matchings of pseudonyms based on the outcomes ({`true`,`false`}) of `runcsprot` queries (as above). As a result, for each pair of distinct pseudonyms p_1, $p_2 \in P^{**}$, $\mathcal{A}$ will be able to compute the probability P_{p_1,p_2} that $f(p_1) = f(p_2)$ based on these observations (assuming that $\mathcal{A}$ makes optimal use of the information provided). $\mathcal{A}$ also takes into account the probability distribution $\mathcal{D}$ used by the Challenger to select the user during `runpeprot` queries.

We now define $\bar{P}$ to be the maximum of these probabilities, i.e.

$$\bar{P} \stackrel{def}{=} \max_{\substack{p_1,p_2 \in P^{**} \\ p_1 \neq p_2}} (P_{p_1,p_2}).$$

We can now define the notion of pseudonym unlinkability.

DEFINITION 4 *A sound pseudonym system is said to offer pseudonym unlinkability iff no $\mathcal{A}$ can win Game 4 with probability greater than $\bar{P} + \epsilon(k)$ for any negligible function ϵ.*

An example scenario of how the two types of deduction might be applied in order to calculate $\bar{P}$, is given in the Appendix.

2.5 Discussion

In real life, colluding organisations could come up with many more effective strategies in order to correlate pseudonyms. Examples include attacks that take into account information such as the time or the geographical location of events that occur in the system. These attacks, however, are not captured by the model, simply because they lie at a different level of abstraction. Protection against, say, timing attacks, de-anonymising traffic analysis or social engineering, is required irrespectively of which particular pseudonym system is being used. The only adversarial strategies to correlate pseudonyms that are inherent in the system, and therefore lie at the same level of abstraction, are the following.

1 If some user is asked for but fails to produce a credential of a given type, the colluding organisations know that none of the pseudonyms on which a credential of that type was previously issued belongs to that user.

2 If some user successfully shows a credential of a given type on one of his pseudonyms, the colluding organisations know that at least one of the pseudonyms on which a credential of that type was previously issued belongs to that user.

These strategies are captured by the probability bound $\bar{P}$. A pseudonym system cannot protect against these strategies without breaching one of its essential properties: that of credential non-transferability. In other words, if a (sound) pseudonym system satisfies Definition 4, this means that the probability that pseudonyms can be successfully linked does not exceed the given bound (by a non-negligible quantity), provided that no 'out-of-scope' attacks place.

2.6 Indistinguishability of pseudonyms

We now establish our second privacy property, namely the notion of indistinguishability of pseudonyms and show that it is a necessary condition for pseudonym unlinkability.

Consider the following game between a Challenger and a polynomial time (and space) adversary $\mathcal{A}$. First, the Challenger chooses a sound pseudonym system and a security parameter k. On input k, he runs `init` and gives the set U of users to $\mathcal{A}$. $\mathcal{A}$ then chooses two users $u_0, u_1 \in U$ and gives them to the Challenger. The Challenger now flips an unbiased random bit $b \in \{0,1\}$ and makes u_b execute $\texttt{peprot}_{u,o,p}$ with some organisation $o \in (I \cup V)$. He then gives o's private information (including the protocol view and the resulting pseudonym p) to $\mathcal{A}$.

GAME 5 *(pseudonym indistinguishability): $\mathcal{A}$ outputs a bit $b' \in \{0,1\}$. We say that $\mathcal{A}$ wins the game iff $b' = b$ with probability* $\mathbf{Pr} > 1/2 + \epsilon(k)$, *for any negligible function ϵ.*

DEFINITION 5 *A pseudonym system is said to offer indistinguishability of pseudonyms iff no adversary $\mathcal{A}$ can win the above game.*

THEOREM 1 *If a sound pseudonym system offers pseudonym unlinkability it also offers pseudonym indistinguishability.*

Proof Suppose the converse, i.e. suppose the pseudonym system offers pseudonym unlinkability but does not offer pseudonym indistinguishability. Given $\mathcal{A}^{\mathtt{i}}$, an adversary that breaks pseudonym indistinguishability, we construct $\mathcal{A}^{\mathtt{u}}$, an adversary that breaks pseudonym unlinkability, as follows. While playing Game 4 (unlinkability) with the Challenger, $\mathcal{A}^{\mathtt{u}}$ plays the role of the Challenger in Game 5 (indistinguishability) with $\mathcal{A}^{\mathtt{i}}$.

Choose a negligible function ϵ. Let $\mu(k) = \sqrt{\epsilon(k)/2}$, which, by definition, is also negligible. In Game 4, $\mathcal{A}^{\mathtt{u}}$ corrupts all but two users, say u_0 and u_1, and one organisation, say o, i.e. $(U - \hat{U}) = \{u_0, u_1\}$ and $(I - \hat{I}) \cup (V - \hat{V}) = \{o\}$. Then $\mathcal{A}^{\mathtt{u}}$ issues `runpeprot`(o) queries until three pseudonyms, say p_1, p_2 and p_3, are established between o and $\{u_0, u_1\}$. $\mathcal{A}^{\mathtt{u}}$ does not issue any `runcsprot` queries.

$\mathcal{A}^{\mathtt{u}}$ then plays three instances of Game 5 (indistinguishability) with $\mathcal{A}^{\mathtt{i}}$; in all these games he gives the set of users $U = \{u_0, u_1\}$ to $\mathcal{A}^{\mathtt{i}}$. In the first he gives the pseudonym p_1 to $\mathcal{A}^{\mathtt{i}}$, in the second p_2, and in the third p_3 (together with o's private information and corresponding `peprot` views). Denote $\mathcal{A}^{\mathtt{i}}$'s output occurring in the three instances of Game 5 by b_1, b_2 and b_3 respectively. Now, since we have assumed that $\mathcal{A}^{\mathtt{i}}$ breaks pseudonym indistinguishability, we suppose that $\mathcal{A}^{\mathtt{i}}$ wins all instances of Game 5 with probability $1/2 + \delta(k)$, where $\delta(k) > \mu(k)$ for all sufficiently large k.

$\mathcal{A}^{\mathtt{u}}$ now selects $j, j' \in \{1, 2, 3\}$, $j \neq j'$, such that $b_j = b_{j'}$, where the pair (j, j') exists by the pigeonhole principle, and outputs $(p_j, p_{j'})$. Now, since $b_j = b_{j'}$ and $f(p_j), f(p_{j'}) \in \{u_0, u_1\}$, we know that $f(p_j) = f(p_{j'})$ if either $(f(p_j) = u_{b_j}$ and $f(p_{j'}) = u_{b_j})$ or $(f(p_j) \neq u_{b_j}$ and $f(p_{j'}) \neq u_{b_j})$. Hence:

$$\begin{aligned}
\mathbf{Pr}(f(p_j) = f(p_{j'})) &= \mathbf{Pr}(f(p_j) = u_{b_j}) \cdot \mathbf{Pr}(f(p_{j'}) = u_{b_j}) \\
&\quad + \mathbf{Pr}(f(p_j) \neq u_{b_j}) \cdot \mathbf{Pr}(f(p_{j'}) \neq u_{b_j}) \\
&= (1/2 + \delta(k))^2 + (1/2 - \delta(k))^2 \\
&= 1/2 + 2\delta(k)^2 \\
&> 1/2 + 2\mu(k)^2 \text{ (for all sufficiently large } k) \\
&= 1/2 + \epsilon(k)
\end{aligned}$$

where ϵ was assumed to be negligible. Thus $\mathcal{A}^{\mathtt{u}}$ breaks unlinkability, contradicting our assumption, and the result follows. □

2.7 Anonymity of users

Consider a sound pseudonym system that offers pseudonym unlinkability. The owner $u \in (U - \hat{U})$ of pseudonym p $(u = f(p))$ is hidden in the anonymity set $U - \hat{U}$ because, from $\mathcal{A}$'s point of view, any user in that set could potentially be the owner of p. The effective size of the anonymity set, however, depends on the probability distribution $\mathcal{D}$ according to which users are selected during pseudonym establishment. Using the information-theoretic anonymity metric of [Serjantov and Danezis, 2002; Steinbrecher and Koepsell, 2003], this is given by $-\Sigma_{p \in P^{**}} \mathbf{Pr}(f(p) = u) \log_2[\mathbf{Pr}(f(p) = u)]$ and is maximised if $\mathcal{D}$ is the uniform distribution. In this case the effective size of the anonymity set for all pseudonyms is $\log_2 |U - \hat{U}|$. It is worth observing that, in the general case, it makes sense to consider the anonymity of the user *while acting using a particular pseudonym*. In other words, it is likely that the anonymity a user enjoys will depend on the pseudonym under which he is acting.

The above measure of anonymity only applies to a naive adversary; it only takes into account the *a priori* knowledge (i.e. the distribution $\mathcal{D}$). After observing the system for some time, in the sense of Game 4, $\mathcal{A}$ may decrease the unlinkability between pseudonyms. This decrease in unlinkability yields an *a posteriori* probability distribution $\mathcal{D}'$, that $\mathcal{A}$ is able to construct using deductions that he can make due to the scheme's soundness. While it is the distribution $\mathcal{D}'$ that defines the (effective) size of the anonymity set in which users are hidden (while acting under one of their pseudonyms), this does not necessarily mean that a reduction in unlinkability implies a reduction in anonymity in the theoretical definition of the term. Of course, in practice, any linking of pseudonyms is likely to lead to an increased risk of loss of anonymity because of 'out of scope' attacks. As a result, unlinkability is a property of great importance in its own right.

3. FUTURE WORK AND CONCLUDING REMARKS

In this paper we have introduced a complexity theoretic model for anonymous credential systems. We have formally defined the notions of pseudonym owner protection, credential unforgeability, credential non-transferability and pseudonym unlinkability. A key challenge is thus to construct scheme(s) that meet the definitions in this model, and/or to prove, under appropriate assumptions, the security of existing ones. There is, however, room to refine and extend the model itself; determining the probability $\bar{P}$ by which colluding organisations should be bound when trying to correlate pseudonyms, given a specific history of events in the system, is clearly of importance. Naive strategies for computing $\bar{P}$ appear to be of exponential complexity. Hence, incorporating efficient strategies for computing, approximating or bounding $\bar{P}$ into the model is a desirable refinement. It is envisaged that a refined version of the model described above will combine complexity theory and probability theory in order to describe the resulting degrees of unlinkability and anonymity using recently proposed information theoretic metrics [Serjantov and Danezis, 2002; Steinbrecher and Koepsell, 2003]. This should provide further insight into the inherent limits of unlinkability and anonymity in credential systems. We believe that this will also provide insight as to what they have to achieve in order not to be considered the weakest link with respect to the overall system of which they form part. An extended version of the model could capture additional properties of pseudonym systems, for example credentials that can be shown only a limited number of times and anonymity revocation.

Another direction for future research is the analysis of real-world distributions $\mathcal{D}$ of pseudonym-to-user mappings. This might lead to the description of strategies that users might follow, in a realistic setting, in order to maximise the unlinkability of their pseudonyms. Given the statistical properties of the context, this could also lead to descriptions of how long any given pseudonym can be kept before it should be renewed (if the context allows for this).

Acknowledgments

We would like to thank Sattam Al-Riyami, Alex Dent, Caroline Kudla and Kenny Paterson for their helpful comments on earlier versions of this paper.

Appendix: An Example

The following example scenario illustrates how the adversarial strategies are captured by the probability bound $\bar{P}$. For the sake of simplicity, in the example are only one issuer which issues only two types of credential, one verifier and three users. It is assumed that, during the first phase of Game 4 (unlinkability), the adversary corrupts all parties except for the three users, i.e. $I = \hat{I} = \{i\}$, $V = \hat{V} = \{v\}$, $U = \{u_1, u_2, u_3\}$, $\hat{U} = \emptyset$ and $T^* = T_i = \{t_1, t_2\}$.

Table A.1 depicts the queries that $\mathcal{A}$ issues in this example scenario. From the first **runcsprot** query, $\mathcal{A}$ can deduce that $f(p_4) = f(p_1)$ or $f(p_4) = f(p_2)$ or $f(p_4) = f(p_3)$. From the second **runcsprot** query, $\mathcal{A}$ can deduce that $f(p_5) \neq f(p_1)$ and $f(p_5) \neq f(p_2)$ and $f(p_5) \neq f(p_3)$. From the third **runcsprot** query, $\mathcal{A}$ can deduce that $f(p_6) \neq f(p_1)$ and $f(p_6) \neq f(p_2)$ and $f(p_6) \neq f(p_3)$.

Combining the three **runcsprot** queries, $\mathcal{A}$ can deduce, with certainty, that $f(p_4) \neq f(p_5)$ and that $f(p_4) \neq f(p_6)$. It follows that p_5 and p_6 must belong to the two

Table A.1. Example scenario: `runpeprot` queries that returned `true`.

Time	*Query type*	*Org*	*Pseudonym*	*Type*	*Outcome*
1	`runpeprot`	i	p_1	n/a	`true`
2	`runpeprot`	i	p_2	n/a	`true`
3	`runpeprot`	i	p_3	n/a	`true`
4	`runpeprot`	v	p_4	n/a	`true`
5	`runpeprot`	v	p_5	n/a	`true`
6	`runciprot`	i	p_1	t_1	`true`
7	`runciprot`	i	p_1	t_2	`true`
8	`runciprot`	i	p_2	t_1	`true`
9	`runciprot`	i	p_2	t_2	`true`
10	`runciprot`	i	p_3	t_1	`true`
11	`runcsprot`	i	p_4	t_1	`true`
12	`runcsprot`	i	p_5	t_1	`false`
13	`runcsprot`	i	p_6	t_1	`false`

users $\{u_1, u_2, u_3\} - \{f(p_4)\}$. So, the probability P_{p_5,p_6} that $f(p_5) = f(p_6)$ is 1/2. This happens to be the maximum over all distinct pseudonym pairs and thus, in the example, $\bar{P} = 1/2$. In other words, if $\mathcal{A}$, at the end of the game, outputs (p_5, p_6), he has a 50% chance of winning the game. If a (sound) pseudonym system offers pseudonym unlinkability, then no $\mathcal{A}$ should be able to break this bound by a non-negligible quantity.

Notes

1. In certain existing pseudonym systems, credential types are identified with some form of public verification key. These keys are typically published.

2. This is easily achieved by having a unique identifier of each i embedded into all its types T_i.

3. We do not specify the probability distribution according to which the Challenger selects p from the set of pseudonyms u has established, since this should not affect security.

4. This requirement is a technicality that we need in order to define the function f. It practice it can be met by having `peprot` select pseudonyms uniformly at random from a large enough set P. The pseudonym establishment protocols of some existing schemes are of this form.

References

Bellare, M. and Rogaway, P. (1994). Entity authentication and key distribution. In Stinson, D., editor, *Advances in Cryptology — Crypto 93 Proceedings*, volume 773 of *Lecture Notes in Computer Science*, pages 232–249.

Brands, S. (2000). *Rethinking Public Key Infrastructures and Digital Certificates — Building in Privacy.* The MIT Press, Cambridge, Massachusetts.

Camenisch, J. and Lysyanskaya, A. (2001). An efficient system for non-transferable anonymous credentials with optional anonymity revocation. In Pfitzmann, B., editor, *Advances in Cryptology — EUROCRYPT 2001, International Conference on the Theory and Application of Cryptographic Techniques, Innsbruck, Austria, May 6-10, 2001, Proceedings*, volume 2045 of *Lecture Notes in Computer Science*, pages 93–118. Springer Verlag, Berlin.

Chaum, D. (1985). Security without identification: Transaction systems to make big brother obsolete. In *Communications of the ACM*, volume 28, pages 1030–1044.

Chaum, D. and Evertse, J.-H. (1987). A secure and privacy-protecting protocol for transmitting personal information between organizations. In Odlyzko, A. M., editor, *Advances in Cryptology — CRYPTO '86, Santa Barbara, California, USA, 1986, Proceedings*, number 263 in Lecture Notes in Computer Science, pages 118–167. Springer Verlag, Berlin.

Damgard, I. (1990). Payment systems and credential mechanisms with provable security against abuse by individuals. In Goldwasser, S., editor, *Advances in Cryptology — CRYPTO '88: Proceedings*, number 403 in Lecture Notes in Computer Science, pages 328–335. Springer Verlag.

Lysyanskaya, A., Rivest, R. L., Sahai, A., and Wolf, S. (2000). Pseudonym systems. In Heys, H. M. and Adams, C. M., editors, *Selected Areas in Cryptography, 6th Annual International Workshop, SAC'99, Kingston, Ontario, Canada, August 9-10, 1999, Proceedings*, volume 1758 of *Lecture Notes in Computer Science*, pages 184–199. Springer Verlag, Berlin.

Serjantov, A. and Danezis, G. (2002). Towards an information theoretic metric for anonymity. In Dingledine, R. and Syverson, P. F., editors, *Privacy Enhancing Technologies, Second International Workshop, PET 2002, San Francisco, CA, USA, April 14-15, 2002, Revised Papers*, volume 2482 of *Lecture Notes in Computer Science*, pages 41–53. Springer-Verlag, Berlin.

Steinbrecher, S. and Koepsell, S. (2003). Modelling unlinkability. In Dingledine, R., editor, *Privacy Enhancing Technologies, Third International Workshop, PET 2003, Dresden, Germany, March 26-28, 2003, Revised Papers*, volume 2760 of *Lecture Notes in Computer Science*, pages 32–47. Springer-Verlag, Berlin.

PRIVATE INFORMATION STORAGE WITH LOGARITHMIC-SPACE SECURE HARDWARE

Alexander Iliev and Sean Smith
Department of Computer Science, Dartmouth College
{sasho,sws}@cs.dartmouth.edu

Abstract In Private Information Retrieval (PIR), a user obtains one of N records from a server, without the server learning what record was requested.

Recent research in "practical PIR" has limited the players to the user and server and limited the user's work to negotiating a session key (eg. as in SSL)—but then added a secure coprocessor to the server and required the secure coprocessor to encrypt/permute the dataset (and often gone ahead and built real systems).

Practical PIR (PPIR) thus consists of trying to solve a privacy problem for a large dataset using the small internal space of the coprocessor. This task is very similar to the one undertaken by the older Oblivious RAMs work, and indeed the latest PPIR work uses techniques developed for Oblivious RAMs. Previous PPIR work had two limitations: the internal space required was still $O(N \lg N)$ bits, and records could only be read privately, not written.

In this paper, we present a design and experimental results that overcome these limitations. We reduce the internal memory to $O(\lg N)$ by basing the pseudorandom permutation on a Luby-Rackoff style block cipher, and by redesigning the oblivious shuffle to reduce space requirements and avoid unnecessary work. This redesign yields both a time and a space savings. These changes expand the system's applicability to larger datasets and domains such as private file storage.

These results have been implemented for the IBM 4758 secure coprocessor platform, and are available for download.

Keywords: Private information retrieval and storage, oblivious RAM, permutation network, sorting network, Luby-Rackoff cipher

1. INTRODUCTION

Private Information Retrieval (PIR) is a privacy-enhancing technique which has been receiving considerable research exploration, both theoretical and practical. The technique allows a user to retrieve data from a server without the server being able to tell what data the user obtained. It is of interest as a counterbalance to the increasing ease of collecting and storing information about a person's online activities, especially as these activities become a significant part of the person's life.

Examples of where PIR can be useful abound, usually where traffic analysis of encrypted data can yield useful information. A medical doctor retrieving *medical records* (even if encrypted) from a database may reveal that the owner of the record has a disease in which the doctor specializes. A company retrieving a patent from a *patent database* may reveal that they are pursuing a similar idea. Clients of both databases would benefit from the ability to retrieve their data without the database being able to know what they are interested in.

Two rather separate tracks exist in the PIR research record—one focuses on designing cryptographic protocols which achieve PIR by either making use of having the dataset on multiple non-communicating servers [3], or by using techniques based on intractability assumptions without multiple servers [2, 9].

The other track attempts to produce *Practical* PIR schemes [1, 7, 18] that can be integrated into existing infrastructure, by limiting the scheme to the server, and only requiring the client to negotiate a secure session to the server, as is typical in SSL sessions. This is made possible by using a physically protected space at the server—a *Secure Coprocessor* (SCOP) [17].

1.1 Existing Prototype

Our previous work on Practical PIR (PPIR) [7] produced a PPIR prototype running on the IBM 4758 secure coprocessor with Linux [17], and offering an LDAP[1] interface to the outside. We will first describe the background items related to this prototype.

Secure Coprocessors. A secure coprocessor is a small general purpose computer armored to be secure against physical attack, such that code running on it has some assurance of running unmolested and unobserved [22]. It also includes mechanisms to prove that some given output came from a genuine instance of some given code running in an untampered coprocessor [16]. The coprocessor is attached to a *host* computer. The SCOP is assumed to be trusted by clients (by virtue of all the above provisions), but the host is not trusted (not even its root user). The strongest adversary against the schemes presented here is the superuser on the host.

IBM 4758 Secure Coprocessor. The 4758 is a commercially available device, validated to the highest level of software and physical security

[1]Lightweight Directory Access Protocol—the protocol of choice for interfacing to online directories.

scrutiny currently offered—FIPS 140-1 level 4 [19]. It has an Intel 486 processor at 99 MHz, 4MB of RAM and 4MB of FLASH memory. It also has cryptographic acceleration hardware. It connects to its host via PCI (hence we often refer to it as a *card*). Our host runs Debian Linux, with kernel version 2.4.2-2 from Redhat 7.1 as needed by the 4758/Linux device driver.

In production, the 4758 runs the CP/Q++ embedded OS; however, experimental research devices can run a version of Linux (as does the follow-on product from IBM). Linux has considerable advantages in terms of code portability and ease of development—our prototype is written in C++, making extensive use of its language features and the Standard Template Library, and it runs fine on the 4758 with Linux.

PIR using Secure Coprocessors. The model which we follow is that we have available a physically protected computing space at the server. If this space was large enough to hold the whole dataset, the problem would be solved, as clients could negotiate a secure session with it, and then retrieve their data. Since it is physically protected, no one should be able to observe what item the client obtained. Unfortunately practical considerations result in real protected environments being quite small, much too small to hold the entire dataset. Thus, the problem becomes that we want to provide private access to a large dataset while using only a small amount of protected space. This is almost isomorphic to the Oblivious RAM problem [6], which we discuss further in Section 2.

Model. In Figure 1 we show the more concrete setup: we have a dataset of N named items each of size M. The items may be visible to the host; they may also be encrypted (for the SCOP's private key), though why and how they may be encrypted ahead of time is orthogonal to our topic here. A client connects to the SCOP (tunneling via the host) and delivers a request for one of the items. The SCOP is very limited in memory—it is allowed $O(\lg N + M)$ memory, which is the minimum needed to store pointers into the dataset, as well as a constant number of actual data items. Any larger storage, like the actual dataset or pre-processed versions of it, is provided by the host. Thus the SCOP has to make I/O requests to the host in order to service a client request. To be a correct PIR scheme, it must be the case that the host cannot learn anything[2] about client requests from observing the I/O from the SCOP.

Simply encrypting the records does not solve the problem; the server can still learn the *identity* of requested items, and (if the server colludes with a user) can learn what any given record decrypts to. It is also insufficient to only hide

[2]We are assuming that cryptography works; strictly speaking, this scheme is not secure in the information theoretic sense, since the host can still see ciphertext.

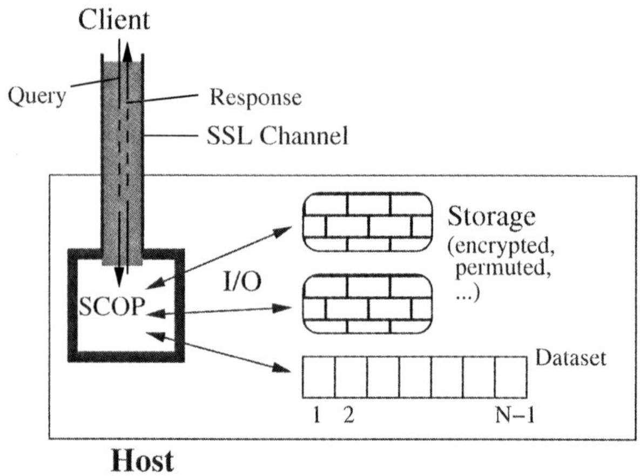

Figure 1. The setup of hardware assisted PIR

the identity of *single* retrievals, as then an attacker could learn the popularity of individual items, and correspondence between requests, eg. "Aphrodite and Boris both retrieved the same data item today".

The Initial PIR with secure coprocessors algorithm. In their initial proposal of using secure hardware for PIR, Smith and Safford kept the dataset unprocessed on the host [18]. Given a request for item i, the SCOP reads *every* item in the dataset, internally keeps item i and returns it to the client at the end. The host only observes that the SCOP touched every record, so it does not learn anything about i. The clear problem is that every retrieval takes $O(N)$ time. (Careful data structures can permit the work to be divided evenly across several devices, but this time bound is still problematic.)

Latest PIR Algorithm. The structure of the algorithm we use was originally developed by Goldreich and Ostrovsky for the Oblivious RAM problem [6]. We note first that it relies on having a dataset of *numbered* items, from 1 to N. It proceeds in retrieval *sessions*, where a session S consists of:

Randomly permuting the contents of records 1 through N. First, the SCOP encrypts each record in the dataset. Then, the SCOP (pseudo)randomly selects a permutation π of $[1..N]$, and relocates the contents of each record r, $1 \leq r \leq N$, to record location $\pi(r)$, changing the encryption along the way. This produces the shuffled[3] dataset of encrypted items D_π. The relocations must

[3]We use permute and shuffle interchangeably, but shuffle always refers to permuting the whole dataset, as opposed to computing $\pi(i)$ for some i

be done so that the host cannot learn which permuted record corresponds to which input record, after having observed the pattern of record accesses during the permutation. Using the terminology of Goldreich et al., the permutation algorithm must be *oblivious*: have the same I/O access pattern regardless of the input (ie. the permutation)[4]. [6].

Servicing $k \ll N$ retrievals. By now, the permuted dataset D_π is available on the host, and the SCOP knows π. The SCOP uses this knowledge to hide the identities of retrieved records. In order to retrieve record r, the SCOP reads in $\pi(r)$ from D_π, and the host does not learn what r can be.

What is left is to hide the relationships between retrieved items, so the host (for example) cannot tell how many times a given item was retrieved. The approach is to copy records which have been accessed into a *working pool* P_S of maximum size k, which is scanned in its entirety for every retrieval. On each retrieval for record r, one record from D_π is added to P_S: either r if it is not already there, or a random untouched record if it is. Thus, records in D_π are accessed at most once.

The implementer can set a a maximum value of k, to put a maximum value on the response time for any given query. However, the shuffling step needs to be fast enough to have a new shuffle ready when P_S reaches that maximum k.

The private shuffle implementation has varied in the literature, and in our prototype we had added a new approach: using Beneš *permutation networks* [21]. A Beneš network can perform any permutation π of N input items by passing them through $O(N \lg N)$ crossbar switches which operate on two items, either crossing them or passing them straight. The connections between the switches are fixed for a given N, only the cross-bar settings differ for different π.

This network is useful for our problem because (1) the SCOP can use cryptography to perform a cross-bar switch on two items resident on the host without the host learning which way the switch went, and (2) by doing this for all the switches in a Beneš network, the SCOP can permute the whole dataset without the host learning anything about the permutation, even though he observes all the record I/O. More specifically, to execute a switch the SCOP reads in the two records involved, internally crosses them or not, and writes them out encrypted under a new key so the host cannot tell if it was a cross or not. Since the network consists of $2 \lg N$ columns of switches with $N/2$ switches each, and the SCOP can execute the switches column by column, he can use one key per column, thus never needing to store more than two keys at a time during the operation.

[4]The access pattern, ie. the sequence and values of I/O operations, will not be identical for all π, but must look identical to a computationally bound observer.

Networks similar to the Beneš are capable of performing other tasks obliviously, again making use of the fact that the SCOP can hide which way a unit operation (on two inputs) went, and by virtue of the fixed structure of the network, the ability to hide the setting of each unit extends to being able to hide the setting of the whole network. We later make use of *sorting* and *merging* networks in this manner.

1.2 Improvements to the Prototype

There are two areas where we saw the potential to improve our prototype: memory usage inside the SCOP, and the ability to update items privately.

Memory usage. Our prototype used two techniques which required $O(N \lg N)$ bits of storage inside the SCOP[5]. One was the storage of a permutation π selected uniformly at random from the set of all $N!$ permutations. The other was the execution of a Beneš network on the data items; in particular computing the switch settings of the network required $O(N \lg N)$ bits[6].

These "memory-hungry" techniques were not a problem for the kind of datasets we were treating, with $N < 2^{13}$ or so, and the memory available in the 4758. However even for $N = 2^{18}$, two objects of $N \lg N$ bits each would need more than 1MB, which begins to strain the 4758's memory. In any case, the memory requirements were, strictly speaking, inconsistent with the desire to have a small protected space.

Updates. Our prototype was really a Private Information *Retrieval* server, and did not have the option for clients to update the contents of data items. This ability could be of interest though, in more interactive applications of the PIR technique, for example if one wanted to build a private filesystem, which could be housed in a remote location but assure a user that nothing about his activities on the filesystem could be gleaned by the remote site.

2. RELATED WORK

Throughout this paper one notices references to Oblivious RAM (ORAM) [6]. This is because that problem has a very similar structure to hardware-assisted PIR, and the mechanisms developed there are for the most applicable here too. The ORAM problem is for a physically shielded but space-limited CPU to execute an (encrypted) program such that untrusted external RAM cannot learn anything about the program by observing the memory ac-

[5]Note that this is less than the $O(NM)$ storage which would be needed to hold the whole database: the size of data items we were working with was at least 1KB.

[6]It is not useful to store the settings on the host, as they are computed in an order dependent on the input, so an adversary could learn about π by observing this order

cess pattern. The CPU corresponds to the SCOP (acting on behalf of clients), and untrusted RAM corresponds to the host. The asymptotically slower solution presented there (square-root algorithm) is what we base our algorithm on.

The asymptotically superior ORAM solution (polylog algorithm), has a $O(\lg^4 N)$ per memory access overhead. An actual operation count reveals that it has a larger actual overhead that the square-root algorithm for about $N < 2^{20}$. Such large dataset sizes are practically infeasible for both algorithms on the hardware we currently have, so we have not experimented with the polylog algorithm.

The ORAM work has covered some of the aims we address in this paper, namely private reading and writing of memory words using a protected CPU with logarithmic in N memory size.

The new contributions over ORAM in this paper are:

- an asymptotically and practically more efficient method of re-shuffling the dataset between sessions (Section 3.2),
- a practically efficient session-transition scheme (Section 4.2),
- permutation using the Luby-Rackoff scheme (which has advantages, for example enabling us to compose and invert pseudo-random permutations) (Section 3.1),
- an actual implementation on commodity secure hardware.

Ostrovsky and Shoup introduced communication-efficient private information storage, the computationally secure version of which is based on the Oblivious RAM algorithm [14].

3. MEMORY USAGE

In this section we present solutions to the high memory needs of the previous prototype. As mentioned before, we had two distinct sources of super-logarithmic memory usage, both of which are addressed.

3.1 Permutation

We need a permutation on the set of integers $\{1, \ldots, N\}$. It should be storable in $O(\lg N)$ space, which rules out the use of a truly random permutation: it requires $O(N \lg N)$ bits of storage. It should also be invertible, which is required by our re-shuffling algorithm (Section 3.2). Because of the storage restriction, we have to settle for a *pseudorandom* permutation, and the one we chose is the Luby-Rackoff-style cipher on $\lg N$-bit blocks, with 7 rounds (LR_n^7) [11].

An L-R cipher (on $2n$-bit blocks) is a *Feistel network* with independent pseudo-random round functions. A Feistel network consists of several iterated rounds $R_i(L, R) = (R, L \oplus f_i(R))$, where

- $L, R \in \{0,1\}^n$ are initialized such that $LR = x$, x being the plaintext,
- f_i are *round functions*, $f_i \in \{0,1\}^n \rightarrow \{0,1\}^n$. Note that they do not have to be permutations for the whole network to be a permutation—this is part of the point in fact, that non-invertible functions are used to produce a permutation.
- $\oplus$ is the bitwise XOR operation.

Luby and Rackoff initially proved chosen-plaintext security with 3 rounds, and chosen-ciphertext security with 4 rounds, in both cases with only a limited number of queries against the cipher oracle.

Recent results have improved the security bounds for higher-round L-R ciphers to state that LR^7_{2n} is indistinguishable from a truly random permutation by an unbounded adversary given m chosen-plaintext queries, where $m \ll 2^{n(1-\varepsilon)}$ [15]. The potential weakness to chosen plaintext attacks (CPA) is significant in our case because the host can mount such an attack by issuing requests to the SCOP (posing as a client), and observing which items in the shuffled dataset the SCOP accesses. In fact the host can harvest up to k chosen-plaintext pairs from the permutation π, where k is the number of retrievals in the session.

A variation on the basic L-R scheme has been conjectured to give a much higher resistance to CPA—unbalanced Feistel schemes which have round functions $f_i \in \{0,1\}^r \rightarrow \{0,1\}^{2n-r}$, where $r \neq n$. In particular Patarin conjectures that an unbalanced L-R scheme (as described, among others, by Naor and Reingold [13, Sect. 6]) on $2n$ bits, using round functions $f_i \in \{0,1\}^{2n-1} \rightarrow \{0,1\}$ (ie. boolean functions on $2n-1$ bits), are secure against CPA given m chosen-plaintext queries, where $m \ll 2^{2n(1-\varepsilon)}$ [15].

For the pseudo-random functions inside the cipher, we use TDES (which is hardware accelerated on the 4758) with expansion and compression to give a function on the required domain.

3.2 Shuffling the Dataset

Once we have established a random or pseudo-random permutation, we need to actually permute the records such that the server cannot learn anything about the permutation. As mentioned before, the Beneš network is not applicable if we are to use only logarithmic space. The algorithm to set its switches for a given permutation has resisted many simplification attempts.

The solution which we came up with takes advantage of the fact that only a small fraction of the dataset is touched during a query session. The untouched items do not need to be reshuffled, only the touched ones do. Informally, the procedure for reshuffling is as follows.

Let the current permutation be π_1. Let T be the touched items at the end of a session, and $\overline{T}$ be the remaining items, untouched. Let the size of T be

k (which is constant in our prototype, so as to limit the query response time). For the next session we generate a new permutation π_2. Also we assume that the indices of the items in T are available in a list L_T in the SCOP. Then we follow the following algorithm:

Reshuffling algorithm.

(i) Re-order the items in $\overline{T}$ so they are sorted by $\pi_2(i)$. We do not need to do this obliviously. We just need to hide what are the indices of T under π_2 (but not under π_1—this is already known).

(ii) Obliviously re-order the items in T so they are sorted by $\pi_2(i)$.

(iii) Obliviously merge the re-ordered T and $\overline{T}$, to give a dataset shuffled under π_2.

This yields savings both in time and space over using a Beneš network to do a full reshuffle. We will first describe in more detail the algorithms used, and then present the resources needed. We assume that we can compute inverse permutations, which is true with Luby-Rackoff style permutations. **Step (i)** is shown in Algorithm 1. **Step (ii)** can be directly performed using a *sorting network*, eg. one of Batcher's networks. However a more efficient approach is to use the Beneš network, after computing the permutation vector for the reordering needed. This can be accomplished using the list L_T, with one sorting step to obtain a sorted list of the indices in T under π_2[7]. **Step (iii)** can be performed using a merging network.

A good reference for sorting and merging networks is found in "Introduction to Algorithms" [4, chap. 27], and at the end of Section 1.1 we explain how such networks can be used to perform operations on a large dataset obliviously.

Notes. Step 6 in Algorithm 1 must take the same amount of time at every execution[8], but this is easy given the sorted array L_{T,π_2}, and takes constant time.

The initial shuffle. For the initial shuffle, which has to re-order all the items obliviously, we resort to the use of Batcher's bitonic sorting network. This method was used in the ORAM work for all shuffles of memory.

Sorting networks sort N items by passing them through a series of *comparators*, which are 2-input units that sort the two inputs. The connections between the comparators are fixed for a given N.

[7]Note that we had to perform this sorting at the start of Algorithm 1 too, so the output of that can be reused.

[8]Or an adversary could use timing attacks to deduce information about the indices of $\overline{T}$ under π_2.

Algorithm 1 Step (i) of the re-shuffle algorithm: Reordering the items in $\overline{T}$ from π_1 to π_2

Require: T is the set of touched records, $\overline{T}$ are the remaining records.
Require: D_{π_1}: the whole dataset under π_1, on the host.
Require: L_T: list of the indices of T, in the SCOP.

$L_{T,\pi_2} \leftarrow$ indices of T under π_2, sorted ▹ *Using L_T*
$\overline{T}_{\pi_2} \leftarrow \emptyset$ ▹ *The destination array (on the host) for the records in $\overline{T}$*
$j \leftarrow 0$ ▹ *j is an index under π_2*
while $j < N$ **do**
  $j \leftarrow$ next index in $\overline{T}$ in order of π_2 ▹ *guided by L_{T,π_2}*
  $r \leftarrow \pi_1(\pi_2^{-1}(j))$ ▹ *r is an index under π_1*
  $R \leftarrow$ `read_from_host` $D_{\pi_1}[r]$
  Tag R with destination j ▹ *But this tag is hidden from the host*
  Append encrypted R to $\overline{T}_{\pi_2}$ ▹ *Recall $\overline{T}_{\pi_2}$ is on the host*
end while

Step	Time cost	Space cost (in bits)
(i)	$O(k \lg k)$ for sorting, $O(N - k)$ for the loop	$O(k \lg N)$ for the indices of T
(ii)	$O(k \lg k)$ for the Beneš network	$O(k \lg N)$ for building and storing the permutation vector, $O(k \lg k)$ for the Beneš network
(iii)	$O(N \lg N)$ for the merging network	$O(\lg N)$ for indices

Table 1. Cost of the reshuffle algorithm. k is the number of queries in a session, same as the size of a touched set. Note that the cost of the merging network in the last step is the dominant one, and that is half the cost of a Beneš network on the same input size. Also the storage needed is $O(k \lg N)$, which is $O(\lg N)$ for constant k (which is how we set k). Even if $k = \sqrt{N}$ as in the ORAM square-root algorithm, the storage required is considerably sublinear.

Batcher's sorters have depth $\frac{\lg^2 N}{2}$, which is appreciably larger than the Beneš network which we have so far used, by a factor of $\frac{\lg N}{4}$, but since we only need to use it once, before the database can be used, this is not a big problem.

Our usage of the bitonic sorting network is very similar to how we used the Beneš network. First we tag each record r with its destination tag $d_r = \pi(r)$, and pass the records through the sorting network, with d_r as the key. We implement a comparator inside the SCOP such that the host cannot tell whether the two records were crossed or not.

4. UPDATES

The problem of evolving our previous design to support private updates of data items reduced to two main tasks: ensuring integrity of data, even against replay attacks[9]; and dealing with the fact that incoming updates render the data in any long-lived preprocessing steps stale: for example a shuffled dataset will be out-of-date by the time the shuffle is done (assuming that shuffles run in parallel to queries, which is necessary to avoid downtime between sessions).

The easy part was modifying the retrieval session to deal with (1) hiding whether a client request is an update or a retrieval, and (2) hiding which item in the working pool is being updated. The approach is to update *all* records in the working pool (but not all records in the dataset) with every request. In particular, for every record r in the pool, the SCOP writes either $\{r\}_K$, or $\{r_{new}\}_K$ if a new value r_{new} is provided by the client. The variable K is a new key generated for this encryption of the working pool only. Given this change of key, the host cannot tell if and where a new record was written. Note that the SCOP does not need to keep the keys for previous versions of the pool.

4.1 Integrity

The integrity of any object stored on the host is assured by first tagging it with a value t which specifies both the *physical* and *temporal*[10] location of the object, and then applying a keyed message authentication code (MAC) to the object and the tag. The location code and MAC are stored with the object on the host. For example, during the last step of a re-shuffle operation (the merging network) we have $t = \langle s, d, i \rangle$, where s is the current shuffle number, d is the depth within the network[11] (both temporal), and i is the item's current actual location in the dataset (physical). Thus, an adversary obviously cannot modify the item's contents undetected, but it also cannot substitute an item from an earlier time (ie. cannot perform a replay attack).

Of more interest is how to compute the temporal location of an object updated during a query session. Within the sth query session, at the end of the ith client request, the query SCOP has built up a working pool of touched records $P_s = \langle r_1, r_1, \ldots, r_i \rangle$. The temporal tag for each record in P_s would then be $t = \langle s, i \rangle$. The notable aspect here is that the SCOP can compute the temporal tag for each object which needs it while maintaining only a fixed small amount of state—s and i in this case. This temporal tagging with small state is the same notion as the "time-labelled" property expounded for some of the Oblivious RAM simulations, and also used to protect against tampering and replay attacks [6].

[9]Replay attacks are where the adversary replaces an item with another one which has a correct checksum/MAC, but comes from a previous execution of the algorithm.

[10]"Temporal" in the sense of where in the timeline of the algorithm the object is located.

[11]The merging network has $\frac{1}{2} \lg N$ levels of $N/2$ independent comparators each, and the depth is the current level number during an execution of the network.

4.2 Session Continuity

The problem of transitioning between query sessions is trivial in the case of read-only PIR: since the database contents are assumed static, several shuffled copies can be produced in advance and used immediately whenever needed—the shuffle data does not go stale. If updates are supported though, pre-shuffling is not an option as the shuffled datasets *will* be stale soon. Even worse, updates will occur between the start and end of a shuffle, requiring them to be incorporated into the output of that shuffle before it can be used. Here we describe our scheme for transitioning between sessions.

Given that we run a shuffle concurrently with a query session, the output of the shuffle will not contain the updates received during that session. We deal with this problem by incorporating the records T_i touched during session i into the working pool of session $i + 1$ from the beginning. This means that session $i + 1$ will touch each record in T_i at every operation, in addition to its own accumulating T_{i+1}. At the end of session $i + 1$, its working pool will contain both T_i and T_{i+1}.

Overview of the algorithm. In Figure 2 we show a diagrammatic representation of the actions of all the components during one full session.

We first note that the working pool of the query session consists of two parts—the set of records touched during that session (which is empty at first), and the ones touched during the last session.

At the end of session $i - 1$, the query SCOP has produced a new touched set T_{i-1}, and the shuffler has produced a new shuffled dataset D_{π_i}. The new session i starts by writing the items in T_{i-1} into D_{π_i} (directly, one by one), and also adding them to its working pool.

The shuffler begins to re-shuffle the dataset D_{π_i}, with touched set T_{i-1}, for use in session $i + 1$ (recall from Section 3.2 that we only need to obliviously reorder the items in a shuffled dataset which have been touched since the last shuffle—these items are now T_{i-1}).

5. EXPERIMENTAL RESULTS

Here we present some performance results from our prototype, whose constitution is described in Section 1.1.

In Figure 3 is shown the running time for the reshuffle operation described in Section 3.2. In Figure 4 we show how long it takes the query SCOP to process queries. Putting these two measurements together gives an idea of what kind of service this prototype can offer. In Table 2 we show the query processing time possible for different N, with two limiting factors: the query processor speed, and the re-shuffle speed (keeping in mind that the query processor can

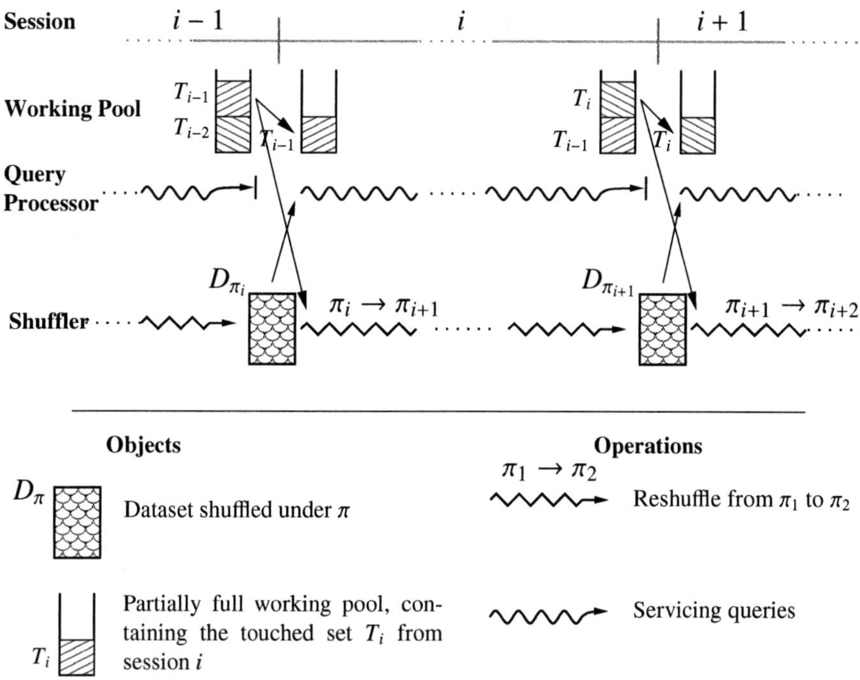

Figure 2. A snapshot of the overall algorithm across one session. At the end of session $i-1$ the shuffler has prepared D_{π_i}, and the query SCOP has a working pool containing the touched sets T_{i-1} and T_{i-2} (see Section 3.2). Then, the shuffler begins a reshuffle with permutation π_{i+1} and with touched set T_{i-1}. The query SCOP begins a new session i with T_{i-1} in its working pool, and filling in its own T_i.

only service $k = 128$ queries before needing a new shuffled dataset from the shuffler).

6. FUTURE WORK AND CONCLUSIONS

We have presented the evolution of our previous work on a hardware-assisted private information retrieval prototype—improved performance in terms of both running time and space, and the ability to update items privately. The prototype gives reasonable performance on dataset sizes up to about 10,000, and can benefit easily from parallelism via extra hardware units.

There are several avenues of interesting and useful further investigations.

We did our prototype work on the IBM 4758, but alternate trusted hardware is emerging. We are particularly interested in exploring the hardened-CPU variations (e.g., [10, 12, 20]), since these devices may provide higher performance, as well as being cheaper and more ubiquitous.

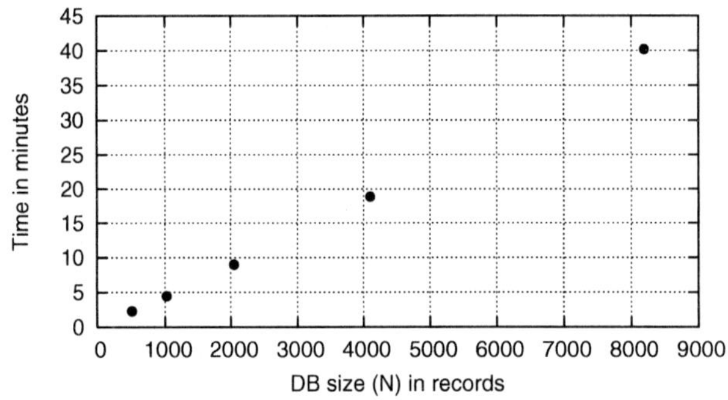

Figure 3. Duration of re-shuffling, for varying dataset sizes. The record size was 850 bytes in all cases. The dominant operation is the oblivious merge, all the others take much less time.

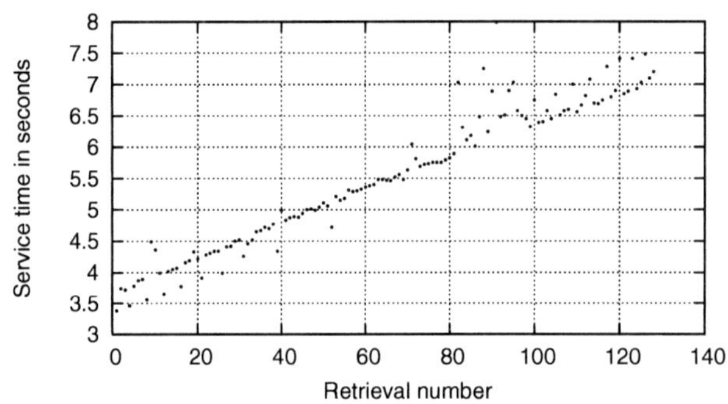

Figure 4. How long does the query SCOP take to service a request? Here are the times during one query session. Recall that the working pool starts with all the items touched during the previous session, in this case 128. The pool accumulates 128 more during the session.

Experiments with the poly-logarithmic oblivious RAM scheme by Ostrovsky [6] could be interesting, for both PIR on larger datasets, and oblivious program execution. Especially now that hardened CPU's, similar to the model used for ORAM, are coming into the picture, the tool of running arbitrary programs obliviously may be practically useful.

As mentioned earlier, private information storage could be a useful primitive for a strongly privacy-protected remote filesystem, providing the "block device" on top of which a filesystem could be built. Relevant here is work analyzing the applicability of block-PIR protocols such as we have described to retrieval of linked structures, eg. web pages [8].

Acknowledgments. This research has been supported in part by the Mellon Foundation, NSF (CCR-0209144), Internet2/AT&T and the Office for Domestic Preparedness, De-

N	Query processor limit	Shuffler limit	Response Time
1024	5.5	2.0	5.5
2048	5.5	4.1	5.5
4096	5.5	8.7	8.7
8192	5.5	18.5	18.5

Table 2. Query response times (in seconds) attainable with different sizes of datasets. The two limit columns show how the respective operations limit the response—the query processor with its average latency (from Figure 4), and the shuffler by virtue of having to complete a whole re-shuffle before the next session can begin. In the $N \geq 4096$ cases, the query SCOP could handle more hits, but a single shuffler is not producing shuffled datasets quickly enough. An easy way out here is to do the merge step of the re-shuffle in parallel, using two or more SCOPs, and gaining linear speedup with the number of SCOPs, as the merging network is actually intended for parallel use. For $N = 1024$, the query SCOP can be always busy and the shuffler will keep up.

partment of Homeland Security (2000-DT-CX-K001). We also thank IBM Research for their assistance with the 4758 secure coprocessors.

This paper does not necessarily reflect the views of the sponsors.

The authors are grateful to Dmitri Asonov, Dan Boneh, Rafail Ostrovsky and the anonymous referees for their helpful comments and discussion.

References

[1] Dmitri Asonov and Johann-Christoph Freytag. Almost optimal private information retrieval. In Dingledine and Syverson [5], pages 209–223. LNCS 2482.

[2] Christian Cachin, Silvio Micali, and Markus Stadler. Computationally private information retrieval with polylogarithmic communication. In *Eurocrypt 1999*, Prague, Czech Republic. Springer Verlag. LNCS 1592.

[3] B. Chor, O. Goldreich, E. Kushilevitz, and M. Sudan. Private information retrieval. *Journal of the ACM*, 45:965–982, 1998.

[4] Thomas Cormen, Charles Leiserson, Ronald Rivest, and Cliff Stein. *Introduction to Algorithms*. McGraw-Hill, second edition, 2001.

[5] R. Dingledine and P. Syverson, editors. *Privacy Enhancing Technologies*, San Francisco, CA, April 2002. Springer. LNCS 2482.

[6] Oded Goldreich and Rafail Ostrovsky. Software protection and simulation on oblivious RAMs. *Journal of the ACM*, 43(3):431–473, 1996.

[7] Alex Iliev and Sean Smith. Privacy-enhanced directory services. In *2nd Annual PKI Research Workshop*, Gaithersburg, MD, April 2003. NIST.

[8] Dogan Kesdogan, Mark Borning, and Michael Schmeink. Unobservable surfing on the world wide web: is private information retrieval an alternative to the MIX based approach? In Dingledine and Syverson [5]. LNCS 2482.

[9] Eyal Kushilevitz and Rafail Ostrovsky. Replication is not needed: Single database, computationally-private information retrieval. In *IEEE Symposium on Foundations of Computer Science*, pages 364–373, 1997.

[10] D. Lie, C. Thekkath, M. Mitchell, P. Lincoln, D. Boneh, J. Mitchell, and M. Horowitz. Architectural Support for Copy and Tamper Resistant Software. In *Proceedings of the*

9th International Conference on Architectural Support for Programming Languages and Operating Systems, pages 168–177, November 2000.

[11] M. Luby and C. Rackoff. How to construct pseudo-random permutations from pseudo-random functions. *SIAM Journal on Computing*, 17(2):373–386, 1988.

[12] P. McGregor and R. Lee. Virtual Secure Co-Processing on General-purpose Processors. Technical Report CE-L2002-003, Princeton University, November 2002.

[13] Moni Naor and Omer Reingold. On the construction of pseudorandom permutations: Luby-Rackoff revisited. *Journal of Cryptology*, 12(1):29–66, 1999.

[14] Rafail Ostrovsky and Victor Shoup. Private information storage. In *ACM Symposium on Theory of Computing*. ACM, 1997.

[15] Jacques Patarin. Luby-Rackoff: 7 rounds are enough for $2^{n(1-\varepsilon)}$ security. In *Advances in Cryptology–CRYPTO 2003*, pages 513–529. Springer-Verlag, Oct 2003.

[16] Sean Smith. Outbound authentication for programmable secure coprocessors. In *7th European Symposium on Research in Computer Science*, Oct 2002.

[17] Sean W. Smith and Steve Weingart. Building a high-performance, programmable secure coprocessor. *Computer Networks*, 31:831–860, 1999.

[18] S.W. Smith and D. Safford. Practical server privacy using secure coprocessors. *IBM Systems Journal*, 40(3), 2001. (Special Issue on End-to-End Security).

[19] National Institute Of Standards and Technology. Security requirements for cryptographic modules. `http://csrc.nist.gov/publications/fips/fips140-1/fips1401.htm`, Jan 1994. FIPS PUB 140-1.

[20] G. Edward Suh, Dwaine Clarke, Blaise Gassend, Marten van Dijk, and Srinivas Devadas. AEGIS: architecture for tamper-evident and tamper-resistant processing. In *Proceedings of the 17th annual international conference on Supercomputing*, pages 160–171. ACM Press, 2003.

[21] Abraham Waksman. A permutation network. *Journal of the ACM*, 15(1):159–163, Jan 1968.

[22] Bennet S. Yee. *Using Secure Coprocessors*. PhD thesis, Carnegie Mellon University, 1994.

TAXONOMY OF MIXES AND DUMMY TRAFFIC

Claudia Diaz and Bart Preneel
K.U.Leuven Dept. Electrical Engineering-ESAT/COSIC
Kasteelpark Arenberg 10, B-3001 Leuven-Heverlee, Belgium
{claudia.diaz; bart.preneel}@esat.kuleuven.ac.be

Abstract This paper presents an analysis of mixes and dummy traffic policies, which are building blocks of anonymous services. The goal of the paper is to bring together all the issues related to the analysis and design of mix networks. We discuss continuous and pool mixes, topologies for mix networks and dummy traffic policies. We point out the advantages and disadvantages of design decisions for mixes and dummy policies. Finally, we provide a list of research problems that need further work.

Keywords: Mixes, Mix Networks, Anonymity, Dummy Traffic

1. INTRODUCTION

The Internet was initially perceived as a rather anonymous environment. Nowadays, we know that it is a powerful surveillance tool: anyone willing to listen to the communication links can spy on you, and search engines and data mining techniques are becoming increasingly powerful. Privacy does not only mean confidentiality of personal information; it also means not revealing information about who is communicating with whom. Therefore, anonymity needs to be implemented at the communication and application layer in order to effectively protect the users' privacy.

Mixes are a basic building block for anonymous applications. In this paper we present an analysis of mixes and dummy traffic. We discuss all the issues that need to be taken into account when analyzing or designing mixes and dummy policies for mix networks. This paper intends to be a starting point for those who are new to the field of anonymous services as well as a support for designers of mixes and dummy policies. We also point out the problems that remain unsolved in this field.

Road-map of the Paper. Section 2 introduces the basic concept of a mix. Section 3 presents the distinction between the two main families of mixes: continuous and pool mixes. Section 4 discusses the issues related to continuous

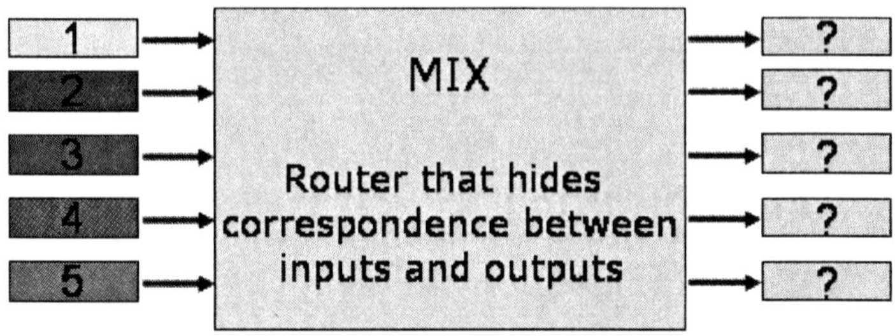

Figure 1. Mix

mixes, while Section 5 analyzes pool mixes. Section 6 presents the different topologies for a mix network. Dummy traffic is presented in Section 7. Finally, Section 8 summarizes the different aspects that need to be taken into account when designing mixes and dummy policies, and Section 9 presents the conclusions and open problems.

2. WHAT IS A MIX?

Mixes were proposed by Chaum [Chaum, 1981] in 1981. The mix takes a number of input messages, and outputs them in such a way that it is infeasible to link an output to the corresponding input (or an input to the corresponding output). In order to achieve this goal, the mix changes the *appearance* (by encrypting and padding messages) and the *flow* of messages (by delaying and reordering). A picture of a mix can be seen in Figure 1.

Changing the appearance of the message (in order to provide *bitwise unlinkability*) can be achieved with the currently available cryptographic primitives, such as randomized encryption schemes and padding schemes. Also, cryptography solves the problem of the integrity checks of the messages, needed to ensure that the contents of the message have not been modified during the transmission. Therefore, these issues are not discussed in this paper.

We need to change the flow of messages in order to make the linking of an input and an output difficult for an attacker. Modifying the flow of messages is not an easy problem, especially when the delay of the messages is constrained by real-time requirements. In this paper, we give an overview on the options that have been explored in order to anonymize the flow of messages, and we discuss the advantages and disadvantages of these designs.

2.1 Anonymity Metrics for a Mix

How to measure the degree of anonymity offered to the users of a mix? An attacker may deploy passive attacks (i.e., traffic analysis [Serjantov and Sewell,

2003]) or active attacks (e.g., the *blending* or $n - 1$ attack, analyzed in detail in [Serjantov et al., 2002]) in order to identify the sender (or recipient) of a message.

The attacker can typically obtain probabilistic relationships between the inputs and the outputs of a mix. Under certain conditions (for example, low traffic, or active attacks), the attacker may be able to narrow down the set of possible senders (recipients) of a message. In other cases, one of the users will appear as having a very high probability of being the sender of a particular message. In order to achieve a good level of anonymity, we should prevent the attacker from obtaining such probability distributions.

Based on the definition for anonymity proposed by Pfitzmann and Kohntopp in [Pfitzmann and Kohntopp, 2000], two information theoretic models were independently proposed by Diaz *et al.* in [Diaz et al., 2002] and by Serjantov and Danezis in [Serjantov and Danezis, 2002]. These models measure the anonymity provided by a mix towards an attacker. Note that it is essential to clearly specify the power of the attacker before applying the anonymity metric.

The anonymity is measured using the concept of *entropy* (i.e., uncertainty), taking into account the probabilistic information that an attacker is able to obtain from the system.

These metrics may be applied to measure the uncertainty of the attacker about the sender of the message, i.e., *sender anonymity*. Analogously, the uncertainty of the attacker regarding the recipient of a message, i.e., *recipient anonymity* may be computed.

One of the limitations of this metric is that the anonymity provided by a mix cannot be computed for the theoretical design, because it needs to take into account the traffic load of the mix and the attack model considered. Therefore, it must be computed either through simulation or using a real setting. This implies that many measurements need to be performed in order to have a good estimate of the degree of anonymity provided by a particular mix. The measurements should take into account different attack models, traffic loads and traffic patterns. Some pratical results have been presented by Diaz *et al.* in [Diaz et al., 2004], where two working remailers have been analyzed (Mixmaster and Reliable). The results show that Mixmaster guarantees a minimum anonymity for all messages, regardless of the traffic load.

3. CONTINUOUS OR POOL MIXES?

The original Chaumian mix [Chaum, 1981] uses the following algorithm to change the flow of messages: it collects n messages and flushes them in a batch. The attacker cannot know which of the n outputs matches a particular input and vice versa. This idea is the basis of *batching mixes*, also called *pool mixes*: a set of messages is collected by the mix and flushed when a certain condition is fulfilled. An analysis of these mixes can be found in Section 5.

A different mix concept was proposed by Kesdogan *et al.* in [Kesdogan et al., 1998]. In this design, the messages are delayed a certain amount of time, and then sent by the mix. The delay of each message is independent from the traffic load. These mixes are discussed in Section 4.

4. CONTINUOUS MIXES

The idea of continuous mixes (also called *Stop-and-Go* mixes) was first proposed by Kesdogan *et al.* [Kesdogan et al., 1998]. In this design, the users generate a random delay from an exponential distribution, and add this delay to the headers of the message. The mix holds the message for the specified delay and then forwards it. The messages are reordered by the randomness of the delay distribution. This mix sends messages continuously: every time a message has been kept for the delay time, it is sent by the mix.

4.1 Reordering Technique

In Kesdogan's original idea, the delay is chosen by the user from an exponential distribution. The exponential distribution has the advantage of being memoryless, but other distributions, such as the uniform distribution (in which the variance of the delay can be larger), may also be taken into account. A thorough study must be carried out in order to find out which design provides the best anonymity properties for the expected working context of the mix (traffic load, traffic pattern, and delay constraints). Nevertheless, Danezis shows in [Danezis, 2004] that the exponential distribution is optimal for continuous mixes.

4.2 Anonymity

Kesdogan *et al.* provide an anonymity study for the *Stop-and-Go* mix in [Kesdogan et al., 1998]. These calculations assume that the incoming traffic pattern can be approximated by a Poisson process. Real traffic arriving to a mix node in a network has been analyzed in [Diaz et al., 2004], and it has been found that the mix incoming traffic pattern is not Poisson and that it cannot be modelled by any known distribution, given that it is very unstable and impredictable.

4.3 Strengths and Weaknesses of the Design

The main advantage of this system is that the delay does not depend on the traffic that arrives to the mix. This means that tight delay constraints can be implemented by this mix, regardless of the current load of the mix (which may be useful for applications in which a small delay is more important than providing a high level of anonymity, such as web browsing applications).

Moreover, when the message is routed through a mix network (see Section 6), the user can choose the amount of time it will take to the message to arrive to every mix on the path (and to the recipient), since he is who chooses the delays of his message at each mix.

On the other hand, the anonymity provided to the users may go to low levels if the number of users decreases during a certain period of time. We must not forget that there is always a tradeoff anonymity / delay, and if we bound the delay we may drop to low levels of anonymity under certain conditions (in this case, low traffic conditions).

This design may be appropriate for systems with stable incoming traffic patterns, in which the anonymity is guaranteed by a (more or less) constant traffic rate. Systems with variable number of users and with changing traffic conditions risk to result in low levels of anonymity during quiet traffic periods, as it is shown in [Diaz et al., 2004].

These mixes are also vulnerable to *blending* or $n-1$ attacks [Serjantov et al., 2002]. This active attack is deployed by an attacker who is able to delay the messages going to the mix. The attacker selects a *target* message he wants to trace, and delays all the other messages. In a continuous mix, this would result in the attacker being able to trace the target message, given that (with an arbitrarily high probability) the attacker can succeed in making the message going through the mix when it does not contain any other messages (the message is not *mixed*). This attack can be prevented, or at least detected, using additional mechanisms. Kesdogan proposes adding a timestamp to the messages (note that the user knows the expected time of arrival of the message to every mix); the mixes discard all messages that contain an old timestamp. Nevertheless, this technique may help detecting a *blending* attack, but it does not prevent it.

Dummy traffic (Section 7) can also be used both to prevent and to detect *blending* attacks. See Section 7.3 to find a description on how dummy traffic can be used to detect and react when a mix is subject to active attacks.

5. POOL MIXES

Pool mixes process the messages in batches. They collect messages for some time, place them in the pool (memory of the mix), and select them for flushing (in random order) when the flushing condition is fulfilled. The aspects that we should take into account when designing and analyzing a pool mix are the *flushing condition* and the *pool selection algorithm*.

Flushing condition. We can distinguish two types of mixes according to the flushing condition: *timed mixes* send messages every fixed internal time, called *timeout*. *Threshold mixes* send messages when they have collected a certain amount of messages, called the *threshold*. Some mix designs, such as Mixmaster [Møller et al., 2003], combine the two mechanisms: they flush when the *timeout* expires only if the *threshold* has been reached. The cycle of collecting and flushing messages is called a *round*.

So far, the mixes that have been implemented have a *fixed* timeout or threshold. It would be interesting to study the properties of mixes that choose the threshold or the timeout from a *random* distribution.

Pool selection algorithm. The performance of a pool mix (in terms of delay and anonymity) is mainly determined by the pool selection algorithm. In Chaum's design, the mix flushes all the messages it contains. Later, the concept of *pool* was added to the mix, extending the original mix to keep a number of messages (instead of flushing all of them). In the first stage, the proposals of mixes keep a fixed number of messages in the pool. Later on, mixes that kept a variable number of messages were designed (e.g., Mixmaster).

Pool algorithms enhance the anonymity (compared to Chaum's mix) by extending the anonymity set size to, potentially, an infinite number of users. Nevertheless, it should be noted that the probability distributions obtained by an attacker trying to trace a message will not be uniform for all senders (or recipients) of messages.

The parameters that should be taken into account when designing a pool selection algorithm are the number of messages kept in the pool (which can be fixed or variable, e.g., percentage of the total number of messages at the time of flushing); and the number of messages sent (which can also be fixed or variable).

Section 8 gives a summary of the relevant parameters in the design of a mix.

5.1 The Generalised Mix Model

The Generalized Mix Model was proposed by Diaz and Serjantov in [Diaz and Serjantov, 2003]. This model can express pool mixes by abstracting of the flushing condition and representing in the graph the pool selection algorithm. The mix is represented at the time of flushing; it shows the percentage of messages contained in the mix that are sent in a round, as a function $P(n)$ of the total number of messages in the mix.

A representation of the flushing algorithm of Mixmaster (designed by Cottrell) is shown in Figure 2. The algorithm is as follows:

- If $0 < n < 45$ do not send any message (i.e., $P(n) = 0$)
- If $45 < n < 129$ send $n - 45$ messages (i.e., $P(n) = 1 - 45/n$)

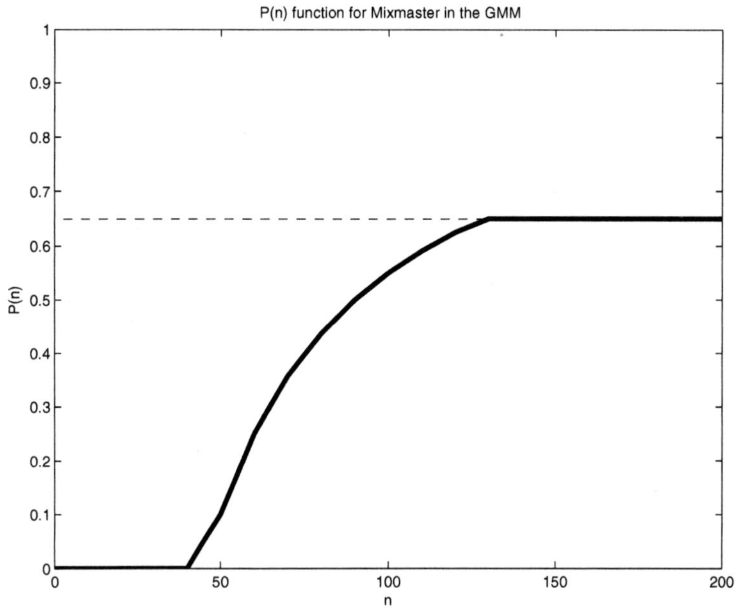

Figure 2. Representation of a Cottrell mix in the Generalised Mix Model

- If $n > 129$ send $0.65 * n$ messages (i.e., $P(n) = 0.65$)

The function that represents the mix in the Generalised Mix Model is very useful to implement anonymity metrics, because it contains all the mix-related data needed to compute the anonymity offered by the mix. It also provides an intuitive idea on the performance of the mix under different traffic loads, which is closely related to this function: high values of the function favor low delays over high levels of anonymity, while low values of the function enhance the anonymity at the cost of larger delays. The model allows for the design of mixes that implement complex pool selection algorithms in an easy and intuitive way.

5.2 Deterministic or Binomial?

The mix function $P(n)$ denotes the probability of sending a message, given that there are n messages in the mix. There are two ways of dealing with this probability. We distinguish between *deterministic* and *binomial* mixes. Note that the value of the function $P(n)$ is independent of the mix being deterministic or binomial.

Deterministic mixes. If a mix is deterministic then the number of messages sent is determined by the number of messages contained in the pool; the mix sends $s = nP(n)$ messages. The only randomness present in the flushing algorithm is the one used to select *which* messages will be sent, but not *how many*. Classical pool mixes fall into this category. Note that, for these mixes, once the number n of messages in the pool is known, the number s of messages sent is determined, and vice versa.

Binomial mixes. Binomial mixes were introduced in [Diaz and Serjantov, 2003]. In these mixes, an independent decision is taken for every message in the pool. A biased coin (its bias is equal to the value of $P(n)$) is thrown for each message, so it is sent with probability $P(n)$. The number of selected messages follows a binomial distribution with respect to the number of messages in the pool. The probability of sending s messages, given that the pool contains n messages is (note that p is the result of the $P(n)$ function for the current round):

$$p(s|n) = \frac{n!}{s!(n-s)!} \cdot p^s \cdot (1-p)^{n-s} \quad .$$

The probability of having n messages in a pool of maximum size N_{max}, given that the mix sends s messages is [Diaz and Serjantov, 2003]:

$$p(n|s) = \frac{p(s|n)}{\sum_{i=s}^{N_{\max}} p(i|n)} \quad .$$

This probabilistic relationship has the following implications: as it was shown in [Diaz and Serjantov, 2003], just by observing the number of outputs of a round, an observer cannot know *exactly* the number of messages contained in the mix; by knowing the number of messages in the pool we cannot determine the number of messages that will be flushed. However, large deviations from the mean values occur with very low probability. This property influences the anonymity metric under certain circumstances, as pointed out by Diaz and Preneel in [Diaz and Preneel, 2004].

5.3 Strengths and Weaknesses of the Design

The main advantage of pool mixes is their ability to adapt to fluctuations in the traffic load. If a good mix function is selected, the mix can compensate a low traffic load by introducing more delay, in order to keep a good anonymity level. These mixes are ideal for applications that do not have tight delay constraints, such as anonymous email.

On the other hand, the delay introduced by a pool mix is not predictable by the sender of the message. This becomes worse when the message is routed through a mix network. Therefore, pool mixes are not appropriate for real-time applications. A comparison between practical pool and continous mixes can be found in [Diaz et al., 2004]

Regarding the vulnerability to *blending* or $n - 1$ attacks, the success of the attacker strongly depends on the details of the mix design. The attacker needs to be able to delay messages going to the mix and also to generate messages that are accepted by the mix (which was not required to attack continuous mixes). We point out the following cases:

- *Threshold mixes* are more vulnerable than *timed mixes* (or mixes that combine the *threshold* with a *timeout*), because the attacker can succeed in emptying the mix from valid unknown messages in a short time by simply flooding the mix with his own messages.

- Mixes that do not have a pool (i.e., they do not keep messages from one round to another) are extremely vulnerable to *n-1* attacks. The attacker can be sure to succeed in tracing the target message, and he only needs to attack the mix for one round.

- Deterministic pool mixes require a stronger effort from the attacker, who needs to attack the mix for several rounds in order to trace a single message. Nevertheless, a powerful attacker is able to successfully trace a message when it goes through one of this mixes.

- Binomial pool mixes are more robust than deterministic pool mixes under *n-1* attacks. The success of the attacker becomes only probabilistic, and the effort required to the attacker grows.

Dummy traffic policies, discussed in Section 7, help preventing and detecting *blending* or *n-1* attacks.

6. MIX NETWORKS

In order to increase the anonymity of a mix system, mixes are usually combined in a mix network. This way, the fact that some mixes are corrupted or controlled by an attacker does not break the anonymity of the users (the anonymity of a message is guaranteed even if only one of the mixes in the path of the message is honest). Also, the reliability of the system is improved, because the failure of a mix does not lead to a denial of service.

6.1 Cascades, Free Route Networks and Restricted Route Networks

The two classical topologies of mix network are cascades and free route networks. In a cascade, the possible paths that a message can follow are predefined (it can be one or more). This is the approach followed by [JAP Anonymity & Privacy,]. In a free route network, users select freely their own path, which may be different for every message. Onion Routing [Goldschlag et al., 1996] and Mixmaster [Møller et al., 2003] are examples of free route mix networks. The advantages and disadvantages of these two topologies have been pointed out by Berthold *et al.* in [Berthold et al., 2000].

More recently, Danezis proposed in [Danezis, 2003] a mix network topology that is somehow in between the two classical designs. In this model, every mix node communicates with a few neighboring others. The goal of this idea is to combine the advantages of cascades and free route networks and overcome the disadvantages.

6.2 Inter-Mix detours

This technique has been proposed in [Gülcü and Tsudik, 1996]. It consists of giving to the mixes the ability to re-encrypt a message at any point of the network and send it through a detour before it goes back to the original path. This increases the latency of the network, but enhances the anonymity of the messages. Nevertheless, we do not have any tools yet that evaluate the effectiveness of this technique and the optimal values for the following parameters:

- Probablity of sending a message through a detour.
- Route length of the detour.
- Route selection of the detour.

7. DUMMY TRAFFIC

A dummy message is a *fake* message introduced in a mix network in order to make it more difficult for an attacker to deploy passive and active attacks. Dummy messages are normally generated by the mixes (although users may also generate dummies, which increases the anonymity level of the mix network and prevents end-to-end intersection attacks [Berthold and Langos, 2002]); they have as destination another mix, instead of a real recipient. Dai proposed the Pipenet system [Dai, 1996] a system in which the traffic is constant: the links between mixes are padded with dummy messages whenever the real traffic is not enough to fill them. This system provides not only anonymity, but also unobservability, since an observer of the network cannot tell whether there are real messages traveling in the network or not. Unfortunately, the system is not practical due to the enormous amount of resources it needs.

The generation and transmission of dummy traffic has a cost, and it is therefore very important to find the right balance on the number of dummies that should be created in a mix network. The rest of this section studies the possible choices we can make when designing a dummy policy.

7.1 Generation of Dummies

The first question that arises when designing a dummy traffic policy is whether the dummies generated should depend on the incoming traffic or not. Generating dummies depending on the traffic load may make a more efficient use of the resources, but this dependency can be exploited by an active attacker to maximize the effectiveness of his attack by generating his own messages in such a way that he minimizes the number of dummies generated by the mix. Therefore, dummy traffic policies that are independent from the traffic load seem to be more secure.

One of the issues that needs to be decided is the average number of dummies we want to generate (for pool mixes we will choose an average number of dummies per round, while in continuous mixes we will generate dummies per fixed time unit). These dummies can be generated following a deterministic or random distribution. Random distributions increase the uncertainty of the attacker, specially when combined with binomial mixes, as pointed out in [Diaz and Preneel, 2004].

Continuous mixes. These mixes may generate a certain number of dummies every period of time, selecting their delay (amount of time they are kept in the mix from their generation until the moment in which they are sent) from a random distribution. This is the approach followed by *Reliable*, one of the mixes that composes the Mixmaster network.

Other dummy policies may be explored, for example, the mix could keep always one dummy inside, and generate a new one (with its corresponding delay) when the dummy is sent. Another policy would be that the mix decides every certain amount of time on whether to generate a dummy or not.

Pool mixes. The design of dummy policies for pool mixes implies making decisions on the following issues:

- The dependency on the traffic load.
- The average number of dummies generated per round.
- The distribution followed to select the number of dummies in a particular round (binomial, uniform, geometrical, etc.).
- Whether the dummies are inserted in the pool or at the output.
- Route length and selection of path for the dummies.

Insertion in the Pool. With this technique, the mix inserts the dummies it generates for a round in the pool. These dummies are treated as real messages by the mix after being placed in the pool.

Insertion at the Output. If the mix is to insert the dummies at the output, then it adds the dummies to the batch of real messages taken from the pool. The mix does not modify the number of messages contained in the pool.

The advantages and disadvantages of these two dummy insertion options have been discussed in [Diaz and Preneel, 2004]. Here, we summarize the conclusions presented in [Diaz and Preneel, 2004]:

- Inserting the dummies in the pool provides less anonymity and less delay that inserting them at the output.

- When dummies are inserted at the output, binomial mixes with a random dummy policy offer more protection against the $n-1$ attack than deterministic mixes.

- Inserting dummies in the pool protects deterministic mixes better than inserting them at the output when an $n-1$ attack is deployed.

7.2 Route Length and Selection of Path

Dummy messages, just like real messages, travel in the mix network going through a number of mixes. The route length of the dummy determines the number of mixes a dummy is going through. Regarding this issue, we should decide on the average number of mixes in the path of the dummy and on the distribution of this route length. Random distributions increase the uncertainty of the attacker with respect to a deterministic distribution (i.e., fixed number of mixes in the path) when the attacker wants to find out whether a message is a dummy or not.

Normally the path of a dummy is selected randomly among the mixes of the network. The last mix in the path of the dummy can be the mix that actually generated it, preventing this way that corrupted mixes can help the attacker (when they are the last in the path of the dummy) providing the information on which messages were dummies. Note that intermediate mixes (i.e., except for the first and last in the path of the dummy) cannot distinguish dummy messages from real messages.

Note that, in order to increase the anonymity provided by the mix, the mix should maximize the number of possible destinations for every message, meaning that the mix should check if it is sending messages to all the possible neighbours. If it is not, then it should generate some extra dummies to send to those mixes. This way, an attacker wanting to trace a message will have to follow more possible paths.

7.3 RGB Dummy Policies

This dummy policy was proposed by Danezis and Sassaman in [Danezis and Sassaman, 2003]. The goal is to detect and counter active attacks (such as the *n-1* attack). The basic idea of this dummy policy is that the mix generates dummies that after being routed through the network are sent back to the mix that generated them. If the mix receives less dummy messages than expected, it may assume that it is subject to an $n-1$ attack, and it reacts by stopping its functioning until the attack is no longer being deployed.

8. SUMMARY

In this section we present a summary of the different aspects that have to be taken into account when designing mixes and mix networks, as shown in Figure 3 and a summary of the parameters of a dummy policy, in Figure 4.

Change appearance of messages	• Select encryption and padding primitives
Change the flow of messages	• Continuous or Pool mix • Real-time constraints?
Pool mixes	• Flushing condition: timed, threshold or a combination of both • Pool selection algorithm (function P(n) in the GMM) • Deterministic or Binomial
Continuous mixes	Delay distribution
Anonymity provided by a mix	• Compute for stable and unstable traffic patterns • Compute for high and low traffic loads • Compute for different attack models
Delay introduced by the mix	• Compute for stable and unstable traffic patterns • Compute for high and low traffic loads
Attacks	Analyze the robustness of the mix against: • Passive attacks (e.g., traffic analysis attacks) • Active attacks (e.g., *n-1* attacks)
Mix network	Topology: • Cascade • Free route network • Restricted route network

Figure 3. Parameters of mixes and mix networks

9. CONCLUSIONS AND OPEN PROBLEMS

In this paper we have presented a thorough analysis of the parameters of mixes and dummy traffic policies, distinguishing between continuous and pool mixes. We have discussed the advantages and disadvantages of different design options. We have introduced anonymity metrics and mix network topologies.

Some of the problems that remain unsolved in this field are:

Dependent on incoming traffic	Yes / No
Dummy generation for continuous mixes	• Average number of dummies • Distribution in time of the dummies
Dummy generation for pool mixes	• Average number of dummies • Distribution of the number of dummies • Insertion in the pool • Insertion at the output
Route length of the dummies	• Average number of intermediate mixes • Distribution of the route length
Selection of the path	• Algorithm to select intermediate mixes • Decide if the last mix in the path is the one that generated the dummy
Attacks	Study if the dummy policy prevents active and active attacks

Figure 4. Parameters of a dummy policy

- The current anonymity metrics can measure the anonymity provided by a mix in a simulation or in a working setting, but we do not have yet theoretical tools that allow us to know the anonymity properties of the mix during the design phase. Nevertheless, we may use simulations in order to see the anonymity that the mix can provide.

- The anonymity metrics are very useful to measure the anonymity provided by a single mix, but they fail to measure the end-to-end anonymity provided by a mix network. An extension to the metric needs to be found in order to have practical tools to measure the anonymity provided by a mix network.

- Much research need to be done in order to solve many dummy traffic related problems. We do not know yet which is the most appropriate distribution for the generation of dummies, the route length they should have in order to optimize the cost/anonymity relationship, whether they should be inserted in the pool of the mix or at the output, whether dummy traffic should depend on the real traffic traveling in the network or not, and how this dependency should be.

- Different mix designs need to be compared in order to find the best performing mixes.

Acknowledgments

Claudia Diaz is funded by a research grant of the K.U.Leuven. This work was also partially supported by the IWT STWW project on Anonymity and

Privacy in Electronic Services (APES), and by the Concerted Research Action (GOA) Mefisto-2000/06 of the Flemish Government.

References

[Berthold and Langos, 2002] Berthold, Oliver and Langos, Heinrich (2002). Dummy traffic against long term intersection attacks. In Dingledine, Roger and Syverson, Paul, editors, *Proceedings of Privacy Enhancing Technologies workshop (PET 2002)*. Springer-Verlag, LNCS 2482.

[Berthold et al., 2000] Berthold, Oliver, Pfitzmann, Andreas, and Standtke, Ronny (2000). The disadvantages of free MIX routes and how to overcome them. In Federrath, H., editor, *Proceedings of Designing Privacy Enhancing Technologies: Workshop on Design Issues in Anonymity and Unobservability*, pages 30–45. Springer-Verlag, LNCS 2009.

[Chaum, 1981] Chaum, David (1981). Untraceable electronic mail, return addresses, and digital pseudonyms. *Communications of the ACM*, 4(2).

[Dai, 1996] Dai, Wei (1996). Pipenet 1.1. Usenet post.

[Danezis, 2003] Danezis, George (2003). Mix-networks with restricted routes. In Dingledine, Roger, editor, *Proceedings of Privacy Enhancing Technologies workshop (PET 2003)*. Springer-Verlag, LNCS 2760.

[Danezis, 2004] Danezis, George (2004). The traffic analysis of continuous-time mixes. In *Accepted submission at PET2004*.

[Danezis and Sassaman, 2003] Danezis, George and Sassaman, Len (2003). Heartbeat traffic to counter (n-1) attacks. In *Proceedings of the Workshop on Privacy in the Electronic Society (WPES 2003)*, Washington, DC, USA.

[Diaz and Preneel, 2004] Diaz, Claudia and Preneel, Bart (2004). Reasoning about the anonymity provided by pool mixes that generate dummy traffic. In *Accepted submission at IH2004*.

[Diaz et al., 2004] Diaz, Claudia, Sassaman, Len, and Dewitte, Evelyne (2004). Comparison between two practical mix designs. Technical report, K.U.Leuven. Submitted to ESORICS 2004.

[Diaz and Serjantov, 2003] Diaz, Claudia and Serjantov, Andrei (2003). Generalising mixes. In Dingledine, Roger, editor, *Proceedings of Privacy Enhancing Technologies workshop (PET 2003)*. Springer-Verlag, LNCS 2760.

[Diaz et al., 2002] Diaz, Claudia, Seys, Stefaan, Claessens, Joris, and Preneel, Bart (2002). Towards measuring anonymity. In Dingledine, Roger and Syverson, Paul, editors, *Proceedings of Privacy Enhancing Technologies Workshop (PET 2002)*. Springer-Verlag, LNCS 2482.

[Goldschlag et al., 1996] Goldschlag, David M., Reed, Michael G., and Syverson, Paul F. (1996). Hiding Routing Information. In Anderson, R., editor, *Proceedings of Information Hiding: First International Workshop*, pages 137–150. Springer-Verlag, LNCS 1174.

[Gulcu and Tsudik, 1996] Gulcu, Ceki and Tsudik, Gene (1996). Mixing E-mail with Babel. In *Proceedings of the Network and Distributed Security Symposium - NDSS '96*, pages 2–16. IEEE.

[JAP Anonymity & Privacy,] JAP Anonymity & Privacy. http://anon.inf.tu-dresden.de/.

[Kesdogan et al., 1998] Kesdogan, Dogan, Egner, Jan, and Buschkes, Roland (1998). Stop-and-go MIXes: Providing probabilistic anonymity in an open system. In *Proceedings of Information Hiding Workshop (IH 1998)*. Springer-Verlag, LNCS 1525.

[Møller et al., 2003] Møller, Ulf, Cottrell, Lance, Palfrader, Peter, and Sassaman, Len (2003). Mixmaster Protocol — Version 2. Draft.

[Pfitzmann and Kohntopp, 2000] Pfitzmann, Andreas and Kohntopp, Marit (2000). Anonymity, unobservability and pseudonymity — a proposal for terminology. In Federrath, H., editor, *Designing Privacy Enhancing Technologies: Proceedings of the International Workshop on the Design Issues in Anonymity and Observability*, pages 1–9. Springer-Verlag, LNCS 2009.

[Serjantov and Danezis, 2002] Serjantov, Andrei and Danezis, George (2002). Towards an information theoretic metric for anonymity. In Dingledine, Roger and Syverson, Paul, editors, *Proceedings of Privacy Enhancing Technologies Workshop (PET 2002)*. Springer-Verlag, LNCS 2482.

[Serjantov et al., 2002] Serjantov, Andrei, Dingledine, Roger, and Syverson, Paul (2002). From a trickle to a flood: Active attacks on several mix types. In Petitcolas, Fabien, editor, *Proceedings of Information Hiding Workshop (IH 2002)*. Springer-Verlag, LNCS 2578.

[Serjantov and Sewell, 2003] Serjantov, Andrei and Sewell, Peter (2003). Passive attack analysis for connection-based anonymity systems. In *Proceedings of ESORICS 2003*.

IDENTITY MANAGEMENT FOR SELF -PORTRAYAL

Toby Baier,[1] and Christian P. Kunze,[2]

[1] *Distributed Systems Group - VSIS, University of Hamburg, Vogt-Kölln-Straße 30, 22527 Hamburg, Germany*

[2] *Distributed Systems Group - VSIS, University of Hamburg, Hamburg (Germany)*
{baier,kunze}@informatik.uni-hamburg.de

Abstract Identity management systems help users to organise their digital profiles in order to communicate parts of them, whenever needed and wanted, to communication partners like internet services or personal contacts. Most current identity management research tries to achieve the highest possible degree of data hiding for best privacy. After sketching some of these projects, this paper presents a different approach where users are assumed to be interested in presenting themselves to selected online communities or internet services for better personalisation, to achieve a consistent reputation, or to establish an application- and service-independent internet society. It thereby stresses the aspect of privacy that persons have the option for self-portrayal. To support this thesis, a survey is presented which shows that many users who actively participate in Internet communities would make high use of such a system. Finally, the project "onefC" is presented which prototypically realises this approach.

Keywords: Digital Identity, Identity Management, Self-Determination, Digital Citizen, Online Communities

1. INTRODUCTION

Many Internet services require personal data of the users to be personalised, optimised or to function at all. Any personalised service obviously needs the identification of the user, most require authentication also. To offer a service which is specifically adjusted to a certain users demands, additional personal information about this user is needed. This is not specific to the Internet, it applies in real life as well: no bank office will grant access to an account without the clients authentication. And in a bookstore, the shop assistant will ask for the customers preferences to offer a personalised selection of books. But while this identity management is familiar in real life, it is hard to be done online. Internet users need to keep track of their login data to any service they use, they need to decide what information they show to communication partners and afterwards remember who knows what about them.

The problem of identity management arises not only during the use of Internet services, but also applies to self-presentation in online communities. People are complex social beings, and the Internet has become an important medium for communication and collaboration. There are many possibilities to coact on the Internet, including simple mailing lists, USENET newsgroups, online blackboards, or sophisticated online portals with several possibilities of interaction. All these subsume to online communities. In each community, the members are presenting themselves by some degree to the other members, otherwise only few interaction would be possible. But if a user has presented herself to one community, she must do it again for every other community she would join. The image one has created can not be transferred, including relations to other members and reputation.

There are two faces of online identity management: one is privacy, the other is self-portrayal. The former is needed to protect personal data from the public or specific third parties, the latter is wanted for convenient use of the Internet and building a consistent, service- and community independent personality. These two objectives should be reached in conjunction, because one does not make sense without the other. A privacy and security oriented identity management system would restrict the users too much in their Internet experience, while a self-portrayal one which disregards security issues is a too great danger to privacy and data protection.

The self-portrayal functionality of an identity management system must offer the following: in a communication session, selected parts of the own identity attributes can be shown either automatically or with user confirmation to the communication partners. The attributes should be transferred in a standard format and with metadata describing the attributes. The system should automatically generate pseudonyms for new contacts who shall not see one of the already existing pseudonyms. These pseudonyms are like identity-parts and can be associated with arbitrary attributes. Short-term or even one-time pseudonyms must be inactivated and archived after use.

Security for identity management means, that others can only see those parts of an identity which they are authorised to. Unauthorised access to any identity data must be prohibited, including unauthorised access to the identity manager itself to prevent identity theft. This also includes the protection during transmission: any data sent over networks must be encrypted. To enhance privacy further, anonymiser networks could be used to prevent third parties to recognise that identity data was transmitted.

The next section briefly introduces some identity management systems or projects which provide some of the identity management functionality. Section 3 explains the motivation for a self-portrayal driven identity management solution in greater detail. After that, the results of a survey about the need of identity management is presented in section 4. Finally, the onefC system developed at University of Hamburg is introduced, followed by a general conclusion.

2. HISTORY AND STATE OF THE ART OF IDENTITY MANAGEMENT SYSTEMS

The beginning of digital identity management (abbreviated as IDM) was set with David Chaums article about "Security without identification" [Chaum, 1985]. Chaum proposes the use of different pseudonyms for different situations, including one-time-pseudonyms and long term pseudonyms for ongoing relationships. The unlinkability of the pseudonyms plays a major role, so that the privacy of the pseudonym holder is not violated. Also, anonymous communication is important, so that the use of the pseudonyms can not be watched.

Since then, identity management systems were seen as privacy enhancing technologies (PET). Accordingly, most active identity management projects have the increase of privacy as their main goal. Mainly commercial IDM approaches have ease of use and personalisation as their targets. In the following, some IDM systems will be presented and explained.

2.1 Commercial projects

There are several commercial projects in the context of identity management. Most aim for single sign-on with internet services. Microsoft's .NET passport and the Liberty Alliance's Project Liberty will be presented hereafter, other projects include Novell's DigitalMe and XNS.org.

2.1.1 Microsoft .NET passport. While .NET passport is not an identity management system in the sense that Chaum predicted it, it is the largest IDM system currently deployed. This is due to the fact that Microsoft forces all 1.5 million users of their free web mail service Hotmail to use .NET passport for authentication. The system aims mainly at single sign-on (authenticate once, use several different services), but also offers to reveal additional personal information to the services. This includes the propagation of credit card numbers for online purchases. All data is stored centrally on a Microsoft server, which makes it vulnerable as a single point of failure and violability. There have already been several cases of system breakdowns and flaws, in which users were authenticated as someone else, reading foreign mail[1]. Next to these security flaws, the coarse data model is the most profound drawback.

2.1.2 Project Liberty. The Project Liberty is an initiative of many companies and non-commercial organisations to establish an infrastructure for online exchange of personal data. The main aspect of it is the concept of "federations". Federations are built between different service providers, which have the possibility of directly sharing user information after the user's consent. User profile information is stored decentrally at the service providers, only in later versions users can manage their data themselves. Direct user to user communication is not in the scope of the project, but due to very sophisticated protocol definitions likely possible.

2.2 Research projects

As mentioned, most research activity on the field of identity management goes into privacy concerns. Only the IDRepository developed at Technische Universität München has community support as a motivation.

2.2.1 DRIM - Dresden Identity Management. The Dresden Identity Management project[2] is an important part of a EU funded integrated project called PRIME (Privacy and Identity Management for Europe). It provides an identity manager (IDMAN) which uses several standard security mechanisms like SSONET for secure connections, AN.ON as an anonymising network adapter, X.509 [3] and XML signatures, and P3P [4] for privacy rule negotiation [Clauß and Köhntopp, 2001]. P3P is also used for actual attribute transfer, although it needed to be extended outside of specification for this.

Security, data-hiding and anonymity services are the main features of DRIM, and the functionality is not hidden from the users, which makes it hard to use for non-security-experts. Also, DRIM concentrates on usage

---

[1] see http://www.epic.org/privacy/consumer/microsoft
[2] http://drim.inf.tu-dresden.de
[3] http://www.ietf.org/html.charters/pkix-charter.html
[4] http://www.w3.org/P3P

of services on the web, direct user to user communication is not covered yet.

2.2.2 iManager. The iManager is part of the ATUS project[5] at University of Freiburg and considers usability to be a most important aspect of privacy enhancing technologies. If the users can not use these tools properly, they will most likely be more hazardous to privacy and security than they help to preserve it. Even more: if PET software does not meet usability standards, people will not use the software at all. Usability aspects of current privacy software like PGP are considered as very confusing. Jendricke states that identity management could be a way to make privacy enhancing technologies more usable and therefore more secure. The iManager tries to provide an easily usable interface [Jendricke and tom Markotten, 2000] .

2.2.3 IDRepository (Cobricks). The Cobricks project[6] at Technical University of Munich contains an own implementation of an identity manager [Koch and Wörndl, 2001]. This is the only current identity management project which has community support as a main aspect. It is designed to help users to join and maintain community affiliations. The IDRepository stores all personal information and is kept decentrally, although the authors suggest to keep it at a trusted third party.

3. MOTIVATION FOR SELF-PORTRAYAL-ORIENTED IDENTITY MANAGEMENT

Since the advent of identity management in 1985, using the Internet has changed dramatically, not alone because far more people have access to it. Latest research shows that two thirds of all US citizens have Internet access [Madden, 2003]. This transformed the Internet from an academic place, which was used only by a few specialists, to a public place where all kinds of communication is done: e-commerce has evolved to an important part of business to business (b2b) transactions, but also for end customers to have a better choice (b2c). Lately, the success of online market places like eBay [7] has led to an even more popular customer to customer (c2c) business. But doing business is of course not the only application for the Internet: just like it was meant to be used in the beginning for academics, the World Wide Web has evolved to

[5]http://www.iig.uni-freiburg.de/telematik/atus
[6]http://www.cobricks.de
[7]http://www.ebay.com

a place for exchange of information for everybody. Online communities develop from plain text USENET newsgroups to highly sophisticated blackboards, where every user can have a detailed private or public profile to store personal information, or with which usage information is associated by the backboard system. Blackboard communities can easily be created using dedicated services[8] or elaborate server components[9] which can be installed on own web servers. Since these communities can be easily joined and left, many have a problem of high user fluctuation. But users who join and leave communities quickly have the disadvantage of earning little or no reputation, since online reputation can not be transferred between communities yet, due to the missing identity representation. Of course, travelling through the space of online communities unknown might be wanted by some users for privacy, secrecy, or negative intentions like fraud or deceit. But many online users put a lot of effort into their online self-portrayal, trying to build a good reputation. The huge number of personal web homepages is a good sign for this [Döring, 1999]. People on the Internet want to be seen, they want to be known.

Peer to peer journalism is a form of information distribution where all users can commit news items. For this it is obvious that reputation and trust plays a major role: the more reputation an author has, and the more people trust in the quality of this authors competency, the more people will actually want to read these news. But since trust and reputation are always bound to persons, it is clear that a definite identification of the users is needed. The onefC project tries to achieve this through identity management.

Privacy is often seen as the protection of personal data from other people or organisations. Then, privacy enhancing technologies (PET) are "a coherent system of information and communication technology measures that protects privacy by eliminating or reducing personal data or by preventing unnecessary and/or undesired processing of personal data; all without losing the functionality of the data system" [Borking and Raab, 2001]. But what is the functionality of the Internet? This can not be reduced to the fact that users can send electronic mail over the Internet – the social collaboration factor offers much more. Here the problem can be seen as a trade-off: "the more I show about myself, the better functionality I get, but also the more people can see my personal data". This includes the possibility that the user is not so much afraid of others seeing their personal data, but very eager to get the best func-

[8]for example http://groups.yahoo.com
[9]for example http://www.phpbb.com

tionality available. So privacy is not only about hiding data, it is also about making the user able to show his data in a reasonable way.

Another important aspect of digital self-portrayal is the fact, that the communication partner receives a portrait or image of the user. Classical identity management systems do not cover this side, because the aim is to hold these images as sparsely detailed as possible. Since self-portrayal identity management enforces user to user (u2u) communication, the management of communication partner images is not only about data mining. This part of identity management can be seen as a semiautomatic addressbook, which stores not only addresses but arbitrary personal information about communication partners in the same way that own personal information is stored.

4. INTERNET USAGE AND SELF-PORTRAYAL SURVEY

As a demonstration that self-portrayal-oriented identity management is a real need of internet users, an exploratory, non-representative survey was done using a web-based questionaire[10]. The link to the questionaire was published on the homepage of the VSIS (distributed and information systems) research group at the University of Hamburg and distributed to many online blackboards. Thus, mainly the target group of the onefC project was reached: long-term Internet users, who spend considerable amounts of their social life and spare time on the Internet. Among the 240 participants 223 make daily use of the Internet, only 9 since less than a year. More than the half (124) have their own web site. Moreover, many of the participants are active in online communities: over 50% write articles in online blackboards more than once a week, 35% even almost daily. 111 of the participants are active in three or more blackboards, only 20 do not use blackboards at all. Three quarters state that they have made personal contacts on the internet. The average age of the participants is 29 years, while the youngest is 14 years old, the eldest 54 years. All in all, this surely does not represent the whole Internet community, but it represents the part of it which may be interested to gain a consistent Internet identity for self-portrayal.

The main part of the questionnaire was a selection of fourteen personal attributes plus two extra fields for self-selected attributes, for which each participant was asked to say whether they would reveal it to more

[10]The questionaire is available at http://vsis-www.informatik.uni-hamburg.de/projects/onefc/umfrage/frag
ebogen-e.phtml (in english, german version is also linked). Any input will be not be considered anymore, though.

than one but not all internet services or communication partners. If they would not reveal them at all or just to one partner, there would be no need for an identity manager and conventional methods of information management would suffice. If the attributes would be shown to anyone, they could as well be published on a personal web site, also here no identity management is needed. The main advantage of identity management is the selective revealing of personal attributes, and the survey was designed to find out for how many of the very active Internet users such a mechanism would be useful.

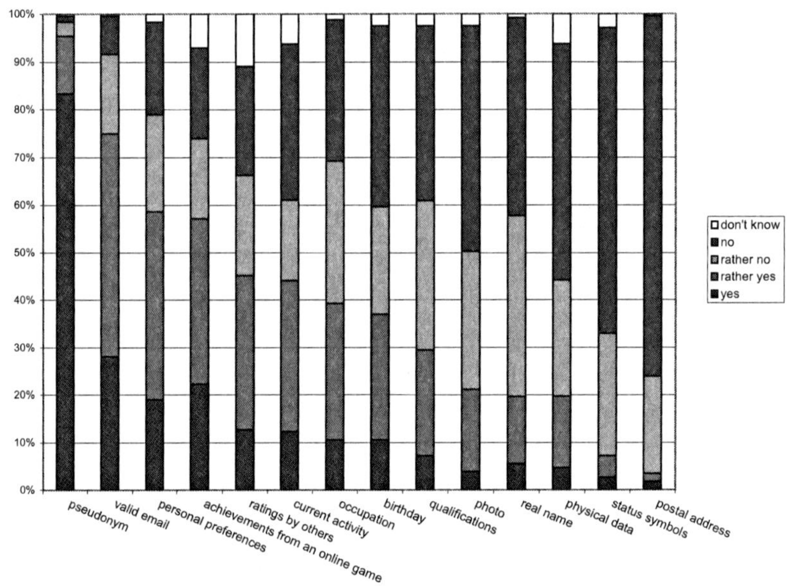

Figure 1. How many participants would reveal each attribute?

To get a representative overview, it was made sure that the selection of the fourteen given attributes was spread from very personal and private ones (like the postal address) to rather public ones (like a pseudonym). The variation can be seen in figure 1, ordered from left to right concerning positive votes. It can be seen that only four of fourteen attributes would be shared to selected communication partners by more than 50% of the participants, but only two attributes would be shared by less than 20%. No attribute would be shared by all nor by none of the participants. This reflects the personal and flexible utilisation of the system: anyone should be able to share whatever attributes she or he wants, there should be no fixed default attributes which can not be extended by users or new services and applications.

The survey revealed that the attributes are more likely to be shared when they have their origin or main functionality on the Internet. This reflects the reluctance of users to reveal real-world attributes of the own identity. Still, some of the real identity would be shown under certain circumstances, presumably to increase trust or to enable real-world interaction like delivery of goods. The disposition to reveal Internet related identity information offers sufficient ground for identity management, though.

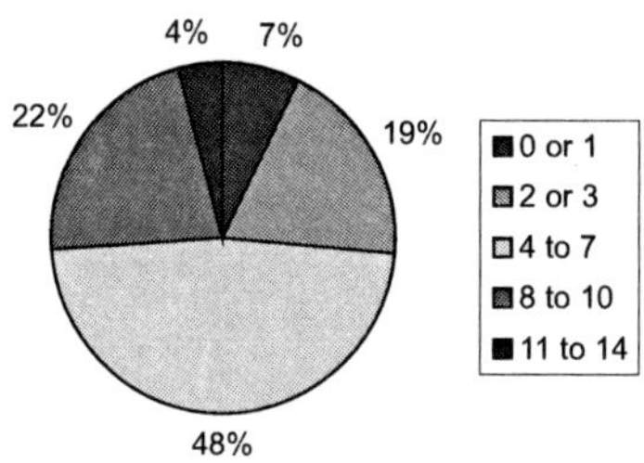

Figure 2. How many attributes would the participants use in an identity management system?

To find out if the participants would actually make use of an identity management system, we analysed how many times each of them said "yes" or "rather yes" to the question whether they would share the given attribute to selected communication partners. The result is shown in figure 2. It can be seen that 26% of the participants would make high use of the system and manage more than the half (8 to 14 of 14) of their attributes with the identity management system. 48% would use such a system for 4 to 7 out of 14 of their attributes, which is still a sensible extent. Our thesis is that for these 74% of the participants, an identity management system would make life on the Internet a lot easier to manage. The remaining 26% would not make much use of such a system.

Another question on the questionaire was "How much are you concerned about your privacy when giving out personal data over the Internet?". While the majority of participants (62%) said to be very or rather concerned about their privacy, these people were almost equally distributed to those who would share many attributes and those who would share rather few attributes. This means that fear about privacy violations was a minor factor for the decisions taken in the main part the survey: the revealing of the given attributes. Remembering the fact that many people would like to reveal attributes from the online world, and realising now that they are equally afraid of losing their privacy, it is clear that there is a real need for identity management.

The attributes entered into the user specified boxes (attribute 15 and 16) were quite interesting too: one participant chose "bank balance" and answered "rather yes". Apparently, she or he saw that if one trusted a system so much as to manage large parts of their identity, one could also enter critical data and be assured that no unauthorised access would be possible.

It needs to be noted that the complex matter of identity management was not explained in detail on the questionaire. Rather, certain situations were explained in which the procedure of identity management was sketched (reveal personal attributes to several selected online communication partners). Maybe the answers would have been different if the participants knew how identity management actually works, including automatically generated short-lived pseudonyms and transparent encryption.

5. PROJECT onefC: AN APPROACH TO AN IDENTITY-ENRICHED SESSION INFRASTRUCTURE

The project "open net environment for Citizens" (onefC) is developing a concept and realisation of an identity-enriched session infrastructure on the basis of self-portrayal. This section presents an overview of the main components of the onefC-architecture. They can be divided roughly into the concept of a digital identity and the management components which assist the user to achieve his needs and goals.

5.1 Representing Users Identities

As the project onefC has the aim to make it possible to be someone on the net, the developed concept of a digital identity covers many aspects of the interpersonal comprehension of identities. [Baier et al., 2003] This comprehension consists of aspects of philosophy, psychology and sociology.

One of the main tasks of the identity is to reliably identify an object or person. This is formalised in the philosophic and mathematic definition of the identity as a binary relation which links any object just to itself. This means it is a special or marginal case of equity. To decide whether the inspected object is in this relation or not, the philosophical term of the moderate numerical identity can be used. It accepts the identity of objects if consecutive characteristics remain even while their state is changing or the object maintains in a continuous but not total change. [Brockhaus, 1989][Henrisch, 1976][Mittelstraß, 1984]

Another aspect of identities is the construction of the single individual with its characteristic attributes. Thereby the identity develops in interactive experiences and relationships in adopted roles in different social contexts. The understanding of being an individual and having the control directs to the unconscious behaviour of presenting the own identity in parts of different size, adapted to the actual figured role and social context. This tends to a newer psychological concept of an identity, which regards it as a complex structure with multiple sets of elements. Every set represents one or more group, role, body or task drawn identity-parts. These parts are organised in a so called "identity patchwork" and are flexibly activated or deactivated depending on the actual context. Each part consists of attributes which contain objective and subjective characteristics of the corresponding person. The objective attributes are similar to entries in a passport - they are more or less verifiable facts like size, age, gender or the appearance as well as achieved skills. The subjective content can cover capabilities in comparison to others, the social appearance, sentiments and moods. [Döring, 1999][Resch, 1998] [Suler, 1996][Turkle, 1999]

The developed identity model maps the "identity patchwork" to a self-referencing data-tree (see figure 3). Each node of the tree represents one identity-part, which is associated with one or more social contexts. These contexts represent common and shared backgrounds of experience in which the corresponding identity node is activated and used for communication. As a consecutive element a unique identifier ties all nodes together. This results in the possibility to identify users across different contexts. Together with the context the unique identifier directs to the part of the identity which has to be activated and thus both imply the presented attributes.

Mapping the identity to a data-tree offers the possibility to use its hierarchical structure for simplifying the construction of the single identity-part. At first the onefC model defines a concept of inheritance to reuse attributes. Each node inherits the attributes of its superior and extends it by adding new one. As it is not always eligible to integrate all characteristics of the superior node, the possibility to conceal particular parts of it is needed. To adapt inherited attributes to the demand of the actual node context, a concept of visibility is introduced. This makes it possible to overwrite the content of characteristics instead of redefining them.

As discussed in section 4, there should be no predefined set of attributes, because the needed ones depend on the actual communication

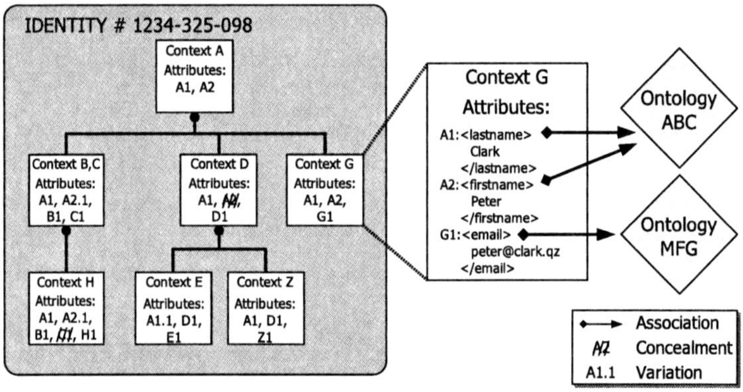

Figure 3. The Identity Model of the Project onefC

context and the user's aims. To cope this, the used attribute model derives from the container concept. It combines meta-data and the explicit content in so called "profile attributes". One of the most important information of the meta-data is the association with an ontology. This makes it possible to use a semiautomatic process to help the user to construct identity-parts for new contexts. To integrate one important aspect of community support, onefC defines the special attribute type of "social-identity attributes". Attributes of this type represent the feeling of being a member of a certain group. With this information the identity-part is banded together with other to a virtual and higher construct: a social identity for this group.

To store and communicate the identity the data-tree is transformed in an XML[11] representation. This leads to the possibility to use the onefC identity model as an exchange format in an open environment.

5.2 Self-Portrayal-Oriented Identity Management

As the term self-portrayal oriented identity management suggests, the onefC architecture is inspired by the social behaviour of presenting the personal identity in accordance with the actual context, role, or situation. It should aid the user to enforce his or her needs and aims. To achieve this, the architecture integrates different core components to a session and identity management system (see figure 4).

The core identity management system consists of the central identity manager and the services the manager uses to provide its functionali-

[11]eXtensible Markup Language, see http://www.w3.org/XML

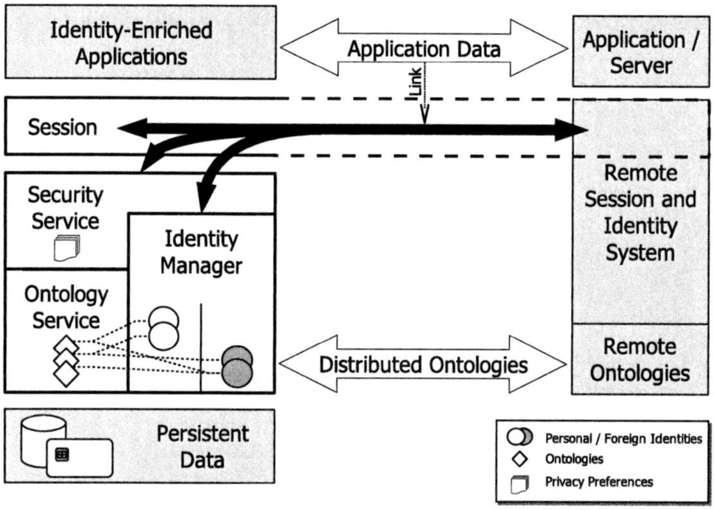

Figure 4. The onefC Identity-Enriched Session Infrastructure

ty. It has been implemented prototypically already [Kunze, 2004]. The management component encapsulates the identities of the user and his communication partners. As the foreign identities are build up from the information provided by the remote identity management systems, they just represent the image the partner has shown in the past and actual communication acts. To enforce the needs and preferences of the identity owner, the identity management component reverts to a security service. This module is based on P3P[12] and APPLE[13] to specify and negotiate privacy aspects before exchanging identity data. While preparing the response to a request the security service has to agree to send any single attribute. This provides the possibility to the user to define as fine grained access rights as he or she needs. This service has also the task to establish safety and trust to a communication act. This is done by using classic techniques like data encryption and signing.

As described in the subsection above, the attributes stored in the identities are associated with ontologies. The management of them is performed by the ontology service which bases on a concept of distributed ontologies. The additional semantic information of the attributes is used in a semiautomatic process to build up new identity-parts for unknown contexts or requested attributes.

[12] http://www.w3.org/P3P/
[13] http://www.w3.org/TR/P3P-preferences/

Identity Management is no end in itself. Since all identity information exchange is done to enrich other communication, a modern session concept was introduced to the onefC architecture. A session is an abstract construct which comprises of a set of communication acts, a representation of the participants and a set of describing attributes. All communication between enabled applications is associated to a session, and sessions are managed using a session manager. The participants of a session are represented using the identities from the identity management system. Some security functionality like encryption or unobservability are handled as attributes of sessions.

6. CONCLUSION

It was shown that privacy is not only about hiding personal data, it includes the option to present oneself to selected communication partners. Identity management is a good solution to support both sides of privacy, data protection on the one hand side, self-portrayal on the other. The presented survey shows that for many active members of online communities, a self-portrayal oriented identity management solution would be of good use. The project "onefC" at University of Hamburg provides a prototype of an identity management system which has self-portrayal as the main motivation. There is already a prototypical example application which uses the onefC-Infrastructure about which will be reported in an upcoming paper. It provides a collaborative filtering service which is personalised with values from onefC identities, while these identities are extended by using the service as well. It can use identity attributes not generated by itself, too.

Future steps include the further development of the onefC infrastructure: the session management component and the ontology infrastructure need to be elaborated. Also, security and privacy mechanisms like P3P and encryption must be further integrated. Large scale evaluation will show how feasible the system is, and how users will actually make use of it.

References

[Baier et al., 2003] Baier, T., Zirpins, C., and Lamersdorf, W. (2003). Digital identity: How to be someone on the net. In *Proceedings of the IADIS International Conference of e-Society*, volume 2, pages 815–820.

[Borking and Raab, 2001] Borking, J. J. and Raab, C. D. (2001). Laws, pets and other technologies for privacy protection. *The Journal of Information, Law and Technology (JILT)*, 1.

[Brockhaus, 1989] Brockhaus, F. A. (1989). *BROCKHAUS ENZYKLOPÄDIE in vierundzwanzig Bänden: Zwölfter Band Kir – LAG.*

[Chaum, 1985] Chaum, D. (1985). Security without identification: transaction systems to make big brother obsolete. *Communications of the ACM*, 28(10):1030–1044.

[Clauß and Köhntopp, 2001] Clauß, S. and Köhntopp, M. (2001). Identity management and its support of multilateral security. *Computer Networks*, 37:205–219.

[Döring, 1999] Döring, N. (1999). *Sozialpsychologie des Internet.* Hogrefe.

[Henrisch, 1976] Henrisch, D. (1976). Identität und Objektivität: eine Untersuchung über Kants transzendentale Deduktion. In *Sitzungsberichte der Heidelberger Akademie der Wissenschaften – Philosophisch-Historische Klasse*, volume 1, page 54 et sqq. Winter.

[Jendricke and tom Markotten, 2000] Jendricke, U. and tom Markotten, D. G. (2000). Usability meets security - the identity-manager as your personal security assistant for the internet. In *Proceedings of the 16th Annual Computer Security Applications Conference*, pages 344–353.

[Koch and Wörndl, 2001] Koch, M. and Wörndl, W. (2001). Community support and identity management. In *Proc. European Conf. on Computer Supported Cooperative Work (ECSCW 2001)*, pages 319–338. Bonn, Germany.

[Kunze, 2004] Kunze, C. P. (2004). Digitale Identität und Identitäts-Management. *Informatiktage 2003.*

[Madden, 2003] Madden, M. (2003). America's online pursuits: The changing picture of who is online and what they do. http://www.pewinternet.org.

[Mittelstraß, 1984] Mittelstraß, J. (1984). *Enzyklopädie Philosophie und Wissenschaftstheorie 2.* Wissenschaftsverlag.

[Resch, 1998] Resch, F. (1998). Zur präpsychotischen Persönlichkeitsentwicklung in der Adoleszenz. *Psychotherapeut*, 43(2):111–116.

[Suler, 1996] Suler, J. (1996). Identity Management in Cyberspace. web-site. *http://www.rider.edu/users/suler/psycyber/identitymanage.html*, Abruf am 06.10.2002.

[Turkle, 1999] Turkle, S. (1999). *Leben im Netz: Identität in Zeiten des Internet.* Rohwolt Taschenbuch Verlag.

PRIVACY PRESERVING ONLINE REPUTATION SYSTEMS

Marco Voss
Darmstadt University of Technology, IT Transfer Office (ITO), Wilhelminenstr. 7, 64283 Darmstadt, Germany
voss@ito.tu-darmstadt.de

Abstract Reputation systems evolve as a mechanism to build trust in dynamic electronic societies. However, they are also a danger to privacy because they monitor a user's behavior. At the same time reputation systems offer the possibility to limit the information a user has to give away during a transaction to ensure accountablity. Privacy preserving reputation systems solve the conflict between anonymity and accountability. This paper examines privacy problems of current reputation systems and classifies them with respect to the location of stored information. Requirements for reputation systems that provide privacy protection are derived from this analysis. As result a new privacy preserving online reputation system is presented that uses locally stored coins to represent reputation information.

Keywords: Anonymity, privacy, accountability, trust, reputation

1. INTRODUCTION

Reputation systems [24] evolve as a mechanism to build trust in dynamic electronic societies. Especially peer-to-peer systems, anonymous remailer networks, online marketplaces, auction sites and web logs rely more and more on reputation to improve their performance and security or to eliminate unwanted behavior. Classical mechanisms to build trust fail in these scenarios.

Reputation systems monitor the behavior of an entity and provide this information upon request. Then this information can be used to make a decision about the trustworthiness of an entity.

By storing data about former transactions of an entity, reputation systems can represent a danger to a user's privacy. However, reputation can be also a mechanism for privacy, because the amount of information that must be disclosed during a transaction can be limited.

This paper investigates the privacy aspects of reputation systems. These systems are classified with respect to the location of stored information. We present requirements for privacy preserving reputation systems and make a proposal for such a system.

Recommender systems and collaborative filtering are related topics, but their focus is more personalization and the filtering of a list of alternatives than to deal with the behavior of entities. Some research has been undertaken in the field of privacy in recommender systems [23]. Similar problems exist here to prevent faking of ratings.

Throughout this paper the following terminology is used: The subject of reputation is an *entity*. The terms entity, peer, user or node are used synonymously. An entity assumes an *identity* for transacting with others. Consequently, an entity can have more than one identity. *Ratings* or *votes* are the committed opinion of one entity about another and are also used synonymously. *Reputation* is the result of collected ratings after consolidation.

The layout of this paper is as follows: The next chapter summarizes some facts about reputation and reputation systems with emphasis on privacy aspects. Then eBay's feedback system is examined as an example of a well known reputation system in use with a lack of privacy protection. After that a classification of reputation systems is presented. This is followed by listing the identified requirements of a privacy preserving reputation system. Finally a sketch of two proposals of such systems is drawn and the paper is concluded with a summary of our results.

2. REPUTATION

More and more interactions involving humans or companies are handled over the Internet. Its openness allows everyone to participate by opening a web site and offering services. The biggest problems appear if one leaves a closed and established group of users. Then there is insufficient information to decide about the trustworthiness of a unknown peer. There are also no regulations to guarantee proper behavior.

Trust and reputation are objects of research in many disciplines from sociology to economics to computer science. The interpretation of these terms differs from author to author and a common definition is still missing.

Mui et al. [21] give a short overview of different notions of reputation and trust from various disciplines. They also derive a computational model of trust and reputation. This discussion is not repeated here, but a more simple and intuitive definition is used:

> Reputation is the collected information about one entity's former behavior as experienced by others. Trust is a decision made on the basis of reputation.

Reputation systems have two effects: they predict the future based on past behavior and they simultaneously influence the future by giving people the incentive to behave well.

Reputation is tightly coupled with an identity. It has no meaning without this identity. From this point of view reputation is not a tradeable asset. After a restaurant is purchased, the name is rarely changed in order to profit from its former reputation. However, there is no guarantee that the new owner will provide the same quality of service.

If a reputation system is implemented by recording and evaluating the outcomes of an entity's interactions, then this means that reputation is sensitive personal information. One may not want to disclose all information about former transactions, because it may also say something about one's preferences and circumstances.

Most simple reputation systems require that an entity is identifiable at least by a pseudonym (entity B in figure 1). This may require a former registration. Then reputation information for this pseudonym is gathered. This information is processed and consolidated. Finally, it is made available upon request.

This process is represented in the figure by the three components collector, processor and emitter. Another entity, A, uses this information together with its own experience to make a trust decision. If A believes that B is trustworthy enough, it enters the interaction. After completion, A rates B according to the outcome of the interaction. This rating is fed back into the system. With further interactions the reputation data of B is steadily updated.

If reputation is not represented as a single value it may also contain detailed information about past transactions. At least for the lifetime of the pseudonym, an entity's transactions can be linked and the development of its reputation can be monitored.

It is vitally important for an entity not to lose reputation because of false accusation. Many people in the USA are concerned about identity theft. The Federal Trade Commission has already setup a web site with information about how to deal with this crime.

The opposite problem is to prevent lending of identities. If the authentication data is not tightly bound to an entity (using biometrics for instance), it is easy to hand on this data to someone else. Some systems try to prevent this by hard punishments or by including some personal information (like a credit card number) in the authentication data. A

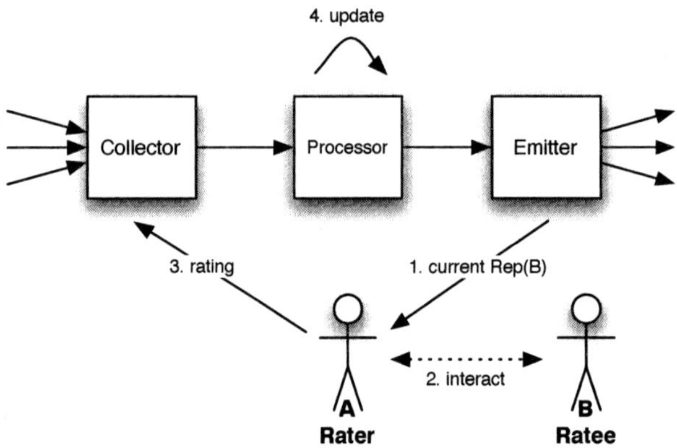

Figure 1. Basic Architecture of Reputation Systems

other issue is to prevent switching of identities without making it too hard to join a reputation system for a newcomer.

Dellarocas [6] analyzes common attacks to compromise reputation systems. He identifies four mayor problems: unfairly high ratings ("ballot stuffing"), unfairly low ratings ("bad-mouthing") and negative or positive discrimination. One of his results is that controlled anonymity can avoid unfairly low ratings and negative discrimination.

2.1 Context and Interdomain Sharing

Reputation is context and domain dependent. It is not clear how a reputation for one context can be transfered to another. A rating earned for having a good understanding of numerical mathematics says nothing about being an honest buyer. This also means that reputation cannot really be captured in a single number. It is more a vector where the elements represent a value for a specific context.

Existing reputation systems are closed and service specific. One cannot transfer a reputation gained in one system to another (e.g. from eBay to Amazon). It would be nice to be able to transfer reputation from one system or domain to another if the context is compatible. This may also involve some normalization of reputation values if the systems have different measures. Single sign-on systems like Microsoft's Passport or the Liberty Alliance project would allow to provide such an interdomain sharing. However, users have strong privacy concerns against such systems.

2.2 Privacy

In this section we will first discuss a general definition of privacy. Then relevant aspects for reputation systems will be stated.

Privacy is a widely and ambiguously used term that is often confused with secrecy, but it means more than only encrypted communication and secure data storage. Communication privacy means that a third party is not able to learn anything about the content of a message exchange between two entities or even that such a communication has happened between them.

Information privacy means that only authorized entities can access and modify information. However, it also means that the owner of personal information should have control over it and that only necessary information has to be disclosed. Goldberg [14] states:

> "Privacy refers to the ability of the individual to control the distribution of information about himself."

Another aspect of privacy is unlinkability. As it is sometimes not possible to avoid disclosure of personal information during transactions with others, the disclosed information should be protected against profiling. Alamäki et al. [1] give a linking-based definition of privacy:

> "A system is privacy-enabled if no party is able to or has the right to link data about a user to its true identity or its other data, unless the user has explicitly allowed it."

Control and unlinkability are two important aspects of privacy that have an impact on reputation systems. The former includes both control of access to reputation information and when it is updated by new votes. Anonymity is a measure for privacy of identity and unlinkability [22]. However, full anonymity reduces accountability if no damage to one's reputation has to be feared.

To whom belongs one's reputation, the operator of the reputation system or the person concerned? Fulda [12] sees reputation as property:

> "Actually, reputation is based on our abilities, capacities, and even physiognomy as modified over the years by every action we take, every behavior we display. Thus, like personal property, reputation is formed by taking natural resources and mixing our labor with it."

In this sense defamation is damaging personal property. Only the interpretation of this record, the opinion other people have about us, belongs to them. Although this position may be extreme and conflicts with freedom of speech, we believe that reputation is sensitive personal information that must be protected and controlled by the user concerned.

This is even more true for online reputation because the amount of information that can be collected and processed is bigger in an online world. If there is only a small possibility to make money out of this, it is guaranteed that it will be abused by marketing (taking spam mails as an example).

Centralized reputation systems like eBay's feedback system [16] collect and store a lot of data about recent transactions. In the case of eBay this data is public and allows the creation of a detailed personal profile about a pseudonym. It is not really difficult to get the email address of an eBay pseudonym to link this information to some identity.

By virtue of containing so much information, reputation systems are a danger to a user's privacy. At worst the collected information can be misused to build a profile of the user's tendencies. Cheating and discrimination can also be a problem if the user lacks control of her reputation.

On the other hand, reputation systems can be a way to provide privacy protection [8]. If one can prove to a partner in a transaction that one has a good reputation in the relevant context there is no need to ask for additional data except the data necessary for fulfilling the transaction.

Chaum [4] already had the vision that anonymous credential systems can promote the protection of privacy. Instead of authentication based access control, one proves authorization by showing possession of an anonymous credential issued by an organization. Brands [3] advances this idea by introducing techniques for a privacy preserving PKI. Any boolean formula can be proved about attributes in a certificate.

What is missing so far is a mechanism to compensate for the decreasing accountablity in systems with strong anonymity. Following the ideas above, we see a privacy protecting reputation system as an extension that allows secure updates to anonymous credentials. This can provide an balance between anonymity and accountability. A digital credential or certificate is something that changes rarely and must be reissued when changed. In contrast, reputation rises and falls according to the owners behavior. If proving and updating a reputation can be done anonymously, it is a perfect mechanism to guarantee a user's privacy. Only necessary information must be disclosed and successive transactions of a single user cannot be linked to each other.

3. CLASSIFICATION OF REPUTATION SYSTEMS

Mui et al. [20] have introduced a typology for reputation systems that concentrates on how the reputation is collected. They subclassify individual reputation into direct and indirect reputation. Direct reputation is derived from direct experiences. Indirect reputation is derived from second-hand information.

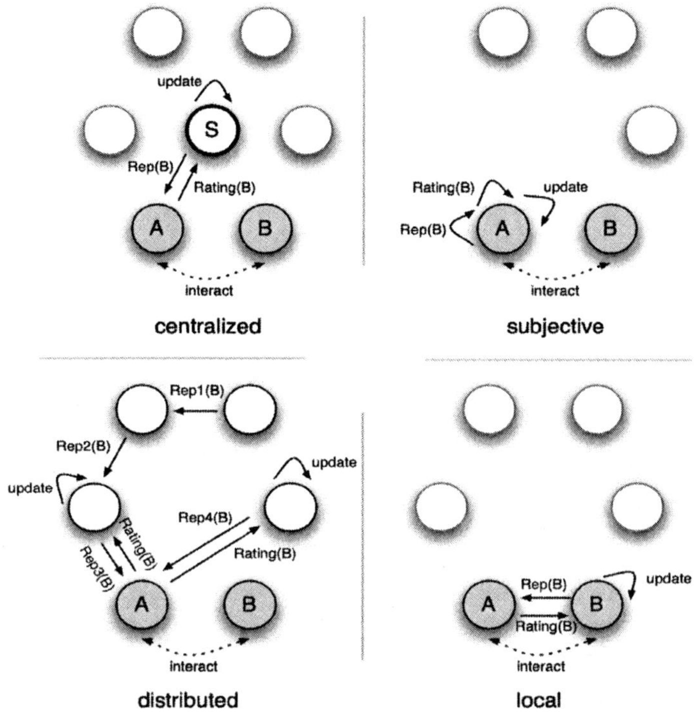

Figure 2. Categorization of Reputation Systems

Their work allows to classify a lot of reputation systems, but it says nothing about the privacy properties. We propose a new categorization according to the place where reputation information is stored. This makes sense if one looks at the privacy aspects resulting from who has control over this information. We found four different classes of storage:

- centralized,
- subjective with no propagation,
- distributed with propagation and
- local storage.

In the following we will describe each class in more detail and state an example system for illustration. Figure 2 gives an overview of this categories.

3.1 Centralized

The centralized approach is very common for reputation systems used for Internet services. Examples are slashdot, web logs, web forums, and auction sites (eBay, Amazon). In the simple case one single central server is responsible for storing and managing all users' reputation data. These systems are easy to implement and follow the need of service providers. They allow users to remain pseudonymous. Anonymity is possible between two users but not between a user and the system.

In scenarios where no central servers exists, like peer-to-peer systems, the role of a central reputation server can be distributed over a certain number of nodes. We still call this a centralized reputation system, because from a privacy perspective it makes no real difference. The propagation of reputation information is restricted to these nodes for synchronization. In [9] each peer node has a number of k designated supervisors that store an updated reputation value after each transaction. One of these act as a main supervising node whereas the others function as a backup. The authors describe how this can be mapped to an overlay peer-to-peer network with a ring structure like Chord [27]: the supervisor nodes can be the immediate successors in the ring topology. [28] describes the same idea but their KARMA system is more like a credit system.

The major drawback is that the central authority has absolute control over the collected data. It can profile the collected data and disclose to a third party. It can swindle or discriminate against users. Even if it is fair, it represents a single point of failure and attack. The latter can be also true in a distributed case. In [9] it is enough to take over the main supervising node to get control over the user's reputation data.

3.2 Subjective

In a subjective model every node stores its own view of the world. For every peer it has interacted with, it creates a record. This record is updated after every transaction according to its result. Nodes do not propagate their opinions about other nodes in order to keep communication low. This also means that every node has a restricted view. Other nodes have to be identifiable over a longer time period in order to track their behavior.

Subjective reputation systems without propagation are good for nodes that interact with a stable number of other known nodes. The number of newly appearing nodes or nodes that change their identification must not be too high. No trusted authority is needed.

GNUnet [13] is a peer-to-peer framework for anonymous distributed file-sharing that uses a subjective reputation system. There are only two operations in GNUnet's protocol which are relevant: queries and replies. A query consumes network bandwidth and is seen as a loss in reputation, whereas a reply is a way to earn reputation. It calls this an economic model, because nodes can attach a priority to a query which is used as the amount of reputation value which is earned or lost. Each node only evaluates the behavior of other nodes it communicates with.

3.3 Distributed

A distributed reputation system extends the former by propagation of reputation information. It allows a more global view and there is information accessible even for nodes that are not members of the direct neighborhood of the request. Nodes combine their own experiences with the observations of other nodes. Other nodes have to be identifiable over a longer time period in order to track their behavior. More elaborate systems use a weighting of votes according to the voter's reputation.

P2PRep [5] extends the Gnutella protocol [19] by a distributed reputation system. Before a user decides from where to download a resource, it can enquire about the reputation of the offers by polling its peers. This is done by broadcasting a message into the p2p network asking for opinions about a specified peer.

EigenTrust [10] is the most extreme form of a distributed reputation system. It integrates the idea of transitivity. They show that global reputation values correspond then to the left principal eigenvector of a matrix of normalized local reputation values.

3.4 Local Storage

In a reputation system with local storage, every entity saves its own reputation data. It can prove to others that it has received this reputation value. After a transaction the value can be updated by another entity in a secure manner. That means that the receiver of a rating has to accept it even if it is negative. She must not be able to fake votes or to use outdated reputation data and drop unpleasant/negative votes. Additionally, it must be difficult for a group of entities to mutually improve their reputation values.

In [18],[11]and [15] schemes that follow this category are presented.

Agent. Gupta et al. introduce a reputation computation agent (RCA) in a Gnutella-like P2P network [15]. This RCA acts as a trusted third party for issuing an updated reputation of a peer. The RCA is not involved in peer-to-peer interaction. Each peer stores its current reptation signed by the RCA. Requesters create signed receipts for peers serving content that can be exchanged for reputation credit with the RCA. To prevent misuse a RCA keeps a list of all processed receipts. This means that a RCA learns about all the recent transactions of a peer.

Portal. In [11] each peer stores context dependent reputation lists. Each entry in one of these lists consists of a signed questionnaire, the IDs of the involved peers and a signed portal ticket. During negotiation between two peers, a requester checks the received reputation list by verifying the signatures and identities. The completeness of the list is confirmed by asking the portal for a counter of processed transactions. This also guarantees that a peer cannot drop negative votes.

After interaction peers must rate each other. They receive an empty questionnaire from the portal to be filled out. After that they exchange the signed questionnaires and challenges contained in the portal tickets. These challenges are send back to the portal. If the portal has received both values it is assured that both questionnaires have been transmitted. The portal updates the transaction counters.

The portal is involved during the negotiation and rating phase. It only stores counters for processed transactions, but learns also the context and the IDs of involved peers. However, it does not know anything about the ratings.

RCert. In [18] the main concept is a certificate called RCert that contains a signed list of former ratings. A RCert consists of a header and units. The header contains information about the owner. A RCert unit contains a timestamp, rating, id of rater and signature. Updates are appended to the end of the RCert and the whole new content signed by the rater. The integrity (but not completeness) of a RCert can be checked by verifying the signature of the last rater. In the simple version the dropping of an entry can only be discovered by analyzing the transaction frequency.

An extended protocol RCertPX includes the previous raters to guarantee the completeness of the presented reputation certificate. Therefore the current rater contacts the previous rater and asks for a last timestamp. When commiting a new rating the rater must contact the previous rater and request that the last timestamp be revoked.

Except for the PKI used for authentication, no central instance is needed. The whole transaction history is contained in the reputation certificate. This also means that every transaction partner learns all about the former transactions.

Currency. Another approach to implementation is to treat reputation as a digital currency. This can guarantee more privacy if the coins are made in a way such that one sees only their value. Dingledine et al. have [7–8] already stated some open questions related to this scenario. Especially, where this currency comes from and who controls its worth are unsolved topics. Currency is a zero-sum game, but reputation is not. Currency is transferable, whereas reputation is bound to an identity.

3.5 Conclusion

None of the described reputation systems has privacy as its main focus. Especially, centralized and distributed systems hold a lot of sensitive personal data accessible for every participant. Only systems with local storage can provide the owner full control over reputation information. But also the three presented reputation systems have some severe privacy shortnesses.

4. REQUIREMENTS OF A PRIVACY PROTECTING REPUTATION SYSTEM

After having discussed important properties of reputation and the relevance of privacy, we now summarize the requirements of a reputation system that provides privacy protection.

General requirements:

- It must provide information that allows users to distinguish between trustworthy and untrustworthy peers.
- It should encourage entities to behave trustworthily.
- An entity must not be able to fake a reputation value.
- Negative ratings (not only positive ones) should be supported.
- An entity must not be able to get rid of a negative reputation.
- An entity should have not an interest to switch its identity to cover misbehavior. Switching should not give any advantage.
- A group of colluding entities should not be able to give each other a high reputation value.
- It should not be possible to defame someone without proof.

Privacy releated requirements:

- The amount of additional data contained in the reputation information should be as limited as possible.

- An entity should have control over its reputation information. This includes access control but also control about when this information is updated.
- The identity of a rater should be protected. If possible a rater should be anonymous.
- Also the identity of a ratee should be kept secret.
- Other parties should learn as less information as possible about the transaction between rater and ratee.

5. A COIN-BASED PRIVACY PROTECTING REPUTATION SYSTEM

We are currently working on two approaches to privacy protecting reputation systems. Both favor the local storage of reputation information. The first approach uses local storage with coin-like reputation and a trusted third party. The trusted third party is used to guarantee a correct update of the reputation information even when a rating has been negative. Because this is still ongoing work, we will only give a sketch of the main ideas. The second one relies on local storage with trusted hardware (smart card or TPM based) and will not be presented here.

5.1 Overview

Reputation is represented as coins. The more coins an entity has the more peers have been satisfied by its performance during former transactions. The coins are issued by a trusted third party for positive ratings and are personalized for the receiver. Consequently, coins do not represent a currency: they cannot be traded or cashed.

At the beginning of a transaction an entity gives coins to its peer as collateral. These coins cannot be used by the peer, but only invalidated if handed over to the trusted third party. By this negative ratings are accomplished. If the rater is satisfied by the outcome of the interaction she can give a positive rating. Thereupon the ratee receives a fresh coin from the trusted third party. To prevent ballot stuffing an entity can give another entity a positive rating only once. This is also guaranteed by the trusted third party.

Different contexts can be mapped to different kinds of coins. For instance a seller can have two kinds of coins: one for the quality of goods she sells and another for reliability and timely delivery. Or a person can have received different coins for being a credit-worthy buyer and another kind for being a Linux expert. To simplify the description we deal only with one kind of coins in the following. The protocol can easily be extended to the case with different kinds of coins. We have implemented a first prototype of this scheme using the project JXTA [26] peer-to-peer infrastructure.

5.2 Online Protocol

This paragraph describes the steps of the protocol. Involved are three parties: the rater (A), the ratee (B) and a trusted third party (T). It is an online protocol because interaction with T is required during the transaction.

1 As a first and optional step B proves that its reputation is bigger than a value x. This is done by proving possession of a sufficient number of coins.

2 Before A agrees to start the interaction it requests a number c of coins as collateral.

3 If B agrees it gives the requested number of coins to A. These coins are not tradeable or cashable. The only possible action for A is to invalidate them.

4 A (together with T) has to verify that the presented coins are still valid and not already used in another transaction.

5 The following interaction between A and B is out of scope of the reputation system. For instance B may provide some service to A.

6 According to the outcome of this interaction A decides about a voting for B. This voting should represent A's satisfaction, but A cannot be forced to give a fair rating. Possible values are elements of {+1, 0, -1, ..., -c}.

7 A communicates this rating to T. If the rating is negative A asks T to invalidate r coins.

8 In case of a positive rating T checks whether A has given B a positive rating before. If not T creates a new coin and sends it to B.

5.3 Building Blocks

Registration Authority To participate in the reputation system an entity has to register with a central authority. By this registration the entity receives a pseudonymous identity and a secret to prove possession of this identity. This identity can be used for authentication, but it is only required by the system to personalize coins and to prevent ballot stuffing (see below).

Coin System We require a coin system that allows to personalize coins on generation. It must also provide anonymity and unlinkability. This means that coins cannot be transfered to another identity without sharing the whole secrets of this identity, but possession of a coin can be proved without authentication. T must be able to invalidate coins.

Anonymous Communication There has already been done a lot of research in the field of anonymous communication [2]. Proposed solutions include mix networks and anonymizing proxies. Although not implemented in our scheme we believe that this solutions can be easily integrated as they use common internet protocols as interface.

Anonymous Recognizing To prevent ballot stuffing T must be able to recognize when A and B interact once again. To preserve privacy T should not be able to identify a single peer but only the tuple of A and B. Currently, we have implemented this by using another trusted party V which only function is to help T recognize a tuple A,B. A and B submit a proof of identity encrypted with the public key of V. V checks whether it has already been presented A,B and gives T the corresponding answer. This scheme provides poor privacy if V is corrupt.

Therefore, we are working on a solution that uses commitments and proofs of knowledge. A and B compute together some value and present this with a proof that this value is dependent on A's and B's certified pseudonyms.

5.4 Privacy Aspects

We will now take a closer look at the privacy aspects of our proposed system. Coins limit the amount of information disclosed: only the outcome of former transactions is revealed. Not the partners, not the subject, not the time (if coins don't have a time stamp). Showing possession of coins can be implemented anonymously and unlinkable. An entity can show the same coin several times to the same partner without giving the possibility to link these actions.

The rater only learns that B possesses a number of coins. The trusted third party only learns that someone (B) has given someone else (A) a number of coins as collateral and how many coins should be returned to B, but it does not learn anything about the identities of A and B. This means that the gained information is only useful to generate a profile about the overall behavior in the reputation system.

6. CONCLUSION AND FUTURE WORK

We have presented a new classification of reputation systems which differentiates by where the reputation data is stored. We have also discussed privacy aspects of reputation systems and the identified classes. This was followed by a summary of important requirements for privacy protecting reputation systems. Especially centralized and distributed reputation systems have privacy problems, because sensitive data about an entity's transactions is stored with inadequate protection in these systems. Local storage of reputation provides a solution to this problem and gives the control back to the user. We have sketched the approach we are currently working on that uses locally stored coin-like reputation. Our future work will focus on finalizing the implementation of this system. A simulation based comparison with existing systems will evaluate its efficiency.

References

[1] Alamäki, T., Björksten, M., Dornbach, P., Gripenberg, C., Gyorbíró, N., Márton, G., Németh, Z., Skyttä, T., Tarkiainen, M.: *Privacy Enhancing Service Architectures*, In Proceedings of Privacy Enhancing Technologies 2002, pp. 99-109

[2] Berthold, O., Federrath, H. and Köpsell, S., *Web MIXes: A System for Anonymous and Unobservable Internet Access*, Lecture Notes in Computer Science 2009, pp. 115, 2001

[3] Brands, S.: *Rethinking Public Key Infrastructures and Digital Certificates*, MIT Press, 2000

[4] Chaum D.: *Security Without Identification: Transaction Systems to Make Big Brother Obsolete*, Communications of the ACM, vol. 28 no. 10, October 1985 pp. 1030-1044

[5] Cornelli, F., Damiani, E., Vimercati, S. D. C. D. , Paraboschi, S. and Samarati, S.: *Choosing Reputable Servents in a P2P Network*, In Proceedings of the 11th World Wide Web Conference, Hawaii, USA, May 2002

[6] Dellarocas, C.: *Immunizing Online Reputation Reporting Systems Against Unfair Ratings and Discriminatory Behavior*, ACM conference on Electronic Commerce, 2000

[7] Dingledine, R., Mathewson, N., Syverson, P.: *Reputation in P2P Anonymity Systems*, Workshop on economics of p2p systems, June 2003

[8] Dingledine, R, Mathewson, N., Syverson, P.: *Reputation in Privacy Enhancing Technologies.*, Computers, Freedom, and Privacy, Apr 2002.

[9] Dutta, D., Goel, A., Govindan R., Zhang H.: *The Design of A Distributed Rating Scheme for Peer-to-peer Systems*, Workshop on Economics of Peer-to-Peer Systems, 2003.

[10] Kamvar, S., Schlosser, M., Garcia-Molina, H.: *The EigenTrust Algorithm for Reputation Management in P2P Networks*, 2003

[11] Fahrenhols, D., Lamersdorf, W. *Transactional Security for a Distributed Reputation Management Sytem*, EC-Web 2002, LNCS 2455, pp. 214-223, 2002

[12] Fulda, J.: *Reputation as Property, and its relation to privacy*, Computers and Society, pp. 27-28, March 2001

[13] Grothoff, C.: *An Excess-Based Economic Model for Resource Allocation in Peer-to-Peer Networks*, WI 32003

[14] Goldberg, I.: *A Pseudonymous Communications Infrastructure for the Internet*, 2000

[15] Gupta, M., Judge, P., Ammar, M.: *A Reputation System for Peer-to-Peer Networks*, NOSSDAV'03, June 2003

[16] Houser, D., Wooders, J.: *Reputation in Auctions: Theory, and Evidence from eBay*, 2000

[17] Kinateder, M., Pearson, S.: *A Privacy-Enhanced Peer-to-Peer Reputation System* EC-Web 2003, LNCS 2738, pp. 206-216, 2003

[18] Liau, C. Y., Zhou, X. Bressan S., Tan, K.: *Efficient Distributed Reputation Scheme for Peer-to-Peer Systems*, HSI 2003, LNCS 2713, pp. 54-63, 2003

[19] NN.: *The Gnutella Protocol Specification v0.4*

[20] Mui, L., Halberstadt, A., Mohtashemi, M.: *Notions of Reputation in Multi-Agents Systems: A Review*, In Proc. of Int'l Conf. on Autonomous Agents and Multi-Agents Systems (AAMAS-02), pp. 280-287

[21] Mui, L., Halberstadt, A., Mohtashemi, M.: *A Computational Model of Trust and Reputation*, 35th Hawaii International Conference on System Science (HICSS), 2002

[22] Pfitzmann, A., Köhntopp, M.: *Anonymity, Unobservability, and Pseudonymity - A Proposal for Terminology*, In Designing Privacy Enhancing Technologies – International Workshop on Design Issues in Anonymity and Unobservability 2000, LNCS 2009, pages 1-9. Springer-Verlag, 2001

[23] Ramakrishnan, N., Keller, B., Mirza, B., Grama, A., and Karypis, G.: *Privacy risks in recommender systems*, IEEE Internet Computing, pages 54 62, November 2001

[24] Resnick, P., Zeckhauser, R.: *Reputation Systems*, Communications of the ACM 43, pp. 45-48, 2000

[25] Resnick, P., Zeckhauser, R.: *Trust Among Strangers in Internet Transactions: Empirical Analysis of eBay's Reputation System*, In The Economics of the Internet and E-Commerce, volume 11 of Advances in Applied Microeconomics. Elsevier Science, 2002.

[26] Sun Microsystems, Inc.: *Project JXTA: An Open, Innovative Collaboration*, 2001

[27] Stoica, I., Morris, R., Liben-Nowell, D., Karger, D., Kaashoek, M., Dabek, F., Balakrishnan, H.: *Chord: A Scalable Peer-to-peer Lookup Protocol for Internet Applications*, To Appear in IEEE/ACM Transactions on Networking

[28] Vishnumurthy, V., Chandrakumar, S., Sirer E. *KARMA : A Secure Economic Framework for Peer-to-Peer Resource Sharing*, Workshop on Economics of Peer-to-Peer Systems, 2003

A RISK-DRIVEN APPROACH TO DESIGNING PRIVACY-ENHANCED SECURE APPLICATIONS

Els Van Herreweghen
IBM Research Division, Zurich Laboratory
evh@zurich.ibm.com

Abstract In the context of authorization in distributed systems, security and privacy often seem at odds. Privacy goals motivate the use of privacy-enhanced forms of authorization such as attribute-based, anonymous authorization; the need to identify misbehaving users calls for either identity-based authorization or identity escrow allowing re-identification of users.

We propose a risk-driven design approach for maximizing privacy of users while satisfying security requirements of an application. In this approach, a security measure such as authentication or identity escrow is introduced only if it addresses a concrete risk. The approach helps to identify privacy-friendly solutions as well as trade-offs between privacy and cost considerations. We illustrate our approach with an example application using anonymous credentials.

Keywords: anonymity, privacy, accountability, risk analysis, anonymous credentials

INTRODUCTION

In distributed systems, the authorization of a specific request for access is often based on authentication of the requesting individual using a certificate or credential issued by a trusted entity. Attribute-based authorization is based on the individual proving possession of certified attributes rather than on his identity; attributes can be certified in conventional public-key certificates [9, 8] or in anonymous credentials [5, 4, 6, 7, 12]; proof of ownership of (the secret associated with) such a certificate or credential then proves ownership of the attributes. As attributes need not be associated with a name, attribute-based authorization can be used to increase the privacy of users while maintaining secure authorization.

Security considerations encompass more than only the verification of a user's right to perform a certain action. For many applications, it is perceived that users can misuse their rights in a way which may mandate establishing the user's identity after the fact in order to hold the user accountable for his actions. Re-identification may be achieved by means of an identity escrow entity [1] trusted with the mapping between a certificate or public key and a user's real identity; revealing this mapping may be subject to certain misuse conditions being satisfied. An issue which has received less attention than user accountability is the accountability of credential or certificate issuers towards relying parties accepting these credentials and certificates. Trust management systems (e.g., [2, 8, 11]) define what are valid chains of trust but fail to address the question of liability and verifiability of certificate issuers. When the owner of an online shop says 'I trust the customer's bank'; he probably means: 'The bank has issued certificate practice statements with liabilities for payments based on certificates it issues; the bank is endorsed by an insurance company with appropriate liabilities. Therefore, I trust that I will receive the money associated with a payment based on a certificate issued by the bank.'

Designing systems with maximal security and privacy clearly requires a way of stating security requirements in a way which allows satisfying them with privacy-friendly technologies. Also this issue seems not to have been addressed so far. In requirements engineering (e.g., [16, 15]), security requirements are often stated in terms of mechanisms such as (traditional, identity-based) authentication. Also research in the field of *security patterns* (e.g., [13, 10]) and their use in modelling and analyzing security requirements describes security problems and requirements at a similar level.

With the risk-driven design approach proposed in this paper, we attempt to address the above issues. Our goal is to correctly address security requirements while maximizing users' privacy. The focus on risks allows us to describe security needs in a mechanism-independent way and to satisfy them using privacy-friendly technologies. It also helps us in finding or avoiding hidden trust assumptions between issuers and relying parties. The approach also identifies trade-offs between privacy (or anonymity) and other considerations such as cost.

The principles of our approach are independent of the technology used for authenticating users' access requests. Of course, we can best illustrate them using an authentication mechanism supporting anonymity as well as accountability. We illustrate our approach using the anonymous credential system with conditional re-identification described in [3, 14].

The remainder of the paper is organized as follows. In Section 1, we introduce the anonymous credential system used to illustrate our approach. In Section 2, we introduce our example application and propose a first, ad-hoc, design. In Section 3, we re-design the example application using our risk-driven approach and discuss its advantages. Section 4 concludes the paper.

1. AN ANONYMOUS CREDENTIAL SYSTEM WITH CONDITIONAL RE-IDENTIFICATION

The anonymous credential system with which we illustrate our approach is the one described in [3, 14]. Here, we describe only the basic constructs; for a more in-depth discussion, we refer to [14].

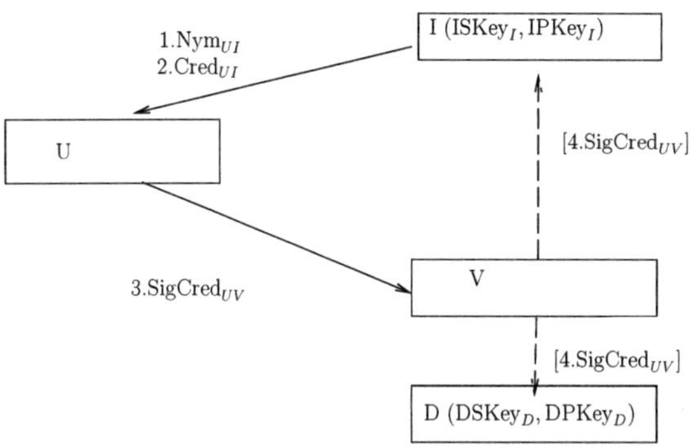

Figure 1. Basic Credential System Protocols

Figure 1 shows a user U (1) establishing a nym (pseudonym) Nym_{UI} with credential issuer I, (2) obtaining a credential Cred_{UI} from I, and (3) proving ownership of that credential to a verifier V by producing a credential-based signature $\mathrm{SigCred}_{UV}$. Such a credential-based signature proves that the signer possesses a credential issued by I. However, it does not contain Cred_{UI} or Nym_{UI} (optional mechanisms allowing to derive Nym_{UI} from $\mathrm{SigCred}_{UV}$ under specific conditions are discussed below). Obtaining a nym or credential and signing with a credential are interactive protocols; representing them as single messages is appropriate for the present discussion.

A credential Cred_{UI} is represented as follows:

$$\mathrm{Cred}_{UI} = \mathrm{Cred}(\mathrm{Nym}_{UI}, \mathrm{IPKey}_I, \mathrm{MultiSig}, \mathrm{Exp})$$

- Nym_{UI} is the nym (pseudonym) under which I knows U. Unless establishing Nym_{UI} involved identity escrow (see below), I cannot link Nym_{UI} to the identity of U.
- IPKey_I is the issuing public key of the issuer; the credential is signed with the corresponding secret key ISKey_I.
- MultiSig being `true` or `false` indicates whether the credential can be used multiple times or only once. When U signs twice with the same one-use credential, the resulting signatures allow I to extract Nym_{UI}. Figure 1 shows V sending SigCred_{UV} to I for double-spending detection. This can be done online, during verification of SigCred_{UV}; offline double-spending detection is less expensive to realize but only allows for after-the fact detection.
- Exp represents a credential expiration time.

U's credential-based signature reflects the parameters and options with which U invoked the signing.

$$\text{SigCred}_{UV} = \text{SigCred}(\text{Cred}_{UI}, \text{Msg}, \text{DeAnCond}, \text{DPKey}_D)$$

represents a signature on Msg (may be `null`, if the goal is authentication without signing a particular message) using Cred_{UI}. The zero-knowledge realization of SigCred_{UV} ensures that SigCred_{UV} cannot be linked to another signature $\text{SigCred}_{UV'}$ with the same Cred_{UI}; SigCred_{UV} only proves (and allows V to prove) that Msg was signed with a (non-expired) credential issued by I, and with parameters DeAnCond and DPKey_D as described in the following.

DPKey_D and DeAnCond are optional parameters related to deanonymization. If DPKey_D is `null`, there is no way of linking SigCred_{UV} back to Nym_{UI}, even with cooperation from I. If DPKey_D is non-`null`, it represents the public key of a deanonymization organization D; with the associated secret key DSKey_D, D can deanonymize the transaction, i.e., extract Nym_{UI} from SigCred_{UV}; Figure 1 shows V sending SigCred_{UV} to D for deanonymization. DeAnCond expresses the condition (signed by U) under which deanonymization by D is allowed. (Of course, fairness and correctness of D's operation are fundamental to users trusting the system. In [14], ways are discussed to motivate such fairness and correctness by making D's actions verifiable.) From SigCred_{UV}, V has a proof that D can deanonymize the signature; when D actually deanonymizes it, D can also prove the correctness of this deanonymization, i.e., D can prove that SigCred_{UV} indeed resulted from showing a credential issued on Nym_{UI}.

Deanonymization thus allows for a conditional linking between a transaction ($\mathrm{SigCred}_{UV}$) and a user's nym (Nym_{UI}). Another feature necessary for realizing re-identification is identity escrow ('signed nym registration' in [14]). Identity escrow is realized by U providing I with a proof of linking between Nym_{UI} and U's real identity with a signature

$$\mathrm{SigNym}_{UI} = S_U(\mathrm{Nym}_{UI}, \mathrm{Msg})$$

where $S_U()$ denotes a signature with a signature private key SSKey_U associated with a public key SPKey_U certified in an 'external' certificate Cert_{CA-U}. This certificate is issued by certification authority CA, who is trusted to either include the real name of the user in Cert_{CA-U} or to reveal it whenever asked. Msg is an optional message; it can, e.g., contain information about U's liability for Nym_{UI}.

When used without identity escrow or deanonymization, the anonymous credential system described allows for fully unlinkable and anonymous attribute-based authorization. The optional features of deanonymization and identity escrow allow for a conditional re-identification with separation of duties between de deanonymizer (D) conditionally mapping a transaction back to a nym and the entity enforcing identity escrow (I) mapping the nym back to an identity. In the following sections, we now use this credential system in the design of secure and privacy-enhanced applications.

2. THE AdsOL ADVERTISEMENT SERVICE

2.1 High-Level Description

AdsOL is an advertisement service accessible through the PrivacyPortal web portal. PrivacyPortal promotes the use of anonymous credentials as the recommended mechanism for any type of authentication. PrivacyPortal offers a Kiosk service to all its members; Kiosk is able to accept an 'external' payment on behalf of AdsOL (or another portal service) and converts it into a payment proof in the form of an anonymous credential.

AdsOL charges users posting advertisements, e.g., by a monthly fee; retrieving and reading advertisements is free of charge. Users posting advertisements can enter pseudonymous contact information such as a temporary or pseudonymous e-mail address obtained from PrivacyPortal's pseudonym email address server. This allows the user who posted an ad to remain anonymous even when contacted by an interested party.

AdsOL does not limit the range of items that can be advertised for. However, if a user posts an illegal (e.g., drugs-related) advertisement, law enforcement (LE) requires a re-identification of the transaction.

U obtaining posting credential from K:
$K \rightarrow U:$ Nym_{UK}
$U \rightarrow K:$ payment, Cert_{CA-U}, $\mathrm{SigNym}_{UK} = S_U(\mathrm{Nym}_{UK}, \ldots)$
$K \rightarrow U:$ $\mathrm{Cred}_{UK} = \mathrm{Cred}(\mathrm{Nym}_{UK}, \mathrm{IPKey}_K, \texttt{true}, \mathrm{Exp}_{UK})$

U posting advertisement to A:
$U \rightarrow A:$ $\mathrm{SigCred}_{UA} = \mathrm{SigCred}(\mathrm{Cred}_{UK}, \texttt{Advert}, \texttt{MisuseCond}, \mathrm{DPKey}_{LE})$

Re-identification:
$LE \rightarrow A:$ need re-identification of `Advert` posting
$A \rightarrow LE:$ $\mathrm{SigCred}_{UA}$
LE: deanonymizes $\mathrm{SigCred}_{UA}$ and obtains Nym_{UK}
$LE \rightarrow A:$ need U related to Nym_{UK}
$A \rightarrow K:$ need U related to Nym_{UK}
$K \rightarrow A:$ U and proof of mapping between U and Nym_{UK}
$A \rightarrow LE:$ U and proof of mapping between U and Nym_{UK}

Figure 2. AdsOL Design

2.2 AdsOL Design

We now propose a first privacy-friendly design satisfying above requirements based on attribute-based authorization using our anonymous credential system; in the next section, we will then show how a risk-driven design can identify more secure and privacy-friendly solutions.

The idea of our solution is the following.

- K (Kiosk) issues a posting credential (a paid subscription to AdsOL) to a user U on condition of having received payment, and having applied identity escrow to the credential (nym);
- A (AdsOL) accepts an advertisement on condition of having received a deanonymizable signature with a posting credential issued by K.

The design is summarized in Figure 2. In a first step, U obtains the posting credential from K as follows. U establishes a nym Nym_{UK} with K, performs the payment and provides K with the identity escrow information ($\mathrm{Cert}_{CA-U}, \mathrm{SigNym}_{UK}$). K then issues the posting credential Cred_{UK} valid for a certain period (Exp_{UK}).

When posting an advertisement, U sends $\mathrm{SigCred}_{UA}$ to A. The advertisement is included as the signed message in $\mathrm{SigCred}_{UA}$; $\mathrm{SigCred}_{UA}$ is deanonymizable by LE on condition `MisuseCond`. Choosing LE as deanonymizing organization may make sense under the assumption that LE anyway has the last word in judging `MisuseCond`; we could also have chosen an independent organization D to deanonymize transactions.

If re-identification is necessary (`MisuseCond` fulfilled), LE asks A for SigCred_{UA} related to the specific `Advert`, deanonymizes it, and asks for the identity of U related to Nym_{UK} (we assume that LE deals with A for obtaining the necessary information). A obtains the provable mapping between U and Nym_{UK} from K and provides it to LE.

2.3 Analysis

In the above design, we directly derived authorization and re-identification requirements from a high-level description of the system. Authorization and (re-)identification ensure that security requirements are fulfilled; the attribute-based and anonymous authorization together with the conditions for re-identification were meant to ensure that these requirements were dealt with in the most privacy-friendly way.

By requiring that every posting transaction be re-identifiable, we assume having excluded A's risk of not being able to re-identify when needed, and having provided LE with a secure means to trace illegal advertisements. Has our design fulfilled these goals?

We have assumed A to be liable towards LE for not being able to re-identify an illegal advertisement. In our design, A trusts K to invest in an identity escrow infrastructure (relationship with CA, verifying SigNym) and to be able to identify a real user associated with a nym. Neither our high-level description nor our design, though, has provided a motivation for K to do so in in the form of a contractual guarantee or liability towards A or LE. Thus, we have reduced the privacy of users (systematic identity escrow and re-identifiability of transactions) without correctly addressing the risk! Even if such liabilities exist, they may not compensate A's potential loss. E.g., if A's operating license gets revoked by LE if an illegal advertisement posting cannot be re-identified, A is likely to decide to act as escrow agent himself. Or, maybe, A will look for ways to prevent illegal advertisements altogether!

On the other hand, we can also stipulate concrete liabilities and exclude A's risk without solving LE's security problem. Assume that A's liability for not being able to re-identify an illegal advertisement is a fine of \$1000 to be paid to LE; and K's liability for not being able to map a nym to an identity is a fine of \$1000 to be paid to A. A has excluded his risk. But, a bribe of \$2000 paid by the misbehaving user may convince K to claim he 'is sorry he lost the user's identity mapping record (including SigNym_{UK}) and is willing to pay the \$1000 to A'. We now provide expensive but unconditional (assuming K is an 'honest' bribee) anonymity to misbehaving users.

The abovc reasoning presents several issues we did not consider in our first design:

- Risks and liabilities should be made explicit without (misplaced) trust assumptions between organizations: A should not have to (blindly) trust K for addressing A's risks and liabilities.
- When addressing a risk, the cost of the risk and its liabilities has to be weighed against the cost of addressing the risk. A fine provides a different motivation for addressing the risk than having to suspend operation. From the point of view of the party (LE) imposing this liability, this of course means that a liability has to motivate the intended result (correct re-identification).
- We have decided to address LE's requirement for re-identification without considering whether it was possible to prevent misuse altogether.

Our risk-driven design in the next section will address these issues.

3. A RISK-DRIVEN DESIGN OF THE AdsOL SERVICE

In this section, we propose a risk-driven approach for satisfying security requirements while maximizing privacy. In this approach, an initial risk analysis is followed by an iterative process of design option analysis, design decisions and residual risk analysis; during this process, we gradually refine the protocols used. By focusing on concrete risks for a specific party, we assure that trust and liability requirements among organizations are made explicit. By identifying potential design options regardless of cost, we can identify the most privacy-friendly solution as well as compromises beween privacy and cost.

Figure 3 illustrates the risk-driven design process for A. 'R' stands for risk, 'O' for option. Ri represents the ith first-level risk; RiOj represents design option j addressing risk i; RiOjRk represents residual risk k within design option RiOj, etc.

3.1 Initial Risk Analysis for AdsOL (A)

What are the initial risks A is exposed to?

- **R1. Not being paid.** A can lose money and even go out of business because it is not paid correctly for advertisements.
- **R2. Fine for illegal advertisement.** A may have to pay `IllegalFine` for an illegal advertisement.

R1. Not being paid
R1O1. *A* accepts external payments
option discarded: infrastructure, cost
R1O2. *K* accepts payment for *A*
R1O2R1. *K* not paying *A*
R1O2R1O1. *A* can prove issuing of a posting credential
option discarded: cannot be realized
R1O2R1O2. *A* can prove use of 'new' posting credential
option discarded: privacy impact too high

← **Change of assumption**: pay-per-subscription → pay-per-posting

R1O2R1O3. *A* can prove use of posting credential
***K*'s analysis** ← *K* requires one-use posting credential with double-spending risk for *A*
R1O2R1O3R1. Not being paid for double-spent posting credential
R1O2R1O3R1O1. Online double-spending detection
R1O2R1O3R1O2. Offline double-spending detection

R2. Fine for illegal advertisement
R2O1. No check
option discarded: cost (fines)
R2O2. Check by *A*
option discarded: cost (residual risk of fines)
R2O3. Check by *LE*
R2O3O1. Requested by user
R2O3O2. Requested by *A*

R3. Suspending operation
risk excluded by R2O3O2

Figure 3. Risk/Options Analysis for *A*

A also needs to determine the consequences of not being able to re-identify an illegal posting. In a real-world system, this may require an interaction with *LE*. We assume that the consequence is suspension of its operation:

- **R3. Suspending operation.**

For the various risks, we now describe the process of design options analysis, design decisions and residual risk analysis which will gradually refine the protocols.

3.2 Design Options Analysis

3.2.1 R1: Not being paid. A addresses this risk by not publishing an advertisement without having received a (guarantee of) payment for it. We consider the following design options:

- **R1O1. A accepts external payments.** A accepts bank transfers, credit card payments etc. from users.
- **R1O2. K accepts payment for A.** K accepts payments from users and issues posting credentials with which the users can post advertisements to A. K, of course, has to forward the payment for every new posting credential to A.

Assuming A prefers not to deal with external payments, we discard R1O1 and further explore R1O2. This decision is represented by underlining design option R1O2 in Figure 3.

Previously, we stated that A and K are different business entities. A thus has to take into account a remaining risk of K not paying A for every posting credential it issues:

- **R1O2R1. K not paying A**

In order to address this risk, A wants a statement from K specifying K's liabilities (e.g., payment to A upon issuing a posting credential); in addition, A wants to be able to prove when a new credential has been issued or is used:

- **R1O2R1O1. A can prove issuing of a posting credential**
- **R1O2R1O2. A can prove use of 'new' posting credential**

R1O2R1O1 cannot be realized as A cannot control K's interactions with users. R1O2R1O2 requires that A can distinguish between multi-use credentials when they are shown. This can only be realized by introducing linkabilities between credential issuing and credential use; that would mean reducing users' privacy in order to solve a trust and liability problem between K and A!

Getting appropriate (proof of due) payment while respecting users' anonymity can only be realized in a model where A charges K for every advertisement posted; as K is only a payment intermediary, this naturally translates into a model where also users pay K per posting as opposed to per subscription.

At this point, we can either backtrack by reconsidering R1O1 which was previously discarded, or by changing our initial assumptions and investigating a pay-per-posting model. In such a model, it suffices that:

- **R1O2R1O3. *A* can prove use of posting credential**

We assume the pay-per-posting model is acceptable to both A and K and thus choose this option. As the change of assumption does not influence any of the earlier considerations or decisions, there is no need for backtracking.

At this point, we have to interleave our discussion with K's independent risk and options analysis. K agrees to A's conditions but of course decides to issue only one-use posting credentials and to not be liable for postings with a double-spent credential.

We now return to A's analysis. A's remaining risk is

- **R1O2R1O3R1. Not being paid for double-spent posting credential**

A now considers either on- or offline double-spending detection:

- **R1O2R1O3R1O1. Online double-spending detection**

- **R1O2R1O3R1O2. Offline double-spending detection**

An online double-spending check is expensive but reduces A's risk to null. (Strictly speaking, the remaining risk for A is K not paying A even if A has proof of K's liability to pay; this should be covered by K's liabilities as already assumed when discussing R1O2R1.) In this case, however, an offline double-spending check may suffice. If a user double-spends a posting credential, he loses anonymity for both advertisements, as K would be able to link the nym revealed from double-spending detection to the user's identity through the identity escrow data. In addition, as soon as double-spending is detected, A can immediately cancel the publication of both advertisements paid for with the credential. Thus, a user can lose more than he can gain by double-spending a posting credential.

Because of the possibility to withdraw the advertisements of a double-spending user, A decides to go for the latter option. Then, for every posting credential correctly verified by A, K needs to either pay A or prove it was double-spent.

So far, we derived a partial solution to the design of A, taking into account the risk R1 of A not being paid. Of the two options for addressing this risk, the first was discarded because of cost reasons. Within the remaining option, we identified the remaining risk by examining trust assumptions between A and K. We chose to change to a pay-per-posting model as it allows to fulfill A's security requirements while allowing more user privacy. K's risk and options analysis then made K to accept being charged for one-use posting credentials without being liable for their double-spending. Within the pay-per-posting model, we investigated the remaining risk (double-spending) and the various ways of addressing it. Between online and offline double-spending detection, the former is more expensive but excludes remaining risk. We chose, however, to implement the latter because it is less expensive while A has good reasons for accepting the residual risk.

We now apply a similar analysis to the remaining initial risk factors. R2 and R3 share a causal event, an illegal advertisement; R3's materialization depends in addition on a second event, A's inability to provide the user's name.

In order to avoid unnecessary backtracking, we want to start with the risk analysis (R2 or R3) which results in the strongest measures against (or: strongest measures preventing) illegal advertisements. If providing the user's name were deemed impossible, R3, being the more severe risk, would lead us to implement the stronger measures; if providing the user's name were trivial or could be realized with no cost to A, R2 would provide us with the stronger measures. In the absence of any of these assumptions, we start with the analysis of R2.

3.2.2 R2: Fine for illegal advertisement (`IllegalFine`). A can address this risk in various ways:

- **R2O1. No check.** A can choose not to address this risk; any message is publicized without screening. This option is discarded because it is deemed too exensive (`IllegalFine`).

- **R2O2. Check by *A*.** A can prevent illegal advertisements by screening and approving every message before it is posted. This is expensive and can prevent most illegal advertisements; however, A has no guarantee that an advertisement which it considers legal is not considered illegal by LE; also this residual risk is deemed too high to accept.

- **R2O3. Check by *LE*.** Illegal advertisements can be excluded if every message, before being published, is approved by LE himself. This is a very expensive solution but completely excludes A's risk if LE's approval is provable (e.g., by a signature); also, given that excluding illegal messages also excludes any re-identification requirements in the system and thus is attractive to users, LE may consider charging the extra cost for this solution to the users.

  - **R2O3O1. Requested by user.** A can require that users only post messages if approved (with a signature) by LE;

U obtaining posting credential from K:
$K \rightarrow U$: Nym_{UK}
$U \rightarrow K$: payment (linked to Nym_{UK})
$K \rightarrow U$: $\mathrm{Cred}_{UK} = \mathrm{Cred}(\mathrm{Nym}_{UK}, \mathrm{IPKey}_K, \mathtt{false}, \mathrm{Exp})$

U obtaining approval from LE:
$U \rightarrow LE$: `Advert`, possibly payment
$LE \rightarrow U$: $S_{LE}(\mathtt{Advert})$

U posting advertisement to A:
$U \rightarrow A$: $\mathrm{SigCred}_{UA} = \mathrm{SigCred}(\mathrm{Cred}_{UK}, S_{LE}(\mathtt{Advert}), \mathtt{null}, \mathtt{null})$

Contracts and liabilities:
K: 'I will pay A every time a Cred_{UK} is shown unless I can prove it is double-spent'
A: 'For any advertisement which is considered illegal but not approved by LE, I will pay `IllegalFine` and suspend operation if I cannot provide a mapping with a user'

Figure 4. AdsOL Risk-Driven Design: Protocols and Liabilities

- **R2O3O2. Requested by *A*.** A himself can contact LE for every advertisement posted and charges the extra cost to the user in the form of a higher price per advertisement.

We now assume that users are willing to accept the burden of contacting LE before posting a message to A, as this guarantees them unconditional anonymity of the posting. (Of course, users require the exchange with LE to be anonymous as well!) By choosing R2O3O1, we have completely excluded risk R2 as well as R3.

3.2.3 R3: Suspending Operation. The risk of suspending operation has thus been excluded by excluding illegal message postings.

3.3 Resulting Design

The resulting design is depicted in Figure 4. In order to obtain a one-use (MultiSig=`false`) posting credential, U establishes a nym Nym_{UK} with K and performs a payment. The implementation should ensure that the payment is linked to Nym_{UK}, e.g., by including Nym_{UK} in the signed payment message. Before posting `Advert` to A, U requests a signed approval on `Advert` from LE. LE may request a payment for this service as well. U then posts the approved $S_{LE}(\mathtt{Advert})$ to A in $\mathrm{SigCred}_{UA}$, now without deanonymization.

The contracts and liabilities represent the observations we made during the above analysis. K's liability expresses his financial obligation towards A related to a posting with a non-double-spent Cred_{UK}. A's liability towards LE expresses payment of `IllegalFine` for an illegal advertisement, and A's obligation to suspend operation if the corresponding transaction cannot be re-identified. By not taking liability for illegal advertisements approved by LE and by not accepting non-approved advertisements, A can however exclude these risks.

3.4 Generalization of the Risk-Driven Design Approach

Our risk-driven design of the AdsOL application allowed us to identify a more privacy-friendly solution, although at a potentially higher cost. It also allowed us to identify hidden trust assumptions (between A and K) in our previous design which could have led to undefined liabilities in the event of failed re-identification. We now capture the principles of the approach.

In the above risk-driven design, we have started out with a risk analysis for the entity to be designed (A).

A risk which does not involve liabilities towards another party is an **internal risk**. A not being paid for the service it provides is an internal risk.

An **external risk** is related to a liability towards another party. A's risk to have to pay `IllegalFine` is an external risk. Such risks are typically captured in contracts or liabilities as shown in Figure 4.

A risk can be dealt with in different ways, leading to different design options. Of these options, we can assess trust assumptions, cost and privacy features; these are taken into account when choosing a design option.

Depending on the option chosen, a risk can then be:

- accepted: A accepts the risk of revenue loss due to double-spending.

- transformed (delegated) into a risk for another party: A transforms R1 into a payment liability by K towards A.

- prevented or excluded: a loss of revenue because of a double-spent posting credential can be prevented by an online double-spending check. Note that, what hat seems as prevention, may often be a transformation: with or without online double-spending detection, the initial risk of not being paid (by the user) is only transformed into the risk of not being paid by K; the protocols chosen merely ensure that A can hold K liable in case K refuses to pay A (as expressed with K's liability statement).

The risk/options analysis is an iterative process as a residual risk analysis leads to a new analysis of design options.

In the AdsOL example, we avoided backtracking through design options in order to keep the simplicity of the example. In general, however, the design process tries to optimize a function of cost, privacy and risk. A systematic risk/options analysis is thus likely to involve backtracking; options should be discarded only if they cannot lead to an optimized solution.

The description of the approach presented here is informal. Clearly, development of a real methodology for the risk-driven design needs a formalization of the risks, of the options addressing those risks and of the measures for evaluating them:

- Risks have to be expressed in terms of the occurrence of events; if a risk is external, provability of events plays an important role. E.g., risk R2 can be stated as the existence of a proof of existence, on A's web site, of an illegal message posting for which A cannot prove approval by LE.

- Options addressing a risk can be stated in terms of minimizing or excluding the occurrence of these events. E.g., A's addressing R2 (and R3) consists of preventing anyone to be able to prove the above.

- The analysis of the various design options has to be done based on measurable criteria, e.g., cost estimates of risks and design options.

4. CONCLUSIONS AND FUTURE WORK

In this paper, we have presented and illustrated a risk-driven approach towards designing privacy-friendly and secure applications. Fundamental principles of the approach are the identification of risks without hidden trust assumptions; and a thorough analysis of design options for addressing risks with a focus on prevention.

Our risk-driven design approach provides for a conceptual framework facilitating the correct addressing of security requirements resulting from real risks while enabling identification of the most privacy-friendly solution. However, the development of a real methodology needs a formalization of the risks, of the options addressing those risks and of the measures for evaluating them. These are topics for further research.

References

[1] T. Aura and C. Ellison. Privacy and accountability in certificate systems. Research Report HUT-TCS-A61, Helsinki University of Technology Laboratory for Theoretical Computer Science, 2000.

[2] M. Blaze, J. Feigenbaum, and A. D. Keromytis. Keynote: Trust management for public-key infrastructures (position paper). In *Proc. 1998 Security Protocols Workshop*, volume 1550 of *Lecture Notes in Computer Science*, pages 59–63. Springer-Verlag, 1998.

[3] J. Camenisch and E. Van Herreweghen. Design and implementation of the idemix anonymous credential system. In *Proc. 2002 ACM Conference on Computer and Communications Security*. ACM Press, 2002.

[4] D. Chaum and J.-H. Evertse. A secure and privacy-protecting protocol for transmitting personal information between organizations. In *Advances in Cryptology – CRYPTO '86*, volume 263 of *Lecture Notes in Computer Science*, pages 118–167. Springer-Verlag, 1987.

[5] D. L. Chaum. Security without identification: transaction systems to make big brother obsolete. *Communications of the ACM*, 28(10):1030–1044, 1985.

[6] L. Chen. Access with pseudonyms. In *Cryptography: Policy and Algorithms*, volume 1029 of *Lecture Notes in Computer Science*, pages 232–243. Springer Verlag, 1995.

[7] I. B. Damgård. Payment systems and credential mechanism with provable security against abuse by individuals. In *Advances in Cryptology – CRYPTO '88*, volume 403 of *Lecture Notes in Computer Science*, pages 328–335, 1990.

[8] C. Ellison, B. Frantz, B. Lampson, R. Rivest, B.Thomas, and T. Ylonen. SPKI certificate theory. RFC 2693, Sept. 1999.

[9] International Telecommunication Union. ITU-T recommendation x.509 - the directory: Authentication framework, Aug. 1997.

[10] S. Konrad, B. Cheng, L. Campbell, and R. Wassermann. Using security patterns to model and analyze security requirements. In *International Workshop on Requirements for High Assurance Systems (RHAS)*, 2003.

[11] N. Li, B. Grosof, and J. Feigenbaum. A practically implementable and tractable delegation logic. In *Proc. 2000 IEEE Symposium on Research in Security and Privacy*, pages 27–42. IEEE Computer Society Press, 2000.

[12] A. Lysyanskaya, R. Rivest, A. Sahai, and S. Wolf. Pseudonym systems. In *Selected Areas in Cryptography*, volume 1758 of *Lecture Notes in Computer Science*. Springer-Verlag, 1999.

[13] The Open Group. Technical guide: Security design patterns, Apr. 2004.

[14] E. Van Herreweghen. Designing anonymous applications with accountability using anonymous credentials. Research Report RZ 3526, IBM Research Division, Jan. 2004.

[15] A. van Lamsweerde. Goal-oriented requirements engineering: A guided tour. In *Proc. IEEE International Symposium on Requirements Engineering*, pages 249–262, 2001.

[16] E. Yu and L. Cysneiros. Designing for privacy and other competing requirements. In *2nd Symposium on Requirements Engineering for Information Security (SREIS'02)*, Raleigh, North Carolina, Oct. 2002.

PRIVACY-INVASIVE SOFTWARE IN FILE-SHARING TOOLS

Andreas Jacobsson, Martin Boldt, and Bengt Carlsson
School of Engineering, Blekinge Institute of Technology, S-372 25 Ronneby, SWEDEN
{andreas.jacobsson;martin.boldt;bengt.carlsson}@bth.se

Abstract Personal privacy is affected by the occurrence of adware and spyware in peer-to-peer tools. In an experiment, we investigated five file-sharing tools and found that they all contained ad-/spyware programs, and, that these hidden components communicated with several servers on the Internet. Although there was no exchange of files by way of the file-sharing tools, they generated a significant amount of network traffic. Amongst the retrieved ad-/spyware programs that communicated with the Internet, we discovered that privacy-invasive information such as, e.g., user data and Internet browsing history was transmitted. In conclusion, ad-/spyware activity in file-sharing tools creates serious problems not only to user privacy and security, but also to network and system performance. The increasing presence of hidden and bundled ad-/spyware programs in combination with the absence of proper anti-ad/spyware tools are therefore not beneficial for the development of a secure and stable use of the Internet.

Keywords: Spyware, adware, peer-to-peer, privacy.

1. INTRODUCTION

As the Internet becomes more and more indispensable to our society, the issue of personal information is recognised as decisively important when building a secure and efficient social system on the Internet [3]. Also, in an increasingly networked world, where new technologies and infrastructures, from pervasive computing to mobile Internet, are being rapidly introduced into the daily lives of ordinary users, complexity is rising [15]. As a consequence, vulnerabilities in systems are more eminent and greater in number than ever before. At the same time, the business climate on the Internet is tightening; e-commerce companies are struggling against competitors and frauds. A powerful component in any business strategy is user/customer information. In general, the company with the most information about its customers and potential customers is usually the most successful one [19]. With respect to personal customer information, consumers generally want their privacy to be protected, but businesses, on the other hand, need reliable personal information in order to reach consumers with offers [13]. Undoubtedly, these demands must be satisfied to establish sound e-commerce, and a secure and well-functioning use of the Internet. However, these conflicting goals leave the control of user information at great risk, and a consequence may be that the users feel uneasy about sharing any personal information with commercial web sites. Human activity on the Internet will only thrive if the privacy rights of individuals are balanced with the benefits associated with the flow of personal information [13].

The problem of assuring user privacy and security in a computerized setting is not new, it has been a discussion for more than 30 years now [9]. However, there are some new aspects, that need to be highlighted. In this paper, we intend to explore privacy aspects concerning software components that are bundled and installed with file-sharing tools. Since file-sharing tools are used exclusively when connected to the Internet, users constitute a good foundation for online marketing companies to display customised ads and offers for users. The displayed contents of these offers are sometimes based on the retrieval of users' personal information. Usually, this kind of software operation is considered to be an invasion of personal privacy [8]. One of the most simple and clear definitions of privacy was first proposed in 1890 by Warren and Brandeis in their article "The Right to Privacy" [23], where privacy was defined as "the right to be let alone". In general, privacy is the right of individuals to control the collection and use of information about themselves [3]. In an Internet setting, the extraction of the definition by Warren and Brandeis has come to mean that users should be able to decide for themselves, when, how, and to what extent information about them is communicated to others [7]. Previous work has suggested that malicious software, or malware, set to collect and transmit user information and/or to display ads and commercial offers without the consent of users have been found bundled with file-sharing tools [11] [22]. There are two kinds of software programs that perform such actions: adware displays advertisements, and spyware goes further and tracks and reports on users' web browsing, keystrokes or anything else that the author of the software has some interest in knowing. In reality, this means that software can be adware and spyware at the same time. However, not all adware is spyware and most spyware is not easily detected by displaying ads [11].

Ad-/spyware has gained a lot of space and attention lately. According to the Emerging Internet Threats Survey 2003 [6], one in three companies have already detected spyware on their systems, while 60% consider spyware to be a growing and future threat. Also, 70% of the companies say that peer-to-peer (P2P) file-sharing is creating an open door into their organisation. When it comes to adware, the Emerging Internet Threats Survey, states that adware and the use of file-sharing tools in office hours are devious and offensive threats that frequently evade both firewalls and anti-virus defences [6]. In effect, ad-

/spyware creates problems, not only to user privacy, but also to corporate IT-systems and networks.

In this paper, we investigate what kind of privacy-invasive software that come bundled with five popular file-sharing tools. We also look into the Internet traffic that is being generated by these hidden programs. A discussion concerning the occurrence of ad-/spyware and its effects on privacy and security is undertaken. In the end, we present conclusions and findings.

2. PRIVACY-INVASIVE PROGRAMS AND THEIR IMPLICATIONS

One of the major carriers of ad-/spyware programs are P2P file-sharing tools [16] [22]. P2P refers to a technology which enables two or more peers to collaborate in a network of equals [12] [18]. This may be done by using information and communication systems that are not depending on central coordination. Usually, P2P applications include file sharing, grid computing, web services, groupware, and instant messaging [12] [18]. In reality, there is little doubt that P2P networks furnish in spreading ad-/spyware [16]. Besides legal difficulties in controlling the content of P2P networks, another contributing factor is that the user is forced to accept a license agreement in order to use the software, but the contract terms are often formulated in such a way that they are hard for the user to interpret and understand. The effect is that most users do not really know what they have agreed to, and thus really cannot argue their right to privacy.

The occurrence of ad-/spyware programs in file-sharing tools pose a real and growing threat to Internet usage in many aspects, and to other interested parties than only to end users. Some examples argued on this topic are [6] [16] [22]:

- **Consumption of computing capacity**: Ad-/spyware is often designed to be secretly loaded at system start-up, and to run partly hidden in the background. Due to that it is not unusual for users to have many different instances of ad-/spyware running covertly simultaneously, the cumulative effect on the system's processing capacity can be dramatic. Another threat is the occurrence of distributed computing clients, bundled with file-sharing tools, that can sell the users' hard drive space, CPU cycles, and bandwidth to third parties.

- **Consumption of bandwidth**: Just as the cumulative effect of ad-/spyware running in the background can have serious consequences on system performance, the continual data traffic with gathering of new pop-ups and banner ads, and delivery of user information can have an imperative and costly effect on corporate bandwidth.

- **Legal liabilities**: With the new directives[1] concerning the use of file-sharing tools in companies, it is the company rather than a single user who is legally liable for, for instance, the breach of copyright (e.g., if employees share music files with other peers) and the spreading of sensitive information (e.g., if spyware programs transmit corporate intelligence).

- **Security issues**: Ad-/spyware covertly transmits user information back to the advertisement server, implying that since this is done in a covert manner, there is no way to be certain of exactly what information is being transmitted. Even though adware, in its purest form, is a threat to privacy rather than security, some adware applications have begun to act like Trojan horses allowing installation of further software, which may include malware. Security experts use the term "Trojan horse" for software that carries programs, which mask some hidden malicious functionality, but many web users and privacy experts use it to describe any program that piggybacks another. It is claimed that most of the latter are P2P file-sharing software that emerged as ad-supported alternatives in the wake of Napster's decline. In effect, if a computer has been breached by a Trojan horse, it typically cannot be trusted. Also, there is a type of spyware that has nothing to do with adware, the purpose here is to spy on the user and transmit keystrokes, passwords, card numbers, e-mail addresses or anything else of value to the software owner/author. In reflect, most security experts would agree that the existence of ad-/spyware is incompatible with the concept of a secure system.

- **Privacy issues**: The fact that ad-/spyware operates with gathering and transmitting user information secretly in the background, and/or displays ads and commercial offers that the user did not by him-/herself chose to view, makes it highly privacy-invasive.

Most ad-/spyware applications are typically bundled as hidden components of freeware or shareware programs that can be downloaded from the Internet [22]. Usually, ad-/spyware programs run secretly in the background of the users' computers. The reason for this concealing of processes is commonly argued as that it would hardly be acceptable if, e.g., free file-sharing software kept stopping to ask the user if he or she was ready to fetch a new banner or a pop-up window. Therefore, the client/server routine of ad-/spyware is executed in the background. In practice, there would be nothing wrong with ad-/spyware running in the background provided that the users know that it is happening, what data is being transmitted, and that they have agreed to the process as part of the conditions for obtaining the freeware. However, most users are unaware of that they have software on their computers that tracks and reports on their

Internet usage. Even though this may be included in license agreements, users generally have difficulties to understand them [22].

Adware is a category of software that displays commercial messages supported by advertising revenues [20]. The idea is that if a software developer can get revenue from advertisers, the owner can afford to make the software available for free. The developer is paid, and the user gets free, quality software. Usually, the developer provides two versions of the software, one for which the user has to pay a fee in order to receive, and one version that is freeware supported by advertising. In effect, the user can choose between the free software with the slight inconvenience of either pop-up ads or banners, or to pay for software free of advertising. So, users pay to use the software either with their money or with their time. This was the case until marketers noted three separate trends that pushed the development of adware into a different direction. Standard banner ads on the Internet were not delivering as well as expected (1% click-through was considered good) [22]. Targeted Internet advertising performs much better [21]. While office hours are dead-time for traditional advertising (radio, TV, etc.), many analyses showed a surprisingly high degree of personal Internet usage during office hours [21].

The conclusion was that targeted Internet advertising was a whole new opportunity for the marketing of products and services. All that was required was a method for monitoring users' behaviour. Once the adware was monitoring users' Internet usage and sending user details back to the advertiser, banners more suited to the users' preferences and personality was sent to the users in return. The addition of monitoring functionality turned adware into ad-/spyware, and the means to target advertising to interested parties accelerated. In reality, the data collected by ad-/spyware is often sent back to the marketing company, resulting in display of specific advertisements, pop-up ads, and installing toolbars showed when users visit specific web sites.

Spyware is usually designed with the same commercial intent as adware [20]. However, while most adware displays advertisements and commercial offers, spyware is designed with the intent to collect and transmit information about users. The general method is to distribute the users' Internet browsing history [22]. The idea behind this is that if you know what sites someone visits, you begin to get an idea of what that person wants, and may be persuaded to buy [21]. Given the fact that more than 350 million users have downloaded KaZaa and supposedly also installed it on their computers [4], this enables for customised and personalised marketing campaigns to millions and millions of end users. Moreover, information-gathering processes have been implicated in the rising occurrence of unsolicited commercial e-mail messages (so called spam) on the Internet [6].

Besides the monitoring of Internet usage, there is an even greater danger, namely when spyware is set to collect additional and more sensitive personal information such as passwords, account details, private documents, e-mail addresses, credit card numbers, etc.

3. EXPERIMENT DESIGN

Problem Domain

Programs designed with the purpose of locating and defeating ad-/spyware components are available throughout the Internet. Even so, these programs are not very refined. For instance, there is usually no linking between the identified ad-/spyware processes inside the computers and the corresponding servers outside, on the Internet. Also, there is no anti-ad-/spyware program that analyses what data content is being transmitted to other third parties on the Internet. So, even when using existing software, it is difficult do keep track of what is going on inside the computer, and what nodes outside it that obtain user-oriented information. As a consequence, Internet browsing records and/or credit card numbers could easily be distributed without the user's consent or knowledge.

In this light, the overall research problem for this paper was to explore the nature and occurrence of privacy-invasive software included in file-sharing tools used over P2P networks. On an experiment level, the research problem was divided into the following subquestions:

- What ad-/spyware programs can be found in file-sharing tools?
- What is the content and format of network data generated as a result of ad-/spyware programs involved in Internet communication?
- What is the extent of network traffic generated by such programs?

Even though there may be numerous components bundled with the installation of file-sharing tools, it is primarily the programs engaged in Internet communication that are of interest to us. There are two reasons for this. First, without this delimitation, the experiment data would be too comprehensive to grasp. Second, for ad-/spyware programs to leak personal information, they must be involved in communication over the Internet. This is of course particularly interesting from a privacy perspective.

Throughout this paper, we use the word ad-/spyware as a synonym for both adware and spyware. In general, both adware and spyware are namely considered to be privacy-invasive software. Also, since they typically are closely intervened with each other, and more or less perform similar actions it is problematic to separate adware from spyware [22].

Instrumentation and Execution

The experiment sample consists of the five most downloaded file-sharing tools [4]. The tools are, in order, the standard, freeware versions of KaZaa, iMesh, Morpheus, LimeWire and BearShare. Also, to be sure that the experiment results were derived from the installed file-sharing tools, we set up a reference computer, which was identical to the other work stations, i.e., the same configuration, but with no file-sharing tool installed. The experiment was executed in January 2004 as one consecutive session that lasted three days. This time range was chosen, because we wanted to avoid getting excessive data quantities, but at the same time be able to capture reliable results.

The experiment was carried out in a lab environment on PC work stations equally connected to the Internet through a NAT gateway. We used OpenBSD's packet filter to deny any inbound network requests, which allowed us to protect the work stations from external threats. The packet filter also helped in reducing the network traffic and in doing so, resulting in less data to analyse. By not downloading or sharing any content in the file-sharing tools we further reduced the amount of network data generated. All incoming and outgoing network traffic of the local computer's network interface were dumped into a file using Winpcap.

Hardware were equivalent for all work stations, which also contained byte-identical installations of both the operating system Microsoft Windows 2000 and program applications[2]. In order to reflect work stations in use, they were all set to browse the Internet according to a predefined schedule containing the 100 most visited web sites in the world [1]. This was done through an automatic surf program. Also, ten identical searches (e.g., "lord of the ring", "star wars", and "britney") were carried out in each of the file-sharing tools, but no files were downloaded. In the end of the experiment, several anti-ad-/spyware programs[3] were used to locate any known ad-/spyware programs previously installed.

Binding network communication to programs is a key feature in the experiment. For allowing continuous monitoring and logging of processes and their use of sockets, we developed a program in C++, which was based on Openport. We chose not to use any Win32 firewalls claiming to support outbound filtering on application level for two reasons. First, they fail in allowing real outbound filtering per application, and there are a number of programs capable of penetrating these fake protections [14] [17]. Second, we have no detailed knowledge in the internal workings of such firewalls and therefore cannot foresee what to expect from them. Finally, it should be emphasised that there exist ways for a malicious program to send network data undetected by the monitoring application, due to the architecture of Windows.

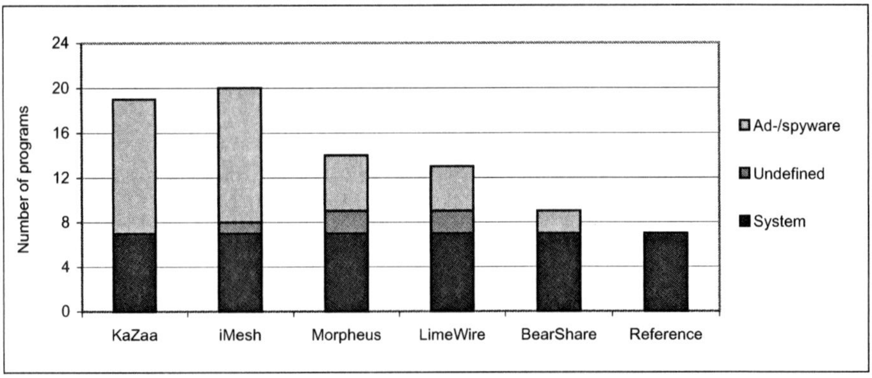

Figure 1. Identified programs in the experiment sample.

Data Analysis

After having performed the experiment, we compiled the data results and set to identify all programs that were bundled with each file-sharing tool. This data was provided by our own process-to-network mapping program in cooperation with the selected anti-ad-/spyware programs. We then isolated the operating system related programs found on the reference work station, since they were considered harmless. Next, we reduced all benign programs handling file-exchange tasks. Remaining were a set of programs that were not related to either the operating system or file-exchange tasks. Further, by using the results from the anti-ad-/spyware tools, we divided the set of programs into two subsets, namely known ad-/spyware programs and unknown programs. The nature of these unknown programs was analysed based on their corresponding network traffic. Also, in some cases we needed additional information and thus turned to Internet resources. Based on this analysis, the remaining ad-/spyware programs were located. In the final step, we divided the retrieved set of ad-/spyware programs into two subsets, namely those involved in Internet communication and those that were not. This analysis was founded on the data from our process-to-network mapping program. In effect, the results from the program analysis lead to a classification of programs as either ad-/spyware programs, system programs or unknown programs.

All data analysis was done in a Unix environment. The data was analysed and filtered using standard Unix programs such as sed, awk, sort, uniq and grep. Much of the analysis was automated using shell scripts and where this could not be done small programs in C were created. To analyse and filter network data, the program Ethereal was used.

In addition, we wanted to see if the corresponding servers were known ad-/spyware servers. Therefore, an effort to map the server names that were involved in Internet communication with a blacklist specifying known ad-/spyware servers [10] was also undertaken.

4. EXPERIMENT RESULTS AND ANALYSIS

Ad-/Spyware Programs in File-Sharing Tools

According to the results, several programs were located for each file-sharing tool (see Figure 1.). Of these programs, we identified 12 ad-/spyware programs for iMesh and KaZaa respectively. Interestingly, these two file-sharing tools were among the two most popular ones [4]. The rates for the other file-sharing tools were five for Morpheus, four for LimeWire and two for BearShare. Also, iMesh, Morpheus and LimeWire contained programs that we were unable to define. However, these programs were all involved in Internet communication.

We discovered that all of the file-sharing tools contained ad-/spyware programs that communicated with the Internet. KaZaa and iMesh included a relatively high amount of such programs. Even so, the anti-ad-/spyware tools defined several other ad-/spyware programs also installed on the computers. Although this was the case, these programs did not communicate with servers on the Internet during the experiment session.

In Table 1., a detailed list of the retrieved ad-/spyware components can be found. As can be seen, the ad-/spyware components were divided into "Adware" respectively "Spyware" based on their actions. Also, we included a category entitled "Download" because some of the ad-/spyware programs included functionality that allowed further software and/or updates to be downloaded and installed on the computers. In addition, programs involved in Internet communication are specified in the category called "Internet". In the column entitled "Host", the five file-sharing tools utilised as carriers of ad-/spyware are listed[4]. In the cases where the empirical results could confirm the recognised view shared by anti-ad-/spyware tools and Internet resources, the x-markers in the table are declared with bolded capital letters.

One reason to why we could not confirm that every ad-/spyware program was involved in Internet communication was that so called Browser Helper Objects (BHO) were installed in Internet Explorer. Malicious BHOs infiltrate the web browser with the intent to access all data generated by Internet Explorer in order to spy on the user and transmit user behaviour to third parties [20]. Such BHOs typically gain the same privileges as its host (i.e., Internet Explorer), which endorse them to penetrate personal firewalls. This means that any possible ad-/spyware traffic distributed via BHOs is highly problematic to detect since it may very well be ordinary browser traffic. In Table 1., we also included two programs, New.Net and FavoriteMan, even though they were

Table 1. Identified ad-/spyware programs.

Name	*Host*	*Adware*	*Spyware*	*Download*	*Internet*
BroadcastPC	M	x	x	x	**X**
KeenValue	K	x	x	**X**	**X**
Morpehus	M	**X**	x	**X**	**X**
BargainBuddy	I, K	x	x	x	
TopMoxie	L, M	x	x	x	
Cydoor	I, K	x	x		**X**
Gator	I, K	**X**	x		**X**
SaveNow	B	**X**	**X**		**X**
BonziBuddy	L	x	x		
Web3000	I	x	x		
ShopAtHomeSelect	I		**X**	**X**	**X**
WebHancer	K		x	x	
BrilliantDigital	K	x		**X**	**X**
MoneyMaker	L, M	**X**		**X**	**X**
Claria	I, K	x			**X**
iMesh	I	x			**X**
WeatherCast	B	x			**X**
CasinoOnNet	L	x			
MyBar	I, K, M	x			
New.Net	I			**X**	**X**
FavoriteMan	I			x	

classified as neither adware nor spyware. However, they allowed for installation of further software, which may be malicious.

The Extent of Network Traffic

The results showed that a significant amount of network traffic was generated, although there was no exchange of files between the file-sharing tools and other peers on the Internet (see Figure 2.). In that light, the amount of network traffic generated in this experiment can be seen as a minimum rate to be expected when running file-sharing tools. Notably, installing Morpheus and LimeWire resulted in a relatively high traffic quote, both when it came to incoming as well as outgoing traffic. On the contrary, iMesh, who also had the largest quantity of bundled programs, represented the least amount of network traffic.

In Figure 2., we included compilations of network traffic for both the installation process and the runtime part per file-sharing tool. In the cases of Morpheus, LimeWire and BearShare, a considerable amount of network activity was generated after the installation. For KaZaa, a significant quantity of network traffic was caused during the installation. In comparison, iMesh

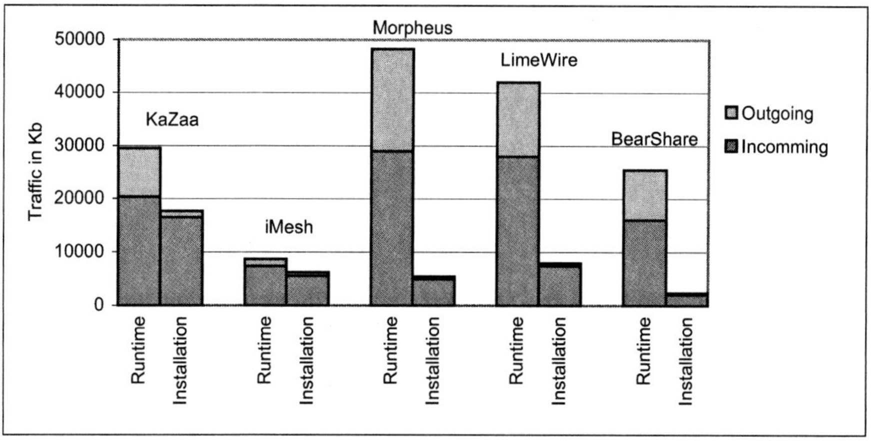

Figure 2. Network data traffic.

produced a notably limited size of network traffic, both during and after installation.

Furthermore, the results suggested a diversity in Internet communication. This is shown in that programs in the file-sharing tools communicated with several different servers on the Internet. Although Morpehus did not contain a particularly great number of bundled programs, it generated notably much network traffic. In reflection, Morpheus communicated with the largest amount of Internet servers, whereas the rates for the other file-sharing tools were in a relatively low accordance with each other. In addition, the results substantiated that most of the invoked servers had domain names. Overall, each of the file-sharing tools contained programs that communicated with known ad-/spyware servers from the specified blacklist [10].

The Contents of Network Traffic

The outgoing network data was in many cases problematic to analyse and understand. In most cases the data was not readable, meaning that it was either encrypted or in a format not graspable. This is also an explanation to why we could confirm only two spyware programs (see Table 1). Although most traffic data was not in clear text, we were able to extract and interpret some of the contents. We discovered that sensitive data such as information about the user (e.g., user name), geographical details (e.g., zip code, region and country) and Internet browsing history records were sent from identified ad-/spyware components to several servers on the Internet. Also, there were other ty of information that were transmitted, for example, machine ID, details about program versions, operating system, etc.

According to the results, one spyware program (ShopAtHomeSelect) was found in the iMesh file-sharing tool. In the experiment, that program transmitted traffic measurement reports and Internet browsing history records to invoked servers on the Internet. Also, in BearShare, one spyware program (SaveNow) transmitted data such as Internet history scores and user-specific information.

The experiment results also reveal one of the methods for ad-/spyware programs to transmit user and/or work station data. In the BearShare tool, the information that was fed into the file-sharing software by the user was redistributed within the tool to one or numerous ad-/spyware programs (SaveNow and WeatherCast) that transmitted the information to servers called upon. This method makes it difficult to map various program components to the actual file-sharing activity. Also, it undermines the ability to control what software objects are useful and legitimate in relation to the redundant or privacy-invasive programs that clog down the computers, systems and networks.

The analysis of the contents of the incoming network traffic was more problematic to conduct than in the case of outgoing traffic. Foremost, because the data quantity was both comprehensive and widespread. Since our focus was on privacy-invasive software, the outgoing traffic content was the most interesting so the efforts were mainly put into that. This, in combination, with vast quantities of incoming network data made it difficult to confirm adware recognised by the anti-ad-/spyware tools and Internet resources. Also, the same discussion concerning the occurrence of BHOs would apply for the unconfirmed adware. However, in the retrieved incoming data, a few interesting results were found.

The retrieved adware programs performed activities such as displaying commercial ads, causing browser banners and pop-ups. In particular, Morpheus and LimeWire proved to contain adware programs that generated much incoming data traffic. In LimeWire, results showed that lists of Internet sites and new programs were retrieved from the Internet by the adware MoneyMaker. In Morpehus, the P2P program itself downloaded and displayed ads and banners.

5. DISCUSSION

With the occurrence of ad-/spyware technology in file-sharing tools, the monitoring of Internet usage has become a common feature. Today, most ad-/spyware programs gather and transmit data such as Internet browsing history records to third parties. That type of information can be correlated to a user and thus employed for marketing purposes.

The experiment has shown that all of the investigated file-sharing tools contained ad-/spyware programs. The ad-/spyware programs that operated inside the computers had an open connection to several Internet servers during the entire experimental session. We know that content-sensitive information was sent, but we may only guess the full extent of information harvesting, because most packets were not sent in clear text. Even though we saw no example of highly sensitive personal information, such as passwords and key strokes, were transmitted by the ad/spyware programs in the experiment, we cannot be sure that these activities were not happening. Spyware may collect and transmit genuinely sensitive information about users such as, e.g., account details, private documents, e-mail addresses, and credit card numbers. The information is secretly sent back to numerous servers owned by companies that make a profit on these activities. Although it is problematic to elaborate on the business ethics of these companies, the occurrence of ad-/spyware programs are reasons enough to question this behaviour. In addition, ad-/spyware programs are responsible for all kinds of unwanted actions. Besides invasion of privacy, they can make the system unstable, degrade system performance, create scores of copies of itself to make removal difficult, and act as security holes in the system.

The actions performed by ad-/spyware programs are approaching the operations of a virus. Since users install them on voluntary basis, the distribution part is taken care of by the file-sharing tools. This makes ad-/spyware programs function like a slowly moving virus without the distribution mechanisms usually otherwise included. The general method for a virus is to infect as many nodes as possible on the network in the shortest amount of time, so it can cause as much damage as conceivable before it gets caught by the anti-virus companies. Ad-/spyware, on the other hand, may operate in the background in such a relatively low speed that it is difficult to detect. Therefore, the consequences may be just as dire as with a regular virus. In addition, the purpose of ad-/spyware may not be to destroy or delete data on the work stations, but to gather and transmit veritably sensitive user information. An additional complicating factor is that anti-virus companies do not usually define ad-/spyware as virus, since it is not designed to cause destruction. Overall, the nature of ad-/spyware substantiates the notion that malicious actions launched on computers and networks get more and more available, diversified and intelligent, rendering in that security is extensively problematic to uphold.

Ad-/spyware enables for the spreading of e-mail addresses that may result in the receiving of spam. Due to the construction of ad-/spyware, it may collect information that concerns other parties than only the work station user. For example, information such as telephone numbers and e-mail addresses to business contacts and friends stored on the desktop can be gathered and distributed by ad-/spyware. In the context that ad-/spyware usually is designed with the purpose of conveying commercial information to as many users as possible, not only the local user may be exposed to negative consequences of ad-/spyware. In other words, the business contacts and friends may be the subjects of ad-/spyware effects such as, e.g., receiving unsolicited commercial e-mail messages. This means that even though my computer may be secure, a breached computer owned by a network neighbour can cause me harm. So, the security of a neighbour very much becomes my own concern.

Besides security issues, ad-/spyware creates intrusion to privacy. An inconvenience commonly argued is that ad-/spyware programs display commercial messages based on the retrieval of personal information fetched without the explicit consent of the users. Even though the offers of these advertising campaigns may be in the interest of some users, there is a fine line between what users in general regard as useful information and what is an intrusion to personal privacy. One thought is that, the more personalised the offers get, the more likely users are to regard them as privacy invaders. If so, what happens when users are presented with advertisements in such an extent that they hardly are able to distinguish the possibly serious offers from all the offers. If users ignore marketing messages, there is evidently a great risk for the success of customer-based e-commerce.

A second privacy concern is the spreading of content that the ad-/spyware distributor did not intend for. One example of this would be a malicious actor that gained control of ad-/spyware servers, and broadcasted offensive unsolicited messages (e.g., adult material, political messages or smearing campaigns, etc.) to a great number of users. Although users may consider regular commercial ads to be harmless, most people react negatively upon frequently receiving repulsive pictures and texts. This suffices for that the ad-/spyware providers need to take their own security with great seriousness. If they lose control of their servers, the damage may be devastating. This could be even more devastating if the ad-/spyware program updates on the company servers were replaced with malicious software. In effect, real and destructive malware (e.g., viruses, Trojans, etc.) could be spread to vast groups of ad-/spyware hosts.

6. CONCLUSIONS

The experiment has shown that all of the investigated file-sharing tools contained ad-/spyware programs. The ad-/spyware programs operating inside the computers had an open connection where the information was secretly sent back to numerous servers owned by companies that make a profit on these activities. Measurements suggested that the carriers of ad-/spyware, file-sharing tools, generated a significant amount of network traffic, even when not exchanging files. The presence of ad-/spyware programs and the network traffic that they generate contribute in over consumption of system and network capacity.

Ad-/spyware is acting like a slowly moving virus, installed on a voluntary basis, with hidden properties problematic to detect and remove. The payload of ad-/spyware may not be to destroy or delete data on the work stations, but to gather and transmit veritably sensitive user information. The distribution part is taken care of by the file-sharing tools with an additional complicating factor; anti-virus companies do not usually define ad-/spyware as virus, since it is not designed to cause destruction.

The nature of ad-/spyware may lead to that not only host users are affected. Ad-/spyware may gather and distribute the details of business contacts and friends resulting in negative consequences to other parties than the infected desktop owner. This means that even though my computer may be secure, a breached computer owned by a network neighbour can cause me harm. So, the security of a neighbour very much becomes my own concern.

Furthermore, the occurrence of ad-/spyware can render in that privacy-invasive messages may be distributed and displayed to large amounts of users. Exposure to messages not chosen by the user, or collection and transmission of user information are two key privacy concerns. In this way, users right to control what, how and when information about themselves is communicated to other parties is almost non-existing. In conclusion, the nature of ad-/spyware programs ignore users' right to be let alone. The increasing presence of hidden and bundled ad-/spyware programs in combination with the abscence of proper anti-ad/spyware tools are therefore not beneficial for the development of a secure and stable use of the Internet.

Notes

1. Examples on legal directives are the "Directive on Privacy and Electronic Communications'" [5] of the European Union, and the "Spyware Control and Privacy Protection Act" [2] of the Senate of California, U.S.
2. These configuration properties were enabled through a self-developed disc cloning system based on standard FreeBSD components.
3. For a detailed list of the programs used, see http://www.ipd.bth.se/aja/PISiFST_Ref.pdf.
4. K is for KaZaa, I for iMesh, M for Morpheus, L for LimeWire and B is for BearShare.

References

[1] Alexa Web Search., http://www.alexa.com/site/ds/top_sites?ts_mode=global&lang=none, 2004-04-27.

[2] California Senate Assembly Bill 1386, United States of America, 2003., http://info.sen.ca.gov/pub/bill/asm/ab_1351-1400/ab_1386_bill_20030904_chaptered.html, 2004-04-27.

[3] M. Caloyannides, "Privacy vs. Information Technology", in *IEEE Security & Privacy*, Vol. 1, No. 1, pp. 100-103, 2003.

[4] C|Net Download.com., http://www.download.com/, 2004-04-27.

[5] Directive 2002/58/EC of the European Parliament and of the Council of 12 July 2002 concerning the processing of personal data and the protection of privacy in the electronic

communications sector (Directive on Privacy and Electronic Communications), 2002., http://europa.eu.int/comm/internal_market/privacy/law_en.htm, 2004-04-27.

[6] Emerging Internet Threats Survey 2003, commissioned by Websense International Ltd., February, 2003., http://www.websense.com/company/news/research/Emerging_Threats _2003_EMEA-de.pdf, 2004-04-27.

[7] S. Fischer-Hübner, "Privacy in the Global Information Society", in *IT-Security and Privacy - Design and Use of Privacy-Enhancing Security Mechanisms*, Lecture Notes in Computer Science LNCS 1958, Springer-Verlag, Berlin Germany, 2000.

[8] S. Garfinkel, *"Database Nation: The Death of Privacy in the 21st Century"*, O'Reilly & Associates Inc., Sebastopol CA, 2001.

[9] E. Grenier, "Computers and Privacy: A Proposal for Self-Regulation", in *Proceedings of the First ACM Symposium on Problems in the Optimization of Data Communications Systems*, ACM Press, New York NY, 1969.

[10] Gorilla Design Studio: The Hosts Files., http://www.accs-net.com/hosts/, 2004-04-27.

[11] M. McCardle, "How Spyware Fits into Defence in Depth", *SANS Reading Room*, SANS Institute, 2003., http://www.sans.org/rr/papers/index.php?id=905, 2004-04-27.

[12] A. Oram, *"Peer-To-Peer: Harnessing the Benefits of a Disruptive Technology"*, O'Reilly & Associates Inc., Sebastopol CA, 2001.

[13] T. Otsuka and A. Onozawa, "Personal Information Market: Toward a Secure and Efficient Trade of Privacy", in *Proceedings of the First International Conference on Human Society and the Internet*, Lecture Notes in Computer Science LNCS 2105, Springer-Verlag, Berlin Germany, 2001.

[14] Outbound., http://www.hackbusters.net/ob.html, 2004-04-27.

[15] L. Palen and P. Dourish, "Unpacking Privacy for a Networked World", in *Proceedings of the ACM Conference on Human Factors in Computing Systems*, ACM Press, New York NY, 2003.

[16] B. Robertsson, "Five Major Categories of Spyware", in *Consumer WebWatch*, October 21, USA, 2002., http://www.consumerwebwatch.org/news/articles/spyware_categories.htm, 2004-04-27.

[17] Robin Keir's FireHole., http://keir.net/firehole.html, 2004-04-27.

[18] D. Schoder and K. Fischbach, "Peer-to-Peer (P2P) Computing", in *Proceedings of the 36th IEEE Hawaii International Conference on System Sciences*, IEEE Computer Society Press, Los Alamitos CA, 2003.

[19] C. Shapiro and H. Varian, *"Information Rules: New Rules for the New Economy"*, HBS Press, Boston MA, 1999.

[20] E. Skoudis, *"Malware - Fighting Malicious Code"*, Prentice Hall PTR, Upper Saddle River NJ, 2004.

[21] J. Sterne and A. Priore, *"E-Mail Marketing - Using E-Mail to Reach Your Target Audience and Build Customer Relationships"*, John Wiley & Sons Inc., New York NY, 2000.

[22] K. Townsend, "Spyware, Adware, and Peer-to-Peer Networks: The Hidden Threat to Corporate Security" (technical white paper), PestPatrol, 2003., http://www.pestpatrol.com/Whitepapers/CorporateSecurity0403.asp, 2004-04-27.

[23] S.D. Warren and L.D. Brandeis, "The Right to Privacy", in *Harvard Law Review*, No. 5, pp. 193-220, 1890-91.

INFUSING PRIVACY NORMS IN DRM

Incentives and perspectives from law

Alex Cameron

LL.M. (Law and Technology) Candidate, University of Ottawa, Canada

Abstract: This paper outlines some basic characteristics of digital rights management (DRM) systems, as well as the ways that DRM systems can threaten user privacy. The author asserts that consent-based privacy laws are alone insufficient to address privacy threats posed by DRM. The author suggests that privacy norms can be infused in DRM design and implementation and that the interests of end-users, DRM engineers and DRM users support striving toward that goal.

Key words: Digital rights management, copyright, privacy, law, legal aspects.

> It is a commonplace that the characteristic virtue of Englishmen is their power of sustained practical activity, and their characteristic vice a reluctance to test the quality of that activity by reference to principles. [...] Most generations, it might be said, walk in a path which they neither make nor discover, but accept; the main thing is that they should march. The blinkers worn by Englishmen enable them to trot all the more steadily along the beaten road, without being disturbed by curiosity as to their destination.
>
> R.H. Tawney, 1921[1]

It seems that engineers and lawyers do not talk to one another enough these days. Driven by the copyright industries and with the blinkers of those industries in place, digital rights management technology is rapidly marching toward copyright owners' utopia of near-perfect control over copyright works. At the same time, driven by the concerns of citizens around the world, lawmakers in many countries are marching toward increased protection of privacy. Soon, these two marches will certainly collide.[2-4]

This paper explores the collision course between DRM and user privacy. Part 1 provides a brief overview of DRM technology and some incentives for its widespread implementation. Part 2 sketches some of varied ways that DRM systems can threaten user privacy. Part 3 asserts that consent-based privacy laws are alone insufficient to address the privacy threats posed by DRM. Finally, Part 4 argues that privacy norms can be infused in DRM design and implementation and that the interests of end-users, DRM engineers and DRM users support striving toward that goal.

1. FRAMEWORK FOR THINKING ABOUT DRM

An open digital networked environment presents a number of challenges for creators and distributors of literary, musical and other works. Although such works are typically protected under existing copyright laws, technology has dramatically increased the difficulty of enforcing those copyrights. Once a work is published, it can usually be copied perfectly and distributed widely without the permission of the owner and often in violation of their legal rights. The most well-known examples of this kind of problem are P2P file-sharing systems.

In response to these new challenges, owners of copyright works have started using DRM systems to level the playing field and to exploit the distribution opportunities that the networked environment offers them. While a detailed review of DRM technologies is unnecessary for the purposes of this paper, it is important to have a general understanding of how DRM works and what factors are motivating its uptake.[i]

1.1 Basic DRM functionality

DRM systems typically travel with copyright works and function like electronic security guards to monitor and control access and use of those works wherever they go. DRM is a form of persistent protection that is tied to works. The following definition of DRM used at a recent IASTED conference captures most of the key concepts:

> [DRM] means the chain of hardware and software services and technologies governing the authorized use of digital content and management of any consequences of that use throughout the entire life cycle of the content. DRM is an access and copy control system for

[i] There are a number of published articles which conduct detailed reviews of DRM technology.[5-7]

> digital content, such that the DRM securely conveys and enforces complex usage rights rather than simple low-level access/copy controls. [...] DRM technologies include a range of functions to support the management of intellectual property for digital resources, such as expression of rights offers and agreements, description, identification, trading, protection, monitoring and tracking of digital content.[8]

In relation to the works that they protect, DRM systems are usually categorized by whether they function to control access, use, or both. Many perform both functions and many utilize a number of different technologies in doing so.[4-7]

DRM systems can also be used to automatically *enforce* legal or contractual rights in relation to works. With DRM, copyright owners are no longer required to enforce their copyrights using the jurisdiction-limited, expensive and time-consuming legal system – by way of licenses with each user, they can efficiently replace the rules of copyright law with their own privately-written and -enforced rules.[9] For example, if a particular user is permitted (for a fee) to listen to a DRM-protected song three times over a 12 hour period but instead tries to listen once and copy part of it, then the DRM system might, among other things, automatically delete the work from the user's computer (assuming the license with the user allowed for that).

Finally, as suggested by the definition above, DRM systems often contain surveillance and reporting functionality which allow copyright owners to track access and use of their works or to single out and profile the activities of particular users. These DRM functions directly implicate user privacy and will be discussed further in Part 2 of this paper.

1.2 Factors motivating DRM

In the basic ways described above, DRM systems promise copyright owners inexpensive, automated and near-perfect control over works of all kinds. If a user does not agree to the owner's rules (which will almost always include payment of a fee), then the user will not be permitted to access or make use of a work. Put another way, DRM allows copyright owners to restrict and in many cases foreclose the possibility of copyright infringement from ever happening.

The copyright industries tell us that their protective technologies are a response to widespread copyright infringement. That is the premise upon which they have lobbied governments to implement legal protections for DRM technology. It is also the premise upon which, for example, the United States passed such legal protections in the controversial *Digital Millennium Copyright Act*.[10] In very general terms, the *DMCA* makes it illegal to circumvent DRM systems or to develop technologies which circumvent DRM. There is no question that DRM is designed to protect against copyright infringement. However, the real promise of DRM and likely the single biggest incentive for its adoption goes far beyond responding to new forms of copyright infringement.

Early in the history of DRM development, Barlow eloquently expressed the idea that DRM would transform "a market where wine is sold in bottles from which everyone may drink infinitely—as is the case with books—into a market where all wine is sold by the sip. Forever."[11] His vision is as true today as it was in 1998. The copyright industries are keenly interested in DRM because it allows them to exploit every conceivable use of a work,[ii] including "paid downloads, subscriptions, pay-per-view and pay-per-listen, usage metering, peer-to-peer, superdistribution, and selling rights instead of the actual content."[12] In a world where DRM systems are pervasive, copyright owners' imagination is the only limit to their ability to exploit content; Stross predicts: "You might be able to read a library book... but your computer will be counting the words you read and monitoring your pulse so that it can bill you for the excitement it has delivered."[13]

DRM promises copyright owners the ability to accomplish through private agreements with users what they cannot accomplish under copyright law.[iii] Even the content that can be exploited using DRM need not be content to which any legal rights attach. DRM can be used to regulate the flow and use of virtually any type of information. To the extent DRM systems can deliver on these promises, they are poised to become the ubiquitous regulators of our ability to access and use copyright works and many other types of information.

2. DRM IMPLICATES PRIVACY RIGHTS

Although there is a growing body of legal and technical literature dealing with the issue, the privacy implications of DRM have not received the careful attention they deserve in light of the potential for a pervasive uptake of DRM. In fact, DRM systems pose a significant threat to user privacy because the fundamental premise of DRM is one of user identification and

[ii] DRM may also allow users to purchase only what they really want (*e.g.* one song) rather than a larger package (*e.g.* a whole album). DRM also allows copyright owners to benefit from profiling users as described in Part 2.

[iii] For example, DRM can allow for an indefinite term of protection. This issue places DRM in direct conflict with copyright concepts of fair use and public domain.[14]

authentication. In other words, the principle job of a DRM system is to regulate who has permission to access and use a work.

By its very nature, DRM functionality requires users to disclose personal information to content providers.[4,15] This information might include their name, email address, age, sex, mailing address, and credit card information. A DRM system would also normally require a user to designate a particular computer from which they will access and use the works; licenses are typically not transferable across different machines. User information must then be tied to a user profile in the DRM system which manages the rights that the user has in relation to various works. Given that DRM systems collect personal information about users in these ways virtually by necessity, there are at least three ways that DRM systems can implicate user privacy.

First, as an integral part of rights management and enforcement functions, many DRM systems will track and report on user activities – owners can use DRM systems "...[to] stay in closer contact with their customers."[16] For example, each time a user requests access or use of a work, the request might be granted only after the identity and request of the user (or device) are verified against the user information database in the DRM system. At these periodic points of interaction between the user and the owner (or distributor), the system may automatically create a record of the interactions. Going one step further, the DRM system might surreptitiously monitor the work or user and report back to the owner regardless of whether or not the user does anything with the rights they have purchased. For example, a DRM system might periodically report back to the owner that the user has not done anything with a purchased work.

Tracking and recording DRM-gathered user information has a deep and broad impact on user privacy. Like other surveillance technologies, monitoring and recording user activities using DRM invades privacy because it interferes with intellectual freedom. Even when a user might not mind others knowing that they accessed or read certain content (which will usually be a very significant privacy concern), the user might not want others to know that they had to read it 20 times, that they highlighted parts of it, that they wrote notes in the margin, that they copied part of it, that they forwarded certain excerpts to their friends with comments, or that all of that cost them a bundle. For many users, knowledge that these or similar kinds of information would be gathered about them would naturally affect the types of content they choose to access and use, as well as how they go about it.[iv] Cohen is particularly troubled by this invasion and argues that intellectual exploration is "one of the most personal and private of activities" and that in

[iv] The important effects of surveillance on the behavior of individuals have been discussed at greater length in a number of articles.[2,3,17]

the invasion, DRM will "create records of behavior within private spaces, spaces within which one might reasonably expect that one's behavior is not subject to observation."[2]

Closely related to its monitoring and reporting capabilities, DRM poses a second threat to privacy because of its capability to profile users. Either by using user information directly or by exporting user information to another system, DRM systems have the potential to create very detailed profiles about users' reading, listening, and watching activities and to tie that information to other information about them.[15,18]

Beyond the *mere potential* for monitoring, recording and profiling, users should have every reason to expect that content owners will exploit those capabilities in DRM. At least in the case of larger commercial copyright owners, owners have a "compelling interest to monitor how purchased works are being used."[18] At a high level, it makes perfect sense that profiling will occur because DRM is motivated by a desire to exploit every conceivable use of a work. With more data about discrete uses served up by DRM, copyright owners and others will simply have more information to feed into and better develop consumer profiling systems already in general use. Detailed and previously unavailable information about how users behave will have significant independent economic value for owners and others. In addition to processing user information for marketing or other purposes, DRM might allow owners to engage in sophisticated user-specific price discrimination.[15,19]

The third privacy threat posed by DRM is perhaps the least obvious and most novel. To the extent that DRM involves controls over our ability to use works, Cohen argues that DRM has significant privacy implications:

> Technologies that force changes in user behavior narrow the zone of freedom traditionally enjoyed for activities in private spaces and activities relating to intellectual consumption. In doing so, they decrease the level of autonomy that users enjoy with respect to the terms of use and enjoyment of intellectual goods.[2]

As Cohen acknowledges, this threat of control requires us to rethink "the nature of privacy and what counts, or ought to count, as privacy invasion in the age of networked digital technologies."[2] However, as DRM continues its ubiquitous march, this kind of "rethinking" about the nature of privacy may be necessary in order to ensure that we have spaces left within which to experience a right of privacy.

3. CONSENT-BASED PRIVACY LAWS AND DRM

Consent is the cornerstone of many if not most privacy regimes around the world.[20-23] Many privacy laws and guidelines include provisions which require organizations to, for example, limit their collection of personal information to information that is necessary for identified purposes.[21,24] In those kinds of provisions, the law presumes that individuals would not consent to information collected for unidentified purposes or beyond what is necessary. Other provisions require organizations to obtain individuals' express consent before they process personal information. Where adequate user consent is obtained, it will usually be a sufficient justification for virtually any processing of personal information.

Thus, privacy regulation is largely premised upon the scope, nature and efficacy of the right of consent provided to individuals – the right to decide whether to consent to the collection and processing of their personal information. It is one of the key rights granted to individuals and it is also one of the key ways that organizations justify their processing of personal information. Consent is a big part of where privacy battles will be won or lost. These features of consent-based privacy laws are important because digital networked environments generally, and DRM systems in particular, cast serious doubt on the efficacy of consent as enabling meaningful privacy regulation.

DRM systems will usually require individuals to consent to some processing of personal information, usually by way of a clickwrap license agreement which incorporates a privacy clause. However, individuals often do not read these agreements which describe what they are consenting to, or even if they do read them, they do not or cannot understand the terms.[v] A law professor, masters' student and law student recently studied several DRM-based content delivery services and came to the following conclusion:

> The ways that information is collected and processed during use of the services examined is almost impenetrably complex. It is difficult to determine exactly what data a service collects, and merely discovering that separate monitoring entities sit behind the services requires a careful reading of the services' privacy policies.[18]

It is also important to note that when content is licensed using DRM, on a case-by-case basis users do not have any say about the owners' privacy terms. The choice typically presented to consumers in a standard form

[v] This problem has several facets. Privacy policies may sometimes be too general or they may be too detailed. There are also special considerations regarding consent in the electronic environment.[25]

clickwrap license is "I agree" or "Cancel". There is no room for negotiation – no consent to the owner's privacy terms means no access to content. If individuals' privacy interests outweigh their desire to access DRM-protected content, then the market might help drive privacy-friendly DRM. On the other hand, to the extent that users agree *en masse* to owners' privacy terms (because they want access to DRM-protected content), DRM has the potential to rewrite privacy law in owners' terms in the same way it stands to rewrite copyright law. Privacy rights would then be dissolved into contract.

Some privacy regimes include provisions which may help address some of the problems posed by DRM systems. For example, some laws have provisions which restrict the ability of data collectors to make user consent a condition of providing wares or services.[21,22] Other privacy rules require a high threshold for obtaining valid consent; for example, the *Directive on data processing* requires "unambiguous"[20] consent and the *Directive on electronic commerce* mandates that certain prescribed information must be conveyed "clearly, comprehensively and unambiguously" to electronic commerce consumers.[26] In the United Kingdom[22] and Canada,[21] the nature of the consent required for processing data is also tied in part to the nature of the information at issue – the more sensitive the information, the more explicit the consent must be.

If respected, these kinds of provisions will help give meaning and effect to the right of consent. Yet, short of more invasive and paternalistic privacy regulation (which can have ramifications of its own as described in Part 4), the law is limited in its ability to remedy the problems posed by DRM so long as it is jurisdiction-limited, difficult to enforce and divorced from the design and implementation of the very technology that threatens it.

4. A ROLE FOR PRIVACY NORMS IN DRM

While using technology to address legal problems rooted in technology is not a novel concept,[27] the following sub-sections attempt to go modestly further. The first briefly discusses existing proposals for achieving privacy-regarding DRM. The second sub-section sketches some of the diverse justifications for why it is in the interests of end-users, DRM engineers and DRM users to strive toward that goal.

4.1 Infusing privacy norms in DRM

With varying degrees of specificity, a number of authors in both law and engineering have suggested ways that privacy norms might be infused into DRM design and implementation. These range from merely raising the privacy question during design[28] to detailed descriptions of how to design DRM to act as "Privacy Rights Management" systems.[29]

Drawing on inter-disciplinary research into technology design, Cohen advocates for a "value-centered" design process for DRM in which privacy would form part of the bundle of values driving DRM design.[2] Going one step further, Cohen argues that privacy law ought to help ensure that privacy is addressed in the process of setting DRM standards, a process which is currently underway. Perhaps as some indication of the soundness of Cohen's suggestion, but on the other side of the coin, it should be noted that a mandate of the Recording Industry Association of America is to "ensure that the protection of musical property rights is built into the relevant standards rather than added as an after-thought."[30] Privacy laws already put forth a number of privacy values but there is limited evidence of those being reflected in DRM systems to date. What is clearly needed for the value-centered approach to be effective is for there to be a meaningful voice for privacy values at the standards-setting table.

Related to the "value-centered" design approach is the idea that privacy can be engineered into DRM through the consideration of privacy principles in the design process. Feigenbaum *et al.* suggest one such approach based on the OECD Guidelines; for example, they suggest that "[a] DRM system should provide easy pseudonymization that can be used to key databases."[31]

The Information and Privacy Commissioner of Ontario published a practical step-by-step guide to injecting privacy into DRM.[32] Aimed at DRM system developers and those who use DRM systems, this guide suggests implementing a system architecture (and code) which respects privacy rules, including "controls around the collection of personal information, linkability, access, use and accountability." One of the interesting ideas mentioned in this guide and developed much further in other technical literature,[29] is the idea that DRM systems can be adapted to protect personal information in the same way that they protect copyright works. These *Privacy Rights Management* systems could offer individuals the same type of monitoring, access and use controls regarding their personal information that DRM systems offer to copyright owners. Using the language of DRM to draw a parallel, under a privacy rights management system individuals are the "owners" and their personal information is the "content".

Notably absent from a number of the proposals described above, however, is a description of the means by which to address the consent-based issues described in Part 3 of this paper. Indeed, one of the proposals identified consent (or what the authors termed "choice") as "one of the most difficult challenges."[31] One of the most interesting approaches to consent is an option-based approach; the following model was developed by Forrester Research:

> At Level 1, visitors choose anonymity, deliberately forgoing the additional benefits offered by personalization and premium content. Retailers build trust by promising not to collect data or use cookies.
>
> With the addition of convenient, targeted content or additional site access, consumers enter Level 2, a one-way communication relationship whereby merchants promise not to initiate contact with the shopper or disseminate personal information to third parties.
>
> In Level 3, consumers agree to two-way communication with retailers. At this stage, visitors share more personally identifying information in exchange for proactive notifications of specials from the retailer. [...]
>
> Level 4 is considered a trusting relationship, whereby shoppers seek advice and active solicitations from their merchants, including deals offered by established partners.[33]

This multi-tiered approach presents a method by which businesses can develop trusting relationships with their customers. However, the approach also suggests that individuals will be able to make informed decisions about consent by choosing from a variety of options.[34] The very presentation of different options helps individuals understand what they are being asked when their consent is being sought. This is an approach which could be codified in DRM in order to help obtain consent that is unambiguous and informed.

4.2 Incentives for infusing privacy norms in DRM

Justifying a role for privacy law in DRM design and implementation is no easy feat. From the perspective of individual users and those who make and enforce privacy laws, there are no straightforward answers but a number of justifications are available. From the perspective of DRM engineers and DRM system users, the justifications are more nuanced and complex.

4.2.1 Users and lawmakers

On the whole, users and lawmakers would benefit by the infusion of privacy directly in DRM systems. With privacy rules embedded in DRM code, there should be less opportunity for privacy abuse and correspondingly less need for consumer concern about privacy and for actual legal enforcement of privacy rights. There is a serious risk, however, that governments and users may become irresponsible or complacent about privacy under the seemingly protective umbrella of privacy-infused DRM - they may incorrectly assume (to a degree) that code has supplanted law and is adequately addressing user privacy concerns.

Yet, in the same way that DRM may foreclose the possibility of copyright infringement from ever happening, so might it restrict or foreclose the possibility of privacy abuses occurring. For example, if a DRM system does not support surveillance of users, user privacy is likely better respected than if it were supported and the law restricted the practice, or worse, allowed it to occur with user consent. Or DRM might be adapted for use as *Privacy Rights Management*. All of this would be welcome news for users and privacy regulators. Further, if users become more comfortable about their privacy in relation to DRM, then they may reap the benefits of increased DRM ecommerce activity, in the form of the lower prices that may follow such an increase.

Users might also benefit from privacy-infused DRM in the sense that they would incur less time and money costs adopting privacy enhancing technologies (PETs) or in defending against unwelcome marketing such as spam. Or users might be better off from a privacy perspective because they have not shown much interest in PETs, or in paying for PETs, in any event.

There are also a number of potential criticisms that might be directed against embedding privacy in DRM code. For one, the benefits described above assume that the law translates well into code and that the code is actually utilizing the best possible translation of the law. To the extent that the law does not translate well (because for example it includes subjective elements) or that the code does not accurately reflect the law for other reasons, infusing privacy in DRM may do a disservice to users' legal privacy rights.

There is equally a risk that even with relatively good privacy-infused DRM, the only privacy abuses that will be prevented by code are the clear-cut ones that happen infrequently in any event. The grey areas of abuse might go largely unchecked at the code level. This problem would be especially significant if governments and users became complacent about privacy as mentioned above.

These criticisms can be addressed in part by some of the proposals discussed in sub-section 4.1. For example, a DRM standard might require DRM systems to provide users or regulators some degree of access to its privacy architecture so that they can assess what privacy invasive and protective functions the system is actually capable of performing.

4.2.2 DRM engineers

The interests of DRM engineers are in some ways connected to the interests of DRM users because the latter group essentially pays the former to develop DRM systems. One might expect that this dynamic between DRM engineers and DRM users would discourage the infusion of privacy in DRM because DRM users' interests are assumed to typically militate against that. However, the dynamic may sometimes encourage the opposite result. Although DRM users might not have felt a significant squeeze yet, a number of other industries are increasingly feeling public and regulatory pressure to respect privacy. With laws allowing consumers rights of consent, access and the right to file privacy complaints, many businesses are incurring significant privacy compliance costs. This has caused some businesses to carefully reconsider how much personal information they collect up-front in order to reduce potential downstream compliance costs. For others who choose to or must collect a lot of personal information, there is a strong incentive to make privacy compliance more efficient. Thus, DRM engineers who can deliver effective DRM that achieves the result on the privacy side should find a ready market for their products. In the long run, privacy-infused DRM products may also be less costly and more effective overall systems than those to which privacy is added as an after-thought.

There are also three ways that DRM engineers may have independent interests which support including privacy norms in DRM. First, there is an incentive for DRM engineers to produce privacy-infused DRM where a failure to do so would bring negative public or professional attention on them. This is particularly significant for DRM engineers who make more than just DRM products. Wanting to be (or wanting to appear to be) a good corporate citizen is a consideration which may encourage DRM engineers to infuse privacy considerations in DRM design independent of what DRM users may desire. Engineers' professional codes of conduct or ethics may also help encourage the development of privacy-regarding DRM.[36]

A second incentive for DRM engineers to infuse privacy in DRM lies in the possibility that privacy abuses using DRM, if sufficiently serious or pervasive, may lead to the adoption of stronger privacy laws or stepped-up enforcement of current laws. This possibility and its effect on DRM users are discussed further in sub-section 4.2.3 below; the significance of this possibility for DRM engineers lies in the challenges that it may pose for innovation. In other words, stronger privacy laws created by lawmakers who probably do not understand engineers' work could directly interfere with engineers' ability to engage in innovative technological development.

The third way that DRM engineers might have an independent incentive to infuse privacy in DRM relates to the anti-circumvention provisions of the

DMCA and similar legislation.[vi] It is well-known that the *DMCA* has had a significant chilling effect on innovative technological research and development.[37] If DRM was infused with privacy, was widely accepted by end-users as a result and proved to be an effective distribution model, then there might be relatively little motivation for users to attempt to circumvent DRM protections. With little incentive to circumvent and little actual circumvention occurring, there would be less justification for *DMCA*-like legislation, particularly if DRM is pervasively adopted as a means of distribution. Although there are some lofty assumptions and tenuous causal links in this argument, what is suggested here is that undermining the justification for the *DMCA* in this way might help tip the scales to a repeal or reform of the *DMCA*. This would be a welcome move for DRM engineers or others who find that their work is chilled by the *DMCA's* current provisions.

4.2.3 DRM users

For the companies that use DRM systems, there are two key justifications motivating the infusion of privacy in DRM. The first relates to ecommerce uptake generally and the second relates to the potential for stronger privacy laws. A third possible incentive – relating to system cost, effectiveness and privacy compliance efficiency – was discussed above in sub-section 4.2.2.

If consumers believe that neither privacy law nor DRM technology do enough to protect privacy, then they may choose not to engage in ecommerce generally, and specifically they may choose not to purchase DRM-protected content. Businesses that use DRM systems are especially susceptible to this harm because of the potential for DRM to be used across many sectors and its potential to enable significant privacy violations. This is also an important concern for companies who enable DRM implementation and who provide the infrastructure for such commerce. There are therefore a broad range of pressures and incentives for DRM users to infuse privacy into DRM. Indeed, their survival may depend on it.

Closely related to the first justification, DRM users have an incentive to infuse privacy in their DRM systems in order to use their status as a selling feature, to gain a reputational advantage over competitors and to develop more trusting relationships with their customers.[38,39]

The second key justification for infusing privacy in DRM stems from the likelihood that privacy laws or enforcement will be strengthened if there is a continued demand for privacy protection along with a failure in the market to protect privacy. A number of commentators[40,41] have already sounded the

[vi] Australia is the most recent country to agree to implement *DMCA*-like anti-circumvention legislation.[35]

alarm – they say that if immediate steps are not taken to protect privacy, then, like an endangered (if not already extinct) species, there may soon be no privacy left to protect. Although some might argue that it is too late to introduce intrusive legal regulation, it is arguable that more intrusive regulation might be a way of preventing the total destruction of privacy, or at least minimizing the risk of that happening. In the specific area of DRM technologies, there are several recent signs that such intrusive regulation may already be on its way.[26,42,43]

To the extent that DRM systems are designed and implemented without regard for privacy, they may contribute to a consumer distrust of DRM, increased consumer privacy concerns generally and ultimately to stronger privacy laws or increased enforcement of current laws. Stronger privacy laws or enforcement efforts might even be specifically targeted at DRM systems or those who use such systems.[26,42,43] In the short term, the two consumer confidence factors will translate into losses for DRM users and related companies as mentioned at the outset of this sub-section. In the long term, if DRM users survive for very long, stronger or targeted privacy laws will only increase privacy risks and compliance costs for entities that use DRM. In these varied ways, infusing privacy in DRM design and implementation now ought to be a paramount concern for entities that use DRM.

5. CONCLUSION

In exploring the conflict between digital rights management and user privacy, my central objective is relatively modest. My aim is to commence a dialogue between engineers and lawyers, to prevent the solo marches of DRM systems and privacy legislations from a head-on collision. This paper has sketched some of the ways that DRM threatens privacy norms as well as the reasons why those threats cannot be adequately addressed by consent-based privacy laws alone. From the perspectives of three key DRM constituents, a case has been made here for the infusion of privacy norms in DRM design and implementation. That there are already detailed proposals setting out how that goal might be accomplished is a positive development. The issues discussed in this paper should provide useful incentives to implement one or more of those proposals, and to create and implement new ones.

ACKNOWLEDGEMENTS

The author wishes to thank to Dr. Ian Kerr, Canada Research Chair in Ethics, Law and Technology, for his personal encouragement and feedback in the preparation of this paper and for support through the inter-disciplinary research project of which he is Principle Investigator: "On the Identity Trail: Understanding the Importance and Impact of Anonymity and Authentication in a Networked Society" (www.anonequity.org). Thanks also to Vicky Laurens for sharing her insightful comments on an earlier draft.

REFERENCES

1. R.H. Tawney, *The Acquisitive Society* (G. Bell and Sons, London, 1921), p. 1.
2. J. Cohen, DRM and Privacy, 18 *Berkeley Tech. L.J.* 575 (2003).
3. J. Cohen, A Right to Read Anonymously: A Closer Look at "Copyright Management" in Cyberspace, 28 *Conn. L. Rev.* 981 (1996).
4. L.A. Bygrave, in: *Digital Rights Management - Technological, Economic, Legal and Political Aspects*, edited by E. Becker *et al.* (Springer, London, 2003).
5. I. Kerr, A. Maurushat, and C. Tacit, Technical Protection Measures: Part I - Trends in Technical Protection Measures and Circumvention Technologies (2003); http://www.pch.gc.ca/progs/ac-ca/progs/pda-cpb/pubs/protection/tdm_e.cfm.
6. European Commission, Digital Rights: Background, Systems Assessment, A Commission Staff Working Paper, submitted for discussion at a workshop in Brussels on February 28, 2002, on Digital Rights Management (February 2, 2002); http://europa.eu.int/information_society/newsroom/documents/drm_workingdoc.pdf.
7. European Committee for Standardization (CEN) and Information Society Standardization System, Digital Rights Management: Final Report (September 30, 2003); http://europa.eu.int/comm/enterprise/ict/policy/doc/drm.pdf, pp. 27-69.
8. M.I. Yagüe, IASTED International Conference on Communication, Network, and Information Security (2003); http://www.iasted.com/conferences/2003/NewYork/cnis-specsess1.htm.
9. L. Lessig, *Code and Other Laws of Cyberspace* (Basic Books, New York, 1999).
10. *Digital Millenium Copyright Act of 1998*, Pub. L. No. 105-304, 112 Stat. 2860 [*DMCA*].
11. J.P. Barlow, Life, Liberty and the Pursuit of Copyright? (September 17, 1998); http://www.theatlantic.com/unbound/forum/copyright/barlow2.htm.
12. B. Rosenblatt, B. Trippe, and S. Mooney, *Digital Rights Management: Business and Technology* (Hungry Minds/John Wiley, New York, 2001).
13. C. Stross, The Panopticon Singularity; http://www.antipope.org/charlie/rant/panopticon-essay.html.
14. D.L. Burk and J. Cohen, Fair Use Infrastructure for Rights Management Systems, 15 *Harv. J. Law & Tech.* 41 (2001).
15. Electronic Privacy Information Center (EPIC), Digital Rights Management and Privacy; http://www.epic.org/privacy/drm/default.html.
16. Microsoft Corporation, What is Windows Media DRM; http://www.microsoft.com/windows/windowsmedia/WM7/DRM/what.aspx.

17. J. Rosen, *The Unwanted Gaze: The Destruction of Privacy in America* (Random House, New York, 2000).
18. D.K. Mulligan, J. Han and A. J. Burstein, in: *Proceedings of the 2003 ACM workshop on Digital rights management* (ACM Press, New York, 2003), pp. 82-83.
19. A. Odlyzko, in: *Proceedings of the 5th international conference on Electronic commerce* (ACM Press, New York, 2003), pp. 355-366.
20. *Directive 95/46/EC of the European Parliament and of the Council of 24 October 1995 on the protection of individuals with regard to the processing of personal data and on the free movement of such data*, Official Journal L 281, 23/11/1995 pp. 0031-0050, Article 7(a) [*Directive on data processing*].
21. *Personal Information Protection and Electronic Documents Act*, S.C. 2000, c. 5, Schedule 1, Principle 4.3, 4.4, 4.3.3, 4.3.4 [*PIPEDA*].
22. *Data Protection Act 1998*, c.29, Schedule I - III.
23. *Federal Data Protection Act (Bundesdatenschutzgesetz)*, adopted 18 May 2001, published in the Bundesgesetzblatt I Nr. 23/2001, page 904 on 22 May 2001, section 4.
24. Organisation for Economic Co-operation and Development, *Guidelines on the Protection of Privacy and Transborder Flows of Personal Data* (OECD Publications, Paris, 2002), article 7 [OECD Guidelines].
25. V. Gautrais, The Color of E-consent, presented to the *Comparative IP & Cyberlaw Symposium at the University of Ottawa, October 2003*, forthcoming in 1 UOLTJ __ (2004).
26. *Directive 2000/31/EC of the European Parliament and of the Council of 8 June 2000 on certain legal aspects of information society services, in particular electronic commerce, in the Internal Market ('Directive on electronic commerce')*, Official Journal L 178, 17/07/2000, pp. 0001-0016, Article 10.
27. B.L. Smith, The Third Industrial Revolution: Policymaking for the Internet, 3 *Colum. Sci. & Tech. L. Rev.* 1 (2001).
28. R. Dhamija and F. Wallenberg, in: *Proceedings of the First International Mobile IPR Workshop: Rights Management of Information Products on the Mobile Internet*, edited by O. Pitkänen (HIIT Publications, Helsinki, 2003), pp.13-23.
29. L. Korba and S. Kenny, in: *Security and Privacy in Digital Rights Management, ACM CCS-9 Workshop, DRM 2002, Washington, DC, USA, November 18, 2002, Revised Papers*, edited by J. Feigenbaum (Springer, London, 2003).
30. Recording Industry Association of America, Issues: New Media; http://www.riaa.com/issues/audio/newmedia.asp.
31. J. Feigenbaum, *et al.*, in: *Revised Papers from the ACM CCS-8 Workshop on Security and Privacy in Digital Rights Management*, edited by T. Sander (Springer, London, 2001).
32. Information and Privacy Commissioner/Ontario, Privacy and Digital Rights Management (DRM): An Oxymoron? (October 2002); http://www.ipc.on.ca/docs/drm.pdf.
33. M. Pastore, Consumers Fear for Their Online Privacy (November 1, 1999); http://cyberatlas.internet.com/markets/retailing/article/0,,6061_228341,00.html.
34. J. Teh, Privacy Wars in Cyberspace: An Examination of the Legal and Business Tensions in Information Privacy, 4 *Yale J. of Law & Tech.* (2001-2002), p. 94.
35. Office of the United States Trade Representative, Free Trade 'Down Under': Summary of the U.S.-Australia Free Trade Agreement (February 8, 2004); http://www.ustr.gov/releases/2004/02/2004-02-08-factsheet-australia.pdf.

36. ACM/IEEE-CS, *Software Engineering Code of Ethics and Professional Practice, Version 5.2 as recommended by the ACM/IEEE-CS Joint Task Force on Software Engineering Ethics and Professional Practices and jointly approved by the ACM and the IEEE-CS as the standard for teaching and practicing software engineering* (1999); http://www.acm.org/serving/se/code.htm#full.
37. J.P. Liu, The DMCA and the Regulation of Scientific Research, 18 *Berkeley Tech. L.J.* 501 (2003).
38. A. Cavoukian *et al.*, *The Privacy Payoff: How Successful Businesses Build Customer Trust* (McGraw Hill, Whitby, 2002).
39. D. Loukidelis, Thoughts on Private Sector Privacy Regulation (November 2003); http://www.oipcbc.org/publications/speeches_presentations/FIPAPIPAspeech112403.pdf
40. B. Barr, A Tyrant's Toolbox: Technology and Privacy in America, 26 *J. Legis.* 71 (2000).
41. J. Cohen, Privacy, Ideology and Technology: A Response to Jeffrey Rosen, 89 *Geo. L.J.* 2029 (2001), p. 2035.
42. The Office of the Federal Privacy Commissioner (Australia), Media Release: No Sympathy for piracy or privacy bandits (November 20, 2003); http://www.privacy.gov.au/news/media/03_16.html.
43. *Consumers, Schools, and Libraries Digital Rights Management (DRM) Awareness Act of 2003*, S. 1621, 108th Cong. (2003).